PENGUIN BOOKS

# THE BEAUTIFUL AND THE DAMNED

Siddhartha Deb is a novelist who was born in north-eastern India in 1970. His first novel, *The Point of Return*, was a Notable Book of the Year in *The New York Times*, while his second novel, *Surface*, was a finalist for the Hutch Crossword Award in India and a book of the year in the *Daily Telegraph*. His journalism, essays and reviews have appeared in *Harpers*, the *Guardian*, the *Observer*, *The New York Times Book Review*, *Columbia Journalism Review*, *Bookforum*, the *Daily Telegraph*, the *Nation*, *n+1*, *London Review of Books* and *The Times Literary Supplement*. He is the recipient of grants from the Society of Authors and the Nation Institute, and has recently been a fellow at the Radcliffe Institute of Advanced Studies at Harvard University.

D1412973

# The Beautiful and the Damned

## Life in the New India

SIDDHARTHA DEB

PENGUIN BOOKS

PENGUIN BOOKS

Published by the Penguin Group
Penguin Books Ltd, 80 Strand, London WC2R 0RL, England
Penguin Group (USA) Inc., 375 Hudson Street, New York, New York 10014, USA
Penguin Group (Canada), 90 Eglinton Avenue East, Suite 700, Toronto, Ontario, Canada M4P 2Y3
(a division of Pearson Penguin Canada Inc.)
Penguin Ireland, 25 St Stephen's Green, Dublin 2, Ireland (a division of Penguin Books Ltd)
Penguin Group (Australia), 250 Camberwell Road,
Camberwell, Victoria 3124, Australia (a division of Pearson Australia Group Pty Ltd)
Penguin Books India Pvt Ltd, 11 Community Centre, Panchsheel Park,
New Delhi – 110 017, India
Penguin Group (NZ), 67 Apollo Drive, Rosedale, Auckland 0632, New Zealand
(a division of Pearson New Zealand Ltd)
Penguin Books (South Africa) (Pty) Ltd, 24 Sturdee Avenue, Rosebank, Johannesburg 2196, South Africa

Penguin Books Ltd, Registered Offices: 80 Strand, London WC2R 0RL, England

www.penguin.com

First published by Viking 2011
Published in Penguin Books 2012
1

Copyright © Siddhartha Deb, 2011
All rights reserved

The moral right of the author has been asserted

Typeset by Palimpsest Book Production, Falkirk, Stirlingshire
Printed in England by Clays Ltd, St Ives plc

Except in the United States of America, this book is sold subject
to the condition that it shall not, by way of trade or otherwise, be lent,
re-sold, hired out, or otherwise circulated without the publisher's
prior consent in any form of binding or cover other than that in
which it is published and without a similar condition including this
condition being imposed on the subsequent purchaser

ISBN: 978-0-141-03334-1

www.greenpenguin.co.uk

MIX
Paper from
responsible sources
FSC™ C018179

Penguin Books is committed to a sustainable
future for our business, our readers and our
planet. This book is made from paper certified
by the Forest Stewardship Council.

To my mother, Manju Rani Deb

In a State where there is no fever of speculation, no inflamed desire for sudden wealth, where the poor are all simple-minded and contented, and the rich are all honest and generous . . . there are necessarily no materials for such a history as we have constructed . . .

Mark Twain
*The Gilded Age: A Novel of Today*, Mark Twain and Charles Dudley Warner

# Contents

# Introduction

I grew up in Shillong, a small town in the north-eastern hills of India that few people can find on a map. The hills around Shillong ran down to the flooded plains of Bangladesh, an area from where my family had originated but that had become for them, in a common quirk of the twentieth century, a foreign country. In 1947, the year my father graduated from a veterinary college and began working in the north-eastern state of Assam, his village disappeared behind the fresh cartographic lines creating the new, largely Muslim nation of East Pakistan. My father's family, consisting of his illiterate peasant parents, three brothers who were still in school, a widowed sister and an infant nephew, left behind their hut with its pots and pans and settled down in a slum in Gauhati, the largest city in Assam. Perhaps their home went to a family of Muslims who had abandoned their hut, and their pots and pans, in the new nation of India that squatted between East and West Pakistan. In 1971, after a protracted civil war, East Pakistan seceded from West Pakistan to become the nation of Bangladesh. It was around this time that new waves of migrants from Bangladesh, driven by war, genocide, starvation and insecurity, began to land up in the north-eastern hills of India. The local, mostly Christian, population in my hometown of Shillong began to fear that they were being swamped by Bengali-speaking settlers. They began to consider all Bengalis foreigners and so, in another twist of twentieth-century irony, I became a Bangladeshi to them, resident of the land that my father had left and that I had never lived in.

As a teenager, I sometimes travelled to Gauhati, four hours from Shillong by bus. It was the nearest thing we had to a big city, since the closest metropolis, Calcutta, was another 1,200 kilometres beyond Gauhati. But I had to be careful while visiting Gauhati that I wouldn't be pulled off a bus by the police on the way back to Shillong. Because I could be called a Bangladeshi and asked to go back to my place of origin, I always carried with me a certificate from the Deputy Commissioner attesting to the fact that I was an Indian and that Shillong was my home. Without that document, I could be considered anything – a Bangladeshi by Indians and an Indian by Bangladeshis.

When I finally left Shillong, first to live in Calcutta and then in Delhi, the great, urban anonymity offered by cities seemed to have put to rest the question of where I came from. It no longer mattered who I was in terms of place of origin as much as the amount of money I had, whatever its origin. In the mid-nineties, I began working for a newspaper in Delhi, living in an area known as Munirka Gaon, that is to say, Munirka Village. The neighbourhood was located in south Delhi, walking distance from the sprawling campus of Jawaharlal Nehru University. Although south Delhi was an upscale area of the city, Munirka was the remnant of an old village that the city had not fully absorbed. It had become an urban slum of sorts, with buffaloes wallowing in the winding dirt lanes, elderly men sitting around their communal hookah in the evening and women walking around veiled in deference to the patriarchal traditions of the Jat Hindus who were the original residents of Munirka and were gradually transforming themselves from farmers to landlords. The rents charged by these new landlords were low, and the facilities rather rudimentary, making Munirka an attractive place for a spillover of students from the university and for lower-middle-class migrants making their way in Delhi.

At first, I shared a room in a Munirka tenement with three other men, but I eventually moved into a one-room flat of my own. There was no electricity during the day. The building didn't have the requisite permits, and the owner hooked up an illegal connection only at night, when it was less likely that the power board would send a van on the prowl to look for such instances of electricity theft. For all that, the building I stayed in represented a certain lower-middle-class privilege. Behind it were the small huts occupied by working-class families who often livened up the nights with furious shouts and screams as men beat their wives or fought each other in drunken brawls.

The other residents of my building were all men in their twenties, carrying out a wide range of jobs. Naseer, who lived above me, was a 'master cutter' at a garment factory on the outskirts of Delhi. Below were three men, two Sikhs and one Bengali, who were aircraft mechanics. Across from me, in a building that was so close by that we could jump from one balcony to another, there lived Dipu, a bright and anguished man who had been trying for years to pass the examinations for the Indian Civil Service. His room-mate was in training with India's intelligence agency and would be dispatched in a couple of years to a remote village on the border with China.

I had been living in Munirka for some years when I decided to take the GRE exams as a preliminary step to applying for a graduate programme in America. Because a passport was the only acceptable form of identification for the exams, I filled out the required documents and handed in my application at the Delhi passport office, not far from where I lived. With a week left to go before the exams, my landlord gave me a crumpled letter that had come from the passport office. My application had been rejected. The police had been unable to find my address and verify that I lived in Munirka, the letter said. I went back to the passport office and showed the letter to a clerk.

'You gave a fake address,' he said. 'That's why the police couldn't find it.'

'But it's the same address that you used to send the letter,' I said.

'So?'

'The postman found it.'

The clerk shrugged. 'Go talk to the police.'

I went to the police and it made no difference. I gave up on the idea of sitting the GRE exams. But then my boss at the newspaper found out that my application had been turned down, and he had a reporter call the minister responsible for passports. I returned to the passport office, where I was led past the long queues into a private chamber, the officer in charge hurriedly issuing me a passport I could use for the exams, which were the next day. The officer was apologetic as he gave me the passport. Because it had to be produced so urgently, it was valid only for one year. But I could come back whenever I wanted to and make it a regular ten-year passport, he said.

So I should have, but another year went by before I had enough money to apply to universities in America. In the summer of 1998, by which time I'd left the newspaper and Delhi and come back to live with my mother in Calcutta, I received a fellowship to a PhD programme at Columbia University. I needed to get the passport extended in order to go abroad, and one July morning, I took a bus from the outskirts of the city to the passport office in Esplanade, joining a line that had formed on the pavement. It was just past seven, but there were already thirty or so people ahead of me. We tried to keep in the shade, away from the sun that burned fiercely even this early in the morning, and as we waited, a few seedy-looking men went up and down the line, asking people if they needed help with their passport applications.

The line grew longer, the day became even hotter and more humid, and as nine o'clock approached, the excitement became palpable. I counted the people in front of me obsessively and figured that I would be all right. Even with the slowest of clerks, I should be able to submit my application before the counters closed at noon. I had prepared my application carefully, the form filled out just so in block letters, my passport photograph glued and not stapled, the picture displaying both ears (a mysterious injunction whose purpose I didn't understand), and with the exact amount in rupees for the application fee.

At nine, the gates opened. There was a sudden swelling of the crowd, an infinitesimal moment of stillness, and then the line collapsed, with people rushing in from every direction to take the stairs leading up to the passport office. The uniformed policeman who had appeared just a little while ago to monitor the queue was nowhere to be seen.

I was so stunned by the unfairness of all this that I didn't move at first, and I was suddenly reduced to a solitary dot on the pavement. Then I dived into the mob. I fought my way upstairs, where I saw, with growing panic, that a new line was forming in front of the single counter that took in passport applications. It was a line that in the composition of its members bore no relation to the one that had existed outside for nearly two hours, and it had grown so long that it already trickled back out of the office, down the stairs and towards the pavement, leaving me with the option of reversing my journey to take my place at the very end.

On another day, or in a different season, without the brutal heat, I might have done so. But that morning I made my way towards the counter, shoved aside two men, ignoring their protests, and planted myself firmly in between. A few seconds later, a hand grabbed me by my shirt and pulled me out of the line. I saw a burly, mustachioed man, pulling back his free hand to punch me. I grabbed his hand with my left and his shirt with my right, and we swayed back and forth for a while as the crowd around us stopped being a mob and transformed back into a peaceful queue, watching us with great interest as sweat dripped from our faces and abuse came out of our mouths. The man wrested one hand free and reached for the back of his trousers. I thought he was a tout going for his knife, and I hurriedly let go and stepped back, still angry, but now scared as well.

Instead of a knife, the man pulled out an identity card, shouting, 'Do you know who I am?'

A policeman in plain clothes, half of me realized with terror, while the other half pulled out an ID card in return, shouting back, 'And do you know who I am?'

I was holding out my press card, which I should have turned in when I quit my job. But I hadn't, and so we glowered at each other, a policeman who had been pretending not to be a policeman staring at a man who was no longer a journalist but pretending to be a journalist.

We had shouted in Bengali, and we were saying something other than what the question seemed to mean. Behind the question, there was an anguish expressed by both the policeman and me, both trying to do the right thing and yet in conflict with each other. This became clear when tempers cooled and we stopped grappling with each other, and in a replay of what had happened in Delhi a year before, the policeman led me into an officer's chamber to get my passport renewed. Yet even though we may not have intended it, when we shouted, 'Do you know who I am?' we were asking the question in a profoundly literal sense. Did I know who he was, a man trying to maintain order in the line – afraid that *I* was a tout with a knife in his back pocket – doing a hopeless job assigned him by his boss? And did he know who I was, breaking the line only after I had tried to follow the rules, wanting nothing more than the passport that was supposedly my right as a citizen of the country?

The outsourcing office was in Noida, a gridwork of factories and offices connected to Delhi by a new four-lane highway suspended over the sluggish, polluted Yamuna river. It was next door to Resistoflex ('Vibrating Control Systems Since 1947'), and almost hidden behind a row of parked trucks. The office had once been part of a factory; the building was unpainted and exposed at the back, although the front had been done up in the requisite international corporate style, with granite steps leading up to the glass doors. The company handled customer service calls from countries around the world, with shifts in the evening and at night to handle queries from Australia, Great Britain and the United States.

After taking tests and being interviewed for a couple of hours, I was finally led into the office of the man with the authority to hire me. The other employees in the company had referred to him as 'Wing Commander Ghosh', and one of them told me that he liked to push candidates to see how they reacted under stress.

The wing commander was a slight, dark and rather intense-looking man whose computer screen saver flashed images of small aircraft at me. As I answered the wing commander's questions, I realized that the right sleeve of his suit jacket was pinned back. The wing commander was missing an arm. I became distracted as soon as I realized this, finding myself unable to stop thinking about how he had lost an arm, adding this to the images of aircraft on his screen saver and beginning to imagine a terrible accident that had ended the man's air force career.

The company needed people, however, and even in my distracted state, I passed the wing commander's stress test. He wanted to hire me right away, although the salary and benefits he was offering seemed rather low by industry standards. There was also the fact that the company, in spite of the talk of faraway Western countries, seemed suspiciously like a family business. But what concerned me most of all, for reasons I could not possibly reveal to the wing commander, was that I needed to know if I would be serving British customers.

The wing commander stared at me firmly. 'The biggest business now,' he said, 'with lots of performance incentives, is in the American process. If you are willing to work in that, you will be calling American homeowners and persuading them to remortgage their houses.' I didn't quite understand what he was talking about, so he explained further. 'You will be calling on behalf of banks that are our clients and are offering the homeowners better loans. Your job is to get people to change their mortgages from their old banks to the new ones. This is the work of the future, my boy.'

Six years after leaving for New York with my passport, I was in Delhi again, trying to get a job in what had become India's best-known industry. I had travelled to the West, to Columbia University, where I'd written a novel. I had left the university to settle into the precarious rhythm of a writer's life, coming back home whenever I could afford to, often to gather material for a feature article. This trip, in January 2004, was centred around my most prestigious assignment so far, one from the *Guardian* weekend magazine that involved trying to get a job at a call centre so that I could report from the inside on what it was like to do such work.

This was a time when globalization was still proceeding smoothly, without the financial meltdowns and the subprime crises that would suddenly add new meaning to Wing Commander Ghosh's work of the future. It was a time when India was one of the main nodes of globalization, running back offices and customer service centres for companies in the West. There was some anxiety about this phenomenon, mostly from unions in the West that watched jobs disappearing offshore and protested that the work done by Indian call centre staff was inferior, perhaps even carried out by 'convicted felons'. There were a few critics in India too, saying that the work was old exploitation dressed up in a new costume and that the people doing long hours and late nights while assuming Western identities and accents were just 'cybercoolies'.

But such protests seemed marginal when compared to the celebration of call centres in business-friendly circles in both India and the

West. The point was not that the work was bad or the salaries far lower than what Western workers might expect, the boosters said. It was how call centre work was creating a generation of Indian youth who were being empowered by capitalism, people who had begun to break down the old restrictions of caste, class and gender, and who now exemplified the new India where men and women worked together late into the night and partied into the day, and who spent their money at the pubs, discotheques and shopping malls that had been brought to India by the same vigorous capitalism that had given them their jobs.

The Indian call centres, some owned by multinationals and some by home-grown enterprises, had nevertheless become rather sensitive to any scrutiny of their business. Like much of corporate India, they had become so secretive that it was difficult for a journalist to freely observe work in call centres.

The assignment from the *Guardian* meant that I had to put aside the Indian passport I had acquired, and the identity presented in its pages, and create a CV that offered a different identity, one more reasonable for an aspiring call centre worker. In order to take a job where I might have to change my name and accent and become a Western person, I first had to erase most traces of the West from my existing self. In order to become globalized through the call centre, I had to stop being globalized and become a provincial Indian, someone leaving Shillong for the first time to try his luck at the networked outsourcing offices of Noida, Gurgaon and Delhi. In the CV that I created, I retained my name and age, but all the other details were invented. I had already worked night shifts in Delhi while living in Munirka, but that had been at a newspaper. The schoolteacher I put down on my call centre CV was an alternate self, someone who had never left Shillong until now.

These questions about who I was, and who the call centre workers were, seemed to be pieces of a larger puzzle about what India was in its new incarnation. In 1998, just as I was leaving the country, the Hindu right-wing Bharatiya Janata Party had won the national elections and formed a government in Delhi. It was a remarkable success for a party that, just ten years earlier, had possessed only two seats in the parliament. As a college student, I had once run into one of the two BJP members of parliament. I had been waiting for a flight at the airport in Silchar, a small town in Assam, when I saw the portly, somewhat forlorn, figure of Atal Bihari Vajpayee. He too was waiting for the flight to Calcutta, having just finished a trip to the border town of Karimganj where he had gone to rouse local sentiments about illegal immigration into India by poor Muslims from Bangladesh.

By 1998, however, Vajpayee had become the prime minister, a coronation celebrated by carrying out five nuclear tests in the desert sands of Rajasthan. Then, in 2002, the BJP government in the western state of Gujarat, headed by the business-friendly chief minister Narendra Modi, unleashed a pogrom on Muslims that left 2,000 people dead, thousands of women sexually assaulted and thousands of others displaced. On the economic front, Vajpayee's government had continued the process of opening up its markets to foreign multinationals and investors while selling off state-owned assets cheaply to private businesses. An entire elite had been made even richer, while the middle class had become flush with cash, partaking happily of consumer goods like cars and mobile phones. But what was happening to the majority of people in India – the poor, the lower castes, women, Muslims and farmers – was a mystery. They were utterly invisible, edited out of the corporate and government buzz about India, and they resurfaced only when the BJP began its re-election bid in 2004, producing happy faces of the forgotten majority in a campaign it called 'India Shining'.

I went about trying to get work at call centres even as the BJP campaigned furiously in the background. In some sense, I was at the heart of India Shining, in the 'sunrise' industry of the call centres. I took an expensive class in call centre English at the British Council in Delhi, paying more for that brief course of a few weeks than I had for my entire state-subsidized higher education in India. I travelled to recruitment offices in Delhi and the outskirts, where I sat through tests and interviews that often took an entire day while trying to understand something of the lives of the youths who cycled in and out of the recruitment centres. On the surface, many of them were indeed trendy and modern, wearing jeans and carrying mobile phones, but the lives they revealed to me were also filled with frustration and doubt. There was Leena, for instance, from the state of Sikkim, already tired of her job handling customer inquiries about mortgages and loans for an American bank. She had studied literature in college and wanted to become a schoolteacher until the higher salaries of the call centre industry drew her to Delhi. But the city life had turned out to offer her little of the freedom she had expected. She shared a room with five other women at the YWCA hostel, and most of her time was taken up by a job that she liked less and less.

'The customers get irate,' she told me. 'Their transactions often get messed up, and it's my job to pacify them. I understand that they're upset, but they start calling me names, and then it gets really difficult.'

My most extended interaction with call centre workers came when I got a job for HCL BPO, an Indian outsourcing firm that had an office in Noida for handling customer service calls for BT. Over the next two weeks, including one week of training, the days blended into each other. The shifts were nine hours long, and with travel time added in, the job consumed twelve to thirteen hours a day. My mornings began with the honking of the company van outside the apartment I was staying in and they ended around midnight with a similar van depositing me home after the driver, in order to avoid having his monthly salary of 4,000 rupees docked for falling behind schedule, had sped through red lights at eighty kilometres an hour. As for the job itself, that involved taking calls from angry British customers who wanted to cancel their BT Internet accounts, trying to convince them to stay on, first by telling them how inconvenient it would be for them to cancel ('Madam, you will lose your BT email address. What if people try to get in touch with you at that address?') and moving up gradually to offering free technical support or a free month of service.

When on the phone with their British customers, my colleagues were invariably polite, murmuring into their headsets in their idiosyncratic renditions of the Northern Irish accent our trainers had all brought back with them from the BT facility in Belfast. In real life, however, they were a competing bunch of neuroses and afflictions, with an incredibly low tolerance for difference of any kind. There was Pradeep, a soft-spoken, intelligent man who was nevertheless convinced that he would never marry a woman who had worked at a call centre because she was bound to be promiscuous. Swati, a plump woman whose husband also worked at a call centre, agreed. It was hard not to feel sympathy for Swati, who had trouble with her English and was worried about talking to British customers, especially those 'Wellish' people who insisted on speaking in 'Wellish'. And yet she had the habit of making disparaging comments about Muslims, especially to Feroze, one of the men who led us in a training session and whose English was flawless. The only one among my colleagues who disagreed with these common views was Alok, a discontented man with an engineering degree. I ran into him one afternoon during a break. He approached me in a haze of marijuana smoke.

'This call centre work is not a career,' he said, offering me a drag of his reefer along with his wisdom. 'If I start working as an engineer, I'll get half of what I make right now. But in five years, I'll be making more money and have a real job. A friend of mine, a civil engineer, began a couple of years ago with a salary of only five thousand rupees. Now, he's part of the Delhi metro construction project. He's doing something with his life.'

Unlike the accounts in the media, most people in the call centre didn't seem to think they were doing anything with their life. They were trapped in the here and now, and the new work opportunities brought by globalization had given these lower-middle-class youths as much of a sense of vulnerability as of empowerment. They went in and out of the call centre jobs, abandoning them for other work when the long, late-night hours became too oppressive, returning to the call centres when the other jobs they had taken seemed not to offer enough money. They might have been the most visible face of India Shining, but their inner lives, invisible to the world, showed a more complex reality where uncertainty and stasis had as great an influence as the superficial mobility and modernity of their jobs.

By the time I quit my job at the call centre, it seemed to me that the sunrise industry was a rather fake world, dressing up its ordinary routine work in the tinsel of youthfulness. From the Internet terminals scattered along the passageways, to the food courts, the recreation rooms with pool tables and the pictures of workers with American flags painted on their faces, the bigger outsourcing offices gave the impression that they were Western college campuses. But there wasn't much freedom in these outposts of the free world, with their sanctioned fifteen-minute bathroom breaks for every four hours of work. They were places where along with the monotony and stress of the work, the modernity of India became an ambiguous phenomenon rather than a marker of irreversible progress. It seemed that I was not the only one there with a fake identity.

In April 2004, the BJP, in spite of its vigorous India Shining campaign, lost the elections. A few months later, I found myself in the city of Bhopal, in central India, pursuing a forgotten story. I was there to write a piece on the twentieth anniversary of the disaster that happened on the night of 2 December 1984, when a pesticide factory run by the American multinational Union Carbide spewed out toxic fumes and killed at least 3,000 people in twenty-four hours. In the two decades since then, the death toll had reached at least 20,000, while another 100,000 people were estimated by Amnesty International to be suffering 'chronic and debilitating' illnesses caused by the lethal methyl isocyanate (MIC) gas that had leaked out from the factory.

When I arrived in Bhopal in November, I was told that I should meet a man called Abdul Jabbar. Even though no one outside the city had heard of him, he had a reputation in Bhopal as someone who had done the most for victims of the Union Carbide disaster. He ran an organization for women widowed and rendered destitute by the disaster, working from a converted industrial shed in the old quarter of the city. It was a shoddily run place in many ways, with grimy toilets, battered sewing machines, a telephone that was kept, oddly enough, in the kitchen, photographs of Gandhi and lesser-known Indian radicals, an office overflowing with paper, and a verandah where a display case contained hideous stuffed toys that stared at visitors with glassy eyes.

From this strange base quartering an organization with a name that came across as unwieldy whether in full form, acronym or in translation (the Bhopal Gas Peedit Mahila Udyog Sangathan or BGP-MUS or Bhopal Gas-Affected Women's Enterprise Organization), Jabbar and the women sallied out occasionally to picket government officials, demanding the compensation money that had been promised but not delivered twenty years after the event.

The women were mostly working class and usually illiterate. The older ones had lost their husbands in the disaster or its aftermath, while some of the younger ones had been abandoned by their husbands. Jabbar claimed that the organization, which had about 5,000 members, allowed the women to step beyond their traditional roles as victims. But it was also an organization of women centred around a male figure, a place where the women seemed to find a masculine presence that perhaps compensated for the fathers, husbands and sons absent in their lives.

Many of the women had been raised as orthodox Hindus or Muslims, an upbringing they had to struggle with in order to venture beyond the neighbourhood and become members of Jabbar's organization. Some of the Muslim women had got rid of their veils. Many of them remained religious without being orthodox, and only Feroza, who described herself as a 'hard-core Muslim', continued to have a running argument with Jabbar, who retorted, quietly but firmly, that he had no faith in any faith.

Jabbar also claimed to have no faith in the West. He detested multinationals, especially Dow Chemicals, which had since acquired Union Carbide. But he also disliked organizations like Greenpeace that had tried to draw attention to the conditions in Bhopal so many years after the disaster. He did not take money from Western outfits, a position that set him at odds with a vastly more efficient organization called the Bhopal Group for Information and Action. He did not have a website for his organization, although even the local reporters begged him to set one up so that they could have easier access to information. He claimed, when I was first introduced to him, that he didn't speak to Western reporters or to urban, upper-class Indians. He refused to speak in English, even though he seemed to have a

working knowledge of the language. For a soft-spoken man of
benign, even nondescript, appearance – short, pudgy, with a moustache and thick glasses – he was surprisingly truculent, and I came
away from our initial meeting feeling rather disappointed.

A writer visiting a new place and struggling with unfamiliar topics
needs sources who are articulate, people who can point him to the
key issues quickly and who can present the information in an organized way. And when the writer needs the stories of people's lives,
those narratives that insert recognizable, human shapes into large but
abstract conflicts, he or she depends on people who have a sense of
their own trajectories and who are willing to impose form on the
chaos of their experiences and memories. Neither Jabbar nor his
organization seemed to possess such qualities. When I followed my
first visit with a few phone calls to Jabbar, I got some incoherent facts
and figures and a half-hearted invitation to attend one of his weekly
rallies. I began to see why Jabbar and his organization were unknown
outside Bhopal, and why their names had never appeared in the well-
researched *Guardian* and *Nation* articles I had gone through before
coming to Bhopal.

There were, after all, other sources of information in the city, like
the Bhopal Group for Information and Action, where activists led
me swiftly and efficiently to the principal aspects of the situation in
Bhopal. From these people, working in a small office where hum-
ming computers and ringing telephones imparted a sense of efficiency
and seriousness, I learned that activists from the Bhopal Group, along
with people from Greenpeace, had broken into the factory to collect
soil samples. These samples had then been analysed by a Boston-
based environmental laboratory and found to be full of mercury and
arsenic, and the Bhopal Group had the data and reports to show how
the groundwater of all the slums around the factory remained con-
taminated with toxic waste.

In comparison to the people working at the Bhopal Group, Jabbar
seemed like a relic of the past, not really a character in a coherent
story as much as a local demigod of the sort that proliferates in India.
One looked at him in passing, and although a native guide might
insist that this was a powerful deity, it was impossible as an outsider

to enter that realm of local mythologies. It was impossible, in other words, to know anything about Jabbar and his activities without some kind of faith in him, and it was impossible to have that faith in him without the local knowledge.

Nevertheless, one afternoon, I turned up to see the last thirty minutes of Jabbar's Saturday rally. It was a time of the year when both Ramadan and Navratri (a Hindu festival) were being observed, and the audience was thinner than usual. About fifty women and a few men sat on the grass as Jabbar addressed them, standing in front of some ragged and stunted palm trees. He was less rambling as a public speaker, focused but intimate with his audience. When he ended his speech with a slogan, he didn't raise his voice in a shout as Indian politicians tend to do. Instead, he said softly, 'Naya Zamana ...' ('The New Age ...'), a phrase that the women closed emphatically and loudly by leaping to their feet and answering, '... ayega' ('... will come'). The slogan was repeated once – softer and on a downbeat – and even before the response had come, Jabbar had moved away, coiling up the wire trailing from his microphone.

I liked the closing note. It was somehow more effective than a blood-curdling cry would have been. And I liked the way the women had given the slogan both body and soul, with Jabbar no more than a catalyst for their aspirations. I stayed on to talk to some of the women while Jabbar and other organizers ran back and forth among the small crowd. They were planning a trip to Delhi in the coming weeks to lobby the parliament, and it was important to spread the word to get an impressive turnout. At some point, Jabbar came up to me and said that it was a good time to talk, but he had to take care of a small task first.

I accompanied Jabbar across the street to the Ladies' Hospital. An ambulance packed with passengers stood in the driveway. I caught a glimpse of a woman in the back and what looked like a baby in swaddling clothes in her arms. 'Go on to the house,' Jabbar said. 'Drive safely. I'll come later.' Then we walked back to the park, where Jabbar wheeled his Honda scooter out and asked me to climb on. During our ride through the jagged, amorphous quarters of the old city, I discovered that the woman in the ambulance was Jabbar's wife and that she had given birth to a boy the night before. The activist had become a father, a first in his life, a fact that in its intimacy and domesticity seemed a little incongruous with the utopian, large-scale issues discussed in the park, but perhaps less incongruous than the fact that I, a stranger, was being taken to Jabbar's house the same day his wife and son were coming home from the hospital.

As Jabbar negotiated a path through the crowded marketplace, a furniture store caught his eye. He asked me to stay with the scooter while he went into the store, a room open to the street and packed with locally made furniture, most of it cobbled together out of plastic or cheap wood. What had attracted Jabbar's attention was an infant cradle of pink plastic with a mosquito net attached to it. Jabbar bargained briefly, bought the contraption and handed it to me. The cradle had looked small in the store, but as I sat on the back seat of Jabbar's scooter, riding up narrow alleyways and under hobbit-sized bridges, it began to assume gargantuan proportions. I had to shout at Jabbar to stop when I thought we were going to scrape against a wall. With frequent halts when I dismounted to cross particularly narrow stretches, we finally arrived at his house.

What kind of man brings a stranger home when his wife has just given birth? In Jabbar's house, I was introduced to his wife, a Kashmiri woman in her late twenties. She was dressed in a black hijab, her hair covered but her face unveiled, and she looked exhausted from her labour. I saw the baby and encountered a squadron of mosquitoes that made me thankful that the cradle had come with a net. Relatives and neighbours passed in and out so fluidly as to leave little distinction between outdoors and indoors, between sitting room and bedroom. I drank tea and talked to Jabbar's neighbours. They were working-class people who were proud of him, of the fact that he had become a father, of the trees he had got for them to plant in the neighbourhood, which was poor without being squalid. Then it was time for Jabbar to head out again because he wanted me to meet people in the nearby slums.

But the initial question remained in my mind, if inflected differently. What kind of man takes a Hindu stranger home even when the proprieties of a lower-middle-class Muslim background demand an observance of the purdah, and especially when his wife seems uncomfortable not following such convention? And if that seems needlessly traditional, what kind of man doesn't see the necessity, accepted even among modern individuals, of separating the private and the public?

One possible answer – and it was the answer Jabbar gave me when I asked him this – is that the idea of separation, between men and women, Hindus and Muslims, the private and the public, is an artificial one. 'My mother never observed the purdah,' he told me. But the disaster of 1984 had broken down other walls, Jabbar said. For some, it had been a temporary erasure of boundaries as they stopped to help the dying and the injured for a few weeks. For Jabbar, who had at the time been a small contractor drilling borewells, the change had been permanent, marking him out for a life as an activist rather than as a businessman.

Another possible answer – and this was one Jabbar didn't come up with – is that it is an obsessed person, one without a sense of proportion, who doesn't observe the distinctions between private and public life, between the needs of activism and the demands of domesticity. It was an answer that had some interpretative power when it came to Jabbar's life, because Yasmeena was his second wife. Jabbar had been married before to a woman called Rehana, a marriage significant enough a decade after its dissolution for Jabbar, his neighbours and his rival at the Bhopal Group for Information and Action to refer to it.

Rehana had been an early member of Jabbar's organization, a woman from a lower-middle-class Muslim background similar to Jabbar's. She had been in her twenties, a divorced mother of two children, at the time she began working with Jabbar in the organization. A bad-tempered, arrogant woman was how Jabbar's neighbours referred to Rehana, as did Usha and Jamila, two of the women in the organization who had known her. Jabbar spoke about Rehana less emphatically, with a touch of despair that was somewhat unusual for him. He had married her because he had been attracted to her 'radical' personality, he told me, using the English word to emphasize the quality that he had found appealing.

'It wasn't easy for me to convince my family to accept our marriage. Even though she was young and beautiful, you know the kind of stigma our community has against divorced women. And she had two children from her previous marriage, which prejudiced them against her even more. I was young, a man, and they thought I could do better.'

But Rehana's radical nature changed into simple querulousness with marriage. Jabbar said that it had made him so unhappy – her fights with neighbours, with small children – that he had wanted to kill himself. But what made him end the marriage was her newly discovered sense of status. She wanted him to rise socially and economically, to become important, to be more than an organizer.

'I found out – and I found out after a long time, because my comrades kept the fact from me – that if anyone came to see me at home and she answered the door, she would turn them away. She would say, "Come back later, the boss is sleeping." That was something I couldn't accept.'

It sounded annoying but not a serious flaw, I thought. Perhaps she had wanted to spend more time with him. But Jabbar wouldn't accept this argument.

'When she said, "The boss is asleep," she was doing something horrible. The people who come to me for help, I am not their boss. When we organize the afflicted, we have to believe that they are our equals. Otherwise, we become like the politicians and civil servants who are supposedly there to serve us, who are elected by us, paid from our taxes, and yet treat us as their inferiors.

'You will have noticed,' Jabbar continued, 'that when some of the older women speak to us after the rally and want our contact information, I rebuke my associates if they just rattle off the phone number and address. I ask them to write it on a slip of paper and give it to them, because otherwise we're taking advantage of the fact that an elderly, illiterate woman won't remember a phone number or address given out so quickly. She won't know how to write it down and it will make her feel small, make her feel inadequate. But when you write it out and give it to her, you show her that you are not a politician, not an incredibly important person, not her boss. That's what Rehana wouldn't understand, that I didn't choose to do this in order to become a boss, to be someone rich and powerful. The other thing she didn't understand is that organizing doesn't stop at five in the evening. The people who came to my house were often desperate, perhaps about to be evicted, perhaps with a child who had to be admitted to hospital.'

Failed marriages are notoriously tricky narratives even when one of the protagonists isn't an organizer. But when one person is obsessed with work that knows no limits, that involves interacting with suffering and poverty on an everyday basis and that does not lead to easily quantifiable rewards, the person can find his or her work destroying an otherwise resilient relationship. And Jabbar's work, which I observed through long mornings and afternoons spent at his office, the flow of time punctuated by the cry of the muezzin from a nearby mosque, involved an unending set of challenges and rather small victories.

The organization had filed a case in the Supreme Court asking the government to distribute the full amount of the compensation money it had taken from Union Carbide. Two decades after the event, the government had paid out no more than an interim amount of $80 for each person, and even that money had to be divided with corrupt lawyers and officials. People who came to Jabbar for help included those who weren't members of his organization, such as a middle-aged man who showed up one afternoon and began to cry with rage and frustration as he told us his story.

He was a waiter in a tea shop who had been affected by the gas, and the government had recently released his initial payment to the lawyer the waiter had needed to hire to make his compensation case. The lawyer invited the waiter into his chamber and asked him to take half the money and leave the rest as fees. When the waiter protested, saying that he had already paid the fees, the lawyer called in a few men, thrashed the waiter and threw him out. When the waiter tried to file a police report at the local station, the officer in charge laughed at him.

Jabbar's forehead grew furrowed as he heard this story. He asked for the name of the lawyer and called other lawyers to ask them what they thought of the man. When he had verified from a few different sources that the lawyer was known to be both corrupt and violent, he asked the waiter for the name of the police official who had refused to help him. Then he called a senior police officer and told him the story, including the fact that the area police station hadn't done anything. He made an appointment for the waiter with the senior official, hung up, and asked someone to talk the waiter through the procedure he would have to follow when he met the senior police officer.

The whole process took about an hour, in which time Jabbar earned the waiter's gratitude, confirmed his reputation in the slums and tenements of Bhopal as an honest, pugnacious man and achieved nothing in terms of furthering his organization's presence outside the city. It was very different from the way the Bhopal Group for Information and Action was run by Satinath Sarangi, a man whose name came up often as a reference point in Western articles and reports.

I had gone to visit Sathyu (as Sarangi is known) a few days earlier. Sathyu met me at the site where he was putting up a new building for Sambhavna. It would serve both as headquarters for his organization and as an Ayurvedic clinic for gas victims. The new clinic was set back from the crowded roads and settlements of the old city. The red-brick building, Sathyu said, was planned to be ecologically sustainable. It would be kept cool – temperatures in Bhopal reach 110 degrees in the summer – by a complicated system of airflow and by water circulating around the walls. The garden, where we sat and talked while the sun set over the Shyamla Hills in front of us, would be used to grow organic herbs. The patients, when the clinic was in operation, would receive Ayurvedic medicines and massages.

It was as different from Jabbar's chaotic operation as Sathyu was from Jabbar. Tall, bearded, and sporting a ponytail, Sathyu had the look of an ageing Indian rock singer. He wore a turban that was wrapped loosely around his head and a black shirt proclaiming 'Toulouse 27/9/2001, 27/9/2002, 27/9/2003', which he explained to me as commemorating a chemical plant explosion in 2001 in Toulouse, and where he had gone in 2003 to attend a conference.

Sathyu was handsome and articulate, alert to the ways of the world. And while Jabbar didn't like interacting with the West, Sathyu thrived on it, even if his West was the alternative, countercultural West of green, anti-globalization politics. I could see how much such interaction characterized Sathyu's organization, from the Indian Americans and Bard College undergraduates who sat around his office to the design and principles of the new clinic. When Greenpeace came to Bhopal, as they had done in 2002 when they broke into the factory site, they had worked in partnership with Sathyu. Even the clinic, though Sathyu was initially reluctant to talk about financing, had been built with money donated by readers of the *Guardian*.

So when Sathyu said that Jabbar was inefficient and outdated, it was hard to dismiss his charges. They had been colleagues once, in the immediate aftermath of the disaster. At that time, when Union Carbide had swiftly dissociated itself from the local factory (initially refusing to even reveal the composition of the gas because it was a proprietary formula) and senior Indian politicians and officials had fled the city, a large number of disparate personalities, left-leaning political parties and groups had come together under a loose coalition called 'Morcha' (Forum). But Morcha had splintered a few years after the event, when the pressure of the original disaster was no longer available to seal the fissures created by conflicting temperaments and varied ideologies. In that aftermath, when various members of Morcha went their separate ways, Jabbar had become corrupt, Sathyu said. He had amassed large amounts of money and started hobnobbing with the politicians. But what Sathyu said he found especially unforgivable was that Jabbar had treated his first wife, Rehana, very badly.

Sathyu wouldn't elaborate upon these charges, but when I asked him if he missed working with Jabbar, he paused to reflect. 'Jabbar has charisma,' he said. 'I miss that very much. He has an ability to convince a crowd, work them into a frenzy, and he can interact with common people.'

It seemed like a good assessment of Jabbar's strengths. It was also a good assessment, indirectly, of the weakness of Sathyu's organization. It was Sathyu's organization I would turn to when I was far from Bhopal and needed a sense of what was happening around the compensation of victims or attempts by Indian industrialists to pressure the government into giving Dow Chemicals complete legal immunity before it began fully fledged operations in India. Sathyu

had a terrific website where information and reports had been col-
lated and organized neatly. What he didn't have were the working-class
women, slum-dwellers and toothless old men one encountered constantly in Jabbar's office. At the premises of the Bhopal Group for
Information and Action, the gas victims seemed to appear only on
posters on the walls.

In the slums of Bhopal too, in areas where the disaster has had the
greatest fallout, I discovered an inverse relationship between international fame and local knowledge. No one in the slums knew Sathyu
or his organization, but everyone knew Jabbar. You could have efficiency or popular support, international alliances or deep local roots,
it seemed, but not both.

I found this paradox fascinating, especially in the new India, a
place supposed to have become exposed to the world – or, in other
words, the West – through globalization. So I pushed Jabbar, saying
that I could understand why he didn't like Western corporations but
I wanted to know what he had against Greenpeace and Western
NGOs trying to help the people he cared about. Jabbar began to talk
about the arrogance of showing up among impoverished people with
laptops and digital cameras. 'They fly in for a few days,' he said, and
I knew the verb 'fly' was as important here as the phrase 'few days'.
When Jabbar went to Delhi, he didn't even buy a ticket for a reserved
berth, let alone in an air-conditioned coach. He travelled in a 'general' compartment with no assigned seating and no limit to the
number of people who could get on, a free-for-all realm where every
inch of space is claimed by some part of a human body.

'They stay in that fancy hotel, Lake View, where it's five thousand
rupees a night,' Jabbar said.

'It's not,' I told him. 'It's less than half that amount.' But I was
relieved I wasn't staying there: I knew that Jabbar approved of the
fact that I was staying at the more downmarket Indian Coffee House
Hotel.

Jabbar was undeterred by my correction of the room rates at Lake
View. 'It's still half a month's wages for people here. How will poor
people even talk to someone living there, in what looks like luxury,
let alone march with them?' We were talking in Jabbar's office and he

led me up to a photograph that showed a young man with thick glasses and a slim, almost emaciated body. 'That is the picture of someone who was a wonderful comrade.'

The man was Shankar Guha Niyogi, an activist who had tried to organize mill workers in the neighbouring state of Chhattisgarh through the eighties and nineties. The workers had been mostly tribal people, living in tenements and kept in virtual bondage to mill owners and moneylenders.

'When Niyogi came to Bhopal,' Jabbar said, 'he asked me to take him to a market to buy a frock for his daughter. He kept pushing away everything I showed him, saying that he wanted something cheaper. Eventually, I got so frustrated that I asked him what his problem was. We were in an ordinary bazaar, after all, and the frocks were fairly cheap. And what Niyogi told me was, "Jabbar, the people I organize wouldn't be able to afford these for their daughters. If my daughter, who plays with their children, is seen wearing far better clothes, how will they take me seriously? How will they see me as one of them, and not on the side of the owners and the moneylenders?"'

Niyogi was killed in the early nineties by thugs hired by the mill owners, although his wife has stayed on and continues to organize the mill workers. In the late eighties, Jabbar himself had come close to being killed when buying vegetables in the market one day. He was shot in the stomach by a man working for a slum landlord angered by Jabbar's advocacy on behalf of the tenants. The shooter was relatively inexperienced, so his aim faltered at the last minute even though he had got close to Jabbar.

But apart from that single dramatic incident, Jabbar's worries tended to be about prosaic things. He had a weak heart, and our conversations included breaks for the many pills he had to swallow. His organization operated on very little money – and although Sathyu had talked of Jabbar amassing money, I had seen no signs of such money on him, either at work or at home. The women in the organization made a little money from what Jabbar described as 'job work', which meant they made the stuffed toys that nobody bought, and stitched misshapen baseball caps and flags for political parties about to fight an election. Some money came from voluntary subscriptions from the members, and some from contributions made by well-wishers. The Honda scooter Jabbar rode had been bought with money given him by the writer Arundhati Roy. Hartosh, a friend of mine who had been a correspondent in Bhopal for four years, said that he had paid Jabbar's telephone bills on a few occasions.

Yet Jabbar disagreed with my view that he was ill-disposed towards people from the West or from cities like Delhi. 'I don't have anything against Greenpeace,' he said. 'But I want them to come down to my level when they are here. I don't want them to be in a hurry when they get here. I want them to slow down, to spend time with us, to allow us to get to know each other. We are not against the world or disinterested in what's happening elsewhere. Our Saturday rallies are the college we attend to find out more about other people. We have guest speakers who tell us about globalization, about the war in the Middle East, about religion and secularism.' He was pleased about the fact that he had convinced many of the Muslim women in the organization to get rid of the veil, and that he had Hindus and Muslims working closely together in an India that had become increasingly sectarian. 'It's a slow process. It takes time,' he said. 'But time is our ally.'

That seemed like a surprising comment to me. Time was the ally of the bureaucrat, the status quo-ist, I had always thought. Time, we are told, is our great enemy when we wish to effect social change, and it had certainly been the enemy of those people in Bhopal who had seen, over the years, the disaster fade in public memory and their own hopes diminish. Time had taken away the Bollywood good looks I had noticed in an old photograph of Jabbar's and forced him to swallow all those pills. It had made him less efficient than the younger Sathyu and marked him in his inability to exploit the Internet and the new mobility of the world.

One morning, Jabbar came to the hotel where I was staying. There was a coffee shop on the ground floor that was a popular meeting place for local journalists. They gathered there every morning for a couple of hours before heading to their newspaper offices or reporting beats, and Jabbar hoped to meet the journalists and hand out press releases about a compensation case coming up in the Supreme Court. Jabbar was popular with most of the local reporters, but his arrival that morning was upstaged by the appearance of a former chief minister, a Congress politician.

A smooth, fair-skinned man with gold-framed glasses and big teeth, the politician entered with followers and a television crew in tow. The reporters, most of whom I knew and thought of as committed journalists, were suddenly transformed, laughing at every joke the politician made and hanging on to every statement of his — even though he had begun with the announcement that he had come not for a press conference but for an 'intellectual' exchange. When Jabbar approached the table, the politician greeted him affably, but none of the reporters had time for the badly typed press releases Jabbar had brought with him.

It was like watching a force field of power distorting all within its range, twisting the faces of the reporters. Jabbar sat in the shadows, towards the back, waiting for an opportune moment to hand out his press releases. It didn't come. Instead, one of the politician's followers, a man with the ostentatious caste marks of the Brahmin on his forehead, whispered that it was his birthday.

The politician laughed with delight. 'We must celebrate,' he said, rubbing his hands together.

Another minion stepped forward and announced that it was his birthday as well.

'Even better,' the politician said. He snapped his fingers. 'Waiter, come here. Order birthday cakes from the pastry shop in the market.'

One of the reporters leaned forward and informed the politician that the birthday boys were vegetarians and that cakes would contain eggs as an ingredient.

'Eggless cakes, then,' the politician said, and the phrase ran like a refrain through the mouths of reporters and photographers, minions and waiters, as if the man had turned into Solomon solving, in an instant, the most fiendish of paradoxes.

Jabbar and I left just as the pink, eggless cakes arrived, borne high in the air by turbaned waiters and escorted to the table by a couple of the politician's armed security guards. Outside, in the lunchtime chaos of rickshaws, scooters and cars, I remarked to Jabbar that his venture to the hotel had been in vain.

'I'll come back tomorrow,' he said. 'Eventually, they will look at the press releases and write about them. The politician will be gone in an hour, but I will always be around.'

It took me a long time after I left Bhopal to understand that Jabbar had been right. I understood that his slow, stubborn activism was as much a story of the new India as the frenetic milieu of the call centre workers I had written about earlier in the year. I grew increasingly interested in these apparent opposites – visibility and invisibility, past and present, wealth and poverty, quietism and activism – as I returned to India over the next few years and criss-crossed a landscape that was sometimes intimately familiar and sometimes completely unknown. I wanted to write about the lives of individuals: the urban and the rural; the rich, the middle class and the poor; men and women; the technology-driven work that is seen as symptomatic of the new India as well as the exhausting manual labour that is considered irrelevant.

In each case, I tried to get inside the details of the stories of individuals, and although my own opinions are clear enough, I have tried to give every person his or her say. I haven't made anything up, but I am aware that I was the one who chose to pursue these characters and subjects and that my perspective may be as distorting as any, especially as I have chosen to tell only five stories from the countless stories available in a country of one billion people. In all cases but one, I have used real names for the main characters (there are a couple of minor characters whom I haven't named or whose names have been changed, but this is indicated in the text). The only exception among the main characters is Esther, the young waitress portrayed in the final chapter, who asked me to protect her identity.

Inevitably, the process of working on this book turned out to be more complicated than I had assumed. It ended up taking nearly five years from reporting to writing, and India itself changed in some significant ways as I went about my work. Yet I hope this is ultimately a unified narrative, the story of a vast, fascinating and grotesquely unequal country, an account of people who, either as celebrated representatives of the new India or as statistical details of the other, old India, might be able to tell us who they really are.

# The Great Gatsby: A Rich Man in India

*Finding a rich man — the controversial reputation of Arindam
Chaudhuri — the Satbari campus — the Power Brands Awards
Night — the ambassador of the world — cigar therapy — a leadership
seminar — the enemies — the aspirers — the namesake*

1

A phenomenally wealthy Indian who excites hostility and suspicion
is an unusual creature, a fish that has managed to muddy the waters it
swims in. The glow of admiration lighting up the rich and the successful disperses before it reaches him, hinting that things have gone
wrong somewhere. It suggests that beneath the sleek coating of luxury, deep under the sheen of power, there is a failure barely sensed by
the man who owns that failure along with his expensive accoutre-
ments. This was Arindam Chaudhuri's situation when I first met him
in 2007. He had achieved great wealth and prominence, partly by
projecting an image of himself as wealthy and prominent. Yet somewhere along the way he had also created the opposite effect, which
— in spite of his best efforts — had given him a reputation as a fraud,
scamster and Johnny-come-lately.

We'll come to the question of frauds and scams later, but it is indis-
putable that Arindam had arrived very quickly. It had taken him just
about a decade to build his business empire, but because his rise was
so swift and his empire so blurry, it was possible to be quite ignorant
of his existence unless one were particularly sensitive to the tremors
created by new wealth in India. Indeed, throughout the years of
Arindam's meteoric rise, I had been happily oblivious of him,
although once I had heard of him, I began to see him everywhere: in
the magazines his media division published, flashing their bright colours and inane headlines at me from little news-stands made out of

bricks and plastic sheets; in buildings fronted by dark glass where I imagined earnest young men imbibing the ideas of leadership disseminated by Arindam; and on the tiny screen in front of me on a flight from Delhi to Chicago when the film I had chosen for viewing turned out to have been produced by him. A Bombay gangster film, shot on a low budget, with a cast of unknown, modestly paid actors and actresses: was it an accident that the film was called *Mithya*? The word means 'lies'.

Still, I suppose we choose our own entanglements, and when I look back at the time in Delhi that led up to my acquaintance with Arindam, I realize that my meeting with him was inevitable. It was my task that summer to find a rich man as a subject, about the making and spending of money in India. In Delhi, there existed in plain sight some evidence of what such making and spending of money amounted to. I could see it in the new road sweeping from the airport through south Delhi, turning and twisting around office complexes, billboards and a granite-and-glass shopping mall on the foothills of the Delhi Ridge that, when completed, would be the largest mall in Asia. Around this landscape and its promise of Delhi as another Dubai or Singapore, I could see the many not-rich people and aspiring-to-be rich people, masses of them, on foot and on two-wheelers, packed into decrepit buses or squeezed into darting yellow-and-black auto-rickshaws, people quite inconsequential in relation to the world rising around and above them. The beggar children who performed somersaults at traffic lights, the boys displaying menacing moustaches inked on to their faces, made it easy to tell who the rich were amid this swirling mass. The child acrobats focused their efforts at the Toyota Innova minivans and Mahindra Scorpio SUVs waiting at the crossing, their stunted bodies straining to reach up to the high windows.

I felt that such scenes contained all that could be said about the rich in India, and the people I took out to expensive lunches offered me little more than glosses on the above. Mittal, Ambani, Dabur, Swarovski crystals, gold-plated toilets, stud farms, nightclubs, private aircraft. They sounded boring, unlike Arindam, who seemed a little different, with images and contradictions swirling around him:

ponytail, controversy, management guru, bloggers, business school, magazines, Bollywood movies.

'I've spoken to the boss about you,' Sutanu said. 'But the boss said, "Why does he want to meet me?"'

Sutanu ran the media division in Arindam's company. We met at Flames, an 'Asian Resto-Bar' up a steep flight of steps with a forlorn statue of Buddha tucked away in the corner, the view from the restaurant opening out to sanitary-goods stores, franchise eating outlets and large cars being squeezed into minuscule spaces by scruffy parking attendants. Sutanu was in his forties, a dark man with thick, clumpy hair parted to one side, a bushy moustache and glasses, his raffish 1960s air complemented by a bright-blue shirt and a red tie patterned with elephants. He was accompanied by Rahul, a studious-looking young man in kurta and jeans who worked at one of the magazines published by the company. Although they couldn't have been there long, their table gave an impression of a party that had been in progress through the morning and had peaked. It held two packs of Navy Cut cigarettes, a partly empty bottle of Kingfisher beer and a battered smartphone with a black-and-white screen that rang out in insistent drumbeats throughout our conversation.

'The boss is a great man, and sure, his story is interesting,' Sutanu said. 'The question is whether he'll talk to you.'

From what Sutanu told me that afternoon, Arindam was very much a man of the times. He had started out in 1996 with a lone business school called the Indian Institute of Planning and Management. Founded by Arindam's father, it had been – Sutanu said dismissively – a small, run-of-the-mill place located on the outskirts of Delhi. But Arindam had expanded it into nine branches in most of the major Indian cities, and he was now going international. He had an institute in Dubai, had tied up with a management school in Belgium with campuses in Brussels and Antwerp, was opening an institute in London by the end of the year, and would have another one in the United States, in an old factory building in Pennsylvania. And that was just the management institute. Arindam's company, Planman, had a media division that included a newsweekly, *The Sunday Indian*, 'perhaps the only magazine in the world with thirteen editions'. There were three business magazines, a software company, a consulting division that managed the 'HR component of multinationals', and a small outsourcing company. The outsourcing company was small only because it was new, but it already did the entire online content of the *Guardian* as well as the proofreading and copy-editing of the *Daily Mail*.

'There's also a film division, and he's produced a major Bollywood blockbuster,' Sutanu said.

'It was meant to be a blockbuster,' Rahul said quietly. 'But it flopped.'

'Yeah, yeah, no big deal,' Sutanu said. 'He's on other blockbuster projects. He's a man of ideas. So sometimes they flop.' He lit a cigarette and waved it around, the rings on his hand flashing. 'What he's doing, he's using intellectual capital to make his money. But people don't get that and because he's been bad-mouthed so much, he's become suspicious. He's been burned by the media. You know, cynical hacks they are. They make up stories that he's a fraud. A Johnny-come-lately. Everyone asks, "Yaar, but where does all that money come from?"'

There was a moment of silence as we contemplated this question.

'They don't ask these things of other businessmen,' Sutanu continued. 'That's because when the mainstream media does these negative stories on him, just hatchet jobs you know, they're serving the interests of the big industrialists. The industrialists don't like him because our magazines have done critical stories on them. The government doesn't like him and harasses him all the time. They say, "You can't use the word 'Indian' in the name of your management school because we don't recognize your school." That it's forbidden in the constitution to use "Indian" in the name of an educational institution unless it's been approved by the government. Something like that. They send us a letter every six months about this. Then, the elite types are after him. The Doon School, St Stephen's, Indian Institute of Management people. There were these bloggers – a *Business Today* journalist and a man who worked for IBM – who started writing silly stuff about him, saying that the institute doesn't give every student a laptop as promised in the advertisements. You want to know how he makes money? It's simple. There are two thousand students who pay seven lakhs[1] each. The operating costs are low – you know how much teachers get paid in India. So the money gets spun off into other businesses.'

We ate hot and sour soup and drank more beer, our conversation widening out into discussions about careers, lives and the unforgiving city of Delhi. Rahul, who had been a television journalist, told us a story about covering the war in Iraq and being arrested by Saddam Hussein's Republican Guard while crossing over the border from Jordan.

When it was time to depart, I felt reluctant to break up the drunken afternoon bonhomie. Nevertheless, I asked, 'When do I get to meet Arindam Chaudhuri?'

'The good thing about the boss is that he's a yes or no sort of person,' Sutanu replied. 'You'll find out in a couple of days whether he wants to meet you.'

The couple of days stretched into a week. Now that my interest in Arindam had grown, it was hard to miss his presence. Every newspaper and magazine I came across carried a full-page advertisement for the management school, with Arindam's photograph displayed prominently in the ads. It was the face of the new India caught in close-up view. His hair was swept back in a ponytail, dark and gleaming against a pale, smooth face, his designer glasses accentuating his youthfulness. He wore a blue suit in the picture, and his teeth were exposed in the kind of bright, white smile I associated with American businessmen and evangelists. But instead of looking directly at the reader, as businessmen and evangelists tend to do to assure people of their trustworthiness, Arindam was gazing at a distant horizon, as if along with the business he was promoting, there was some other elusive goal on his mind.

Beneath the picture, there was information about the Indian Institute of Planning and Management, with nine campuses in seven cities that encircled the Indian subcontinent and left vacant only a small

1 One lakh is 100,000. A crore is 100 lakhs or 10 million.

stretch of unconquered territory in the east. There were few details about the programme or admission requirements, but there were many small, inviting photographs of the Delhi campus: a swimming pool, a computer lab, a library, a snooker table, Indian men in suits and a blonde woman. Around these pictures, in text that exploded into a fireworks display of italics, exclamation marks and capital letters, were the perks given to students: 'Free Study Tour to Europe etc. for 21 Days', 'World Placements' and 'Free Laptops for All'. Stitching these disparate elements together was a slogan. 'Dare to Think Beyond the IIMs', it said, referring to the elite, state-subsidized business schools, and managing to sound promising, admonishing and mysterious at the same time.

I kept pestering Sutanu, calling and text-messaging him. Then it was done, an appointment made, and I entered the wonderland to meet Arindam Chaudhuri, the man in the picture, the management guru, the media magnate, the business school entrepreneur, the film producer, the owner of IT and outsourcing companies, to which we should add his claims of being a noted economist and author of the 'all-time best-sellers' *The Great Indian Dream* and *Count Your Chickens Before They Hatch*.

## 2

Arindam was a few shades darker than his picture, with glossy hair tied back in a ponytail. He wore a blue pinstriped suit, with a white shirt open a third of the way down his smooth, shaved chest. There were rings on his fingers and bright, sparkling stones on the frame of his designer glasses. He sported silver cufflinks on his sleeves, and argyle socks and shiny pumps on his feet. I felt under a mild sensory assault from all those glittering surfaces, but they were accompanied by a youthfulness that softened the effect. He was thirty-six, younger than me, with a boyish air that was particularly pronounced when he became sarcastic about his critics and rivals and said, 'Wow!'

We were meeting at the Delhi campus of IIPM, in a boardroom that looked out at an open-plan office to one side and to classrooms at the other end. The furniture was in bright shades of red and blue, with a projection screen flickering blankly on one wall. There were about fifty chairs in the room, most of them pushed to one side, and Arindam and I sat at one end of a long table, our chairs swivelled to face each other. The air conditioning was fierce, and after a couple of hours I began to feel cold in my summer garb of a short-sleeved shirt and cotton trousers, but Arindam went on speaking, slowing down only slightly when a worker brought us chicken sandwiches on paper plates and cups of Coca-Cola.

Like most of the new rich in India, Arindam hadn't started from scratch. He had inherited his management institute from his father, Malay Chaudhuri, who began it in 1973. But the original institute had hardly been cutting edge. The office, in a house in south Delhi, had been a family bedroom at night. As for Gurgaon, where the institute was located, 'it was the least developed place on earth'. I understood why Arindam wanted to emphasize this. Gurgaon, an area just across the Delhi border in the state of Haryana, is now a modern suburb, hosting office parks for multinationals, as well as condominiums and shopping malls. Forty minutes from south Delhi on the new highway, it is a satellite city serving India's upper-tier professional classes, offering a branch of the London department store Debenhams and an Argentinean restaurant serving imported beef. But in the seventies, when Arindam's father ran his management institute in Gurgaon, the place had been little more than an assortment of unpaved roads meandering through fields of wheat, with electricity and phone lines in short supply, a no-man's-land between Delhi and the vast rural hinterland of India where a management school would have seemed like just one more of those strange, minor cults that crop up in India from time to time.

The expansion, the acquisitions and the overdrive started only after Arindam entered the picture. He had wanted to go to college in the United States, but his father convinced him to enrol in the family institute as one of the first students in a new undergraduate programme in management. Before he had even graduated, he was teaching a course at the institute. 'I took advantage of being the director's son,' Arindam said, laughing but making it clear that he had been perfectly qualified to teach his fellow students. Three years after finishing his degree, he started a recruitment consulting firm. His rationale was that by getting into a position where he was hiring people for other companies, he would also be able to find jobs for IIPM graduates with his clients. The placement of IIPM graduates was a pressing problem at the time, and although Arindam would disagree, it remains a problem now, after all his success.

During those early years, however, Arindam's ambitions were disproportionate to his abilities and experience. He started a magazine and a research division, but the magazine closed quickly and his recruitment firm failed to take off. He had nothing to sell except himself. 'In 1997, I announced my first leadership workshop for senior executives under the banner "Become a great leader". My thinking was that if they can take leadership lessons from me, they will give me business. So they came, not realizing from the photos how young this guy was. And then it didn't matter, because that first workshop was a *rocking interactive supersuccess*.' His voice rose, his chin lifted with pride and he looked me in the eyes. 'That is how we built a brand.'

The drive to IIPM's campus, located roughly midway between Delhi and Gurgaon, is a fairly quick one. First come the temples of Chattarpur, modern structures with crenellated, fluted walls, where memories of old Hindu architecture have been transformed into a simple idea of excess. A gargantuan statue of Hanuman, the monkey god, stands with a mace on his shoulder, looking dismissively down at the traffic, while the temples sprawl endlessly on that flat landscape, each the capital of an imaginary Hindu kingdom that has never existed except in this shapeless present.

The road is dusty, sometimes empty, and sometimes crowded with vehicles ranging from small trucks to air-conditioned SUVs. There are occasional clusters of shops and houses, but they disappear quickly, giving way to large stretches of land partitioned off for the very rich. A few boutique hotels appear now and then, looking empty, but the land is mostly colonized by 'farmhouses' – weekend homes for the Delhi rich that celebrate wealth, and where entertainment for the guests can range from an American rock star on a downward career curve to upwardly mobile Ukrainian prostitutes. Nothing of this is visible from the road, of course, with the farmhouses closed off by walls, gates and security guards, and all I saw on my first drive along that route were walls edged with broken glass, the occasional flash of green from a well-tended lawn, the curve of a driveway where a gate had been left open, and a young peasant woman with a suitcase sitting in front of a large farmhouse.

It was amid these hotels and farmhouses that IIPM had its five-acre, high-walled Delhi campus. The gates were kept shut, and the campus had a sleepy air except when Arindam was due to arrive. On those occasions, the security guards hovered around the guardhouse in the front, looking at their watches and fingering their walkie-talkies. The scruffy management students on campus, who, in their odd assortment of blazers and flashy shirts, had the air of men just coming off an all-night wedding party, adjusted their postures, trying not to look as if they were loitering.

Arindam arrived in a blaze of activity, the gates being opened hurriedly for his metallic-blue luxury car, a million-pound Bentley Continental that coasted down the driveway and parked in front of the building lobby. Another flash of blue, another gathering of employees, and then Arindam was inside the building, leaving behind nothing but the frisson of his arrival and the Bentley gleaming in the fierce Delhi sun. The power and the glory! A million pounds! Custom-made in the mother country of England! A Bentley was the ultimate status symbol of the Indian rich – expensive and relatively uncommon. A business journalist, unaware that I knew Arindam, had told me the probably apocryphal story that Arindam had had the special paint scraped off when his car arrived from England, repainting it to a shade of blue that matched one of his favourite shirts.

The campus building was split along two levels. Most of the classrooms were on the basement floor, filled with the chatter of students, some of them dressed in suits if they happened to be attending a class in 'Executive Communications'. The ground floor contained a computer lab, a small library and some classrooms. On the other side of the panopticon boardroom was the open-plan office, with Planman employees at their computers and phones. They were mostly in their twenties and thirties, and although they looked busy, they didn't give the impression of running a global megabusiness. Arindam and his division heads referred to the people behind the desks as 'managerial staff', although when I introduced myself to one of the managers – a balding, middle-aged man – he seemed to be making cold calls, looking up numbers from a database and asking people if they were interested in taking management seminars.

Almost all the Planman employees – 90 per cent of them, according to Arindam – were former IIPM students. The same was true of the faculty members, who tended to morph from students to teachers as soon as they had finished their courses. Many of the faculty members did 'consulting' work for IIPM. Some, like Rohit Manchanda, a short, dapper man in a suit who probably would have been shorter without the unusually high heels of his shoes, taught advertising and headed Planman's small advertising agency. The dean of IIPM, Prasoon Majumdar, a man with a smart goatee, was also economics editor for the magazines published by Planman. Then there were the employees who were family members as well as former students. Arindam's wife, Rajita, a petite woman who drove a Porsche, had been a student of Arindam's before they got married and now taught Executive Communications. Arindam's sister's husband, a young man with shoulder-length hair, shirt left unbuttoned to reveal a generous expanse of chest and carrying a copy of *The Omnivore's Dilemma* when I first met him, was a former student, a faculty member and features and lifestyle editor of the magazines published by Planman.

When Arindam met his division heads, all of whom had been his classmates at IIPM, they joked and chatted for the first hour or so before turning to the work at hand. I sat in on a meeting one morning, and they seemed to derive immense collegial pleasure from demonstrating to me just how close-knit they were. 'We're like the Mafia,' Arindam said.

It was a comparison that had occurred to me, although there were other metaphors that also came to mind. They were like the Mafia in their suspicion of outsiders, like a dot.com in their emphasis on collegiality and like a cult in their belief in a mythology made up of

Arindam's personal history, management theories and the strange ways in which the company functioned. But perhaps all this is simply another way of saying that they were a business, operating through an unquestioning adherence to what their owner said and believed.

Arindam, in our first meeting, had explained to me in a monologue that lasted five hours that his business was built around the 'brand' of Planman Consulting, the group that includes the business school and numerous other ventures from media and motion pictures to a charitable foundation. To an outsider, however, the brand is Arindam. Even if his role is disguised under the description of 'honorary dean' of IIPM, the image of the business school and Planman is in most ways the image of Arindam Chaudhuri. With his quirky combination of energy, flamboyance, ambition, canniness – and even vulnerability – he is the promise of the age, his traits gathering force from their expression at a time in India when everything seems combustible, everyone is volatile and all that is solid melts into air.

### 3

One evening, after receiving a text-message invitation from one of Arindam's many minions, I showed up at the Park Royal Hotel in south Delhi. The auto-rickshaw I had flagged down took me past Select Citywalk, a new shopping mall in its final stages of construction, a pharaonic dream of glass and granite rising amid broken sidewalks where daily-wage labourers huddled under dwarfish tents made from sheets of plastic. The road to the Chirag Delhi crossing was jammed, the traffic squeezed into narrow lanes by a wide aisle in the centre where the government was trying to build a high-speed bus corridor. It remained crowded all the way on to the Ring Road, with buses, cars and motorcycles brawling for space, and I was relieved to get off outside the Park Royal, where a sign forbade auto-rickshaws from entering.

I walked up a steep driveway towards the brutalist, looming structure of the Park Royal. The traffic smog and summer heat gave way to an artificial chill as I stepped past the bowing doormen, and time itself seemed to slow down on the thick carpeting, anxious not to provoke the flashy Indians and foreign tourists wandering around the overpriced restaurants and handicraft shops. I was at the hotel to witness the 'Power Brands Awards Night' sponsored by *4Ps*, one of the three business magazines published by Arindam. The sign in the lobby announcing the event, gold letters arranged on a red board like an unfinished Scrabble game, was pathetically small, and it took me a while to find the place where the event was being staged.

There weren't too many people inside the Royal Ballroom auditorium on the eighth floor, and those attending seemed visibly impatient. The vast chandeliers loomed above rows of empty chairs, and on the stage, a projector played endless clips of motorcycles zooming along deserted highways. Eventually, people began to trickle into the front rows, men in suits whose expressions of self-content seemed to suggest that they were among the power brands being felicitated that night. After a while, a dapper, shaven-headed man showed up onstage to give out the awards. His name was A. Sandip and, in keeping with the multiplicity of roles held by people at Planman, he was a senior executive at the company, editor in chief of all the magazines and dean of the business school. Polite applause followed the handing out of each certificate and plaque, the claps punctuated by clips of revving motorcycles – Yamaha was an event sponsor and one of the power brands being celebrated – and then the ceremony was over. Smoke rose from the stage and a local band began belting out a Hindi pop song, asking the audience to start jiving as they sang.

But where was the audience? The auditorium had emptied out rapidly, while outside, in the passageway, the crowd was thick around the buffet tables laden with Western and Indian food, guests and waiters collaborating in a chaotic dance that involved plates piled with alarmingly red tandoori chicken. At the ends of the passageway, fresh-faced young women waited behind stacks of free Planman magazines, smiling hopefully but in futility; it was always going to be a losing contest with the tandoori chicken. I made my way past the buffet tables to the open-air balcony. It was packed, with people pressed hard against the bar, releasing cigarette smoke into the evening air while far below the traffic honked and swerved its way towards the brightly lit Nehru Place flyover.

Throughout the awards ceremony, Arindam had been standing at the back of the Royal Ballroom. When I returned from the bar, he was still there, shaking hands with people who stepped into the nearly empty auditorium and addressed him in low, conspiratorial voices. Arindam was dressed in blue, his clothes and slicked-back hair giving him a glamorous look amid the Indians and the Japanese (presumably representatives of Yamaha) wearing staid suits or chinos and polo shirts and the IIPM students (or Planman employees) in their uniform-like formals. Even the band – the men in tight jeans and sleeveless shirts, the women in sequinned skirts – couldn't compete with Arindam's star value, serving as no more than a noisy backdrop for the primary business of the evening.

As I watched people circling around Arindam in the Royal Ballroom, it seemed to me that the evening was not so much about the recognition of other companies and products as about making a statement on the Arindam power brand and *his* 4Ps (product, price, place and promotion). This was why Arindam was working instead of lining up for the buffet, shaking hands and exchanging small talk. I hovered near him, receiving swift appraising glances from the strangers delivered to Arindam by an efficient assembly line of ambition. Those meeting him expressed deference, desire and nervousness; some were matter-of-fact, one business tycoon talking to another, as it were; others were proprietorial, expressing mild outrage that he hadn't noticed them yet or that they would have to wait for the person ahead of them to finish; a few, it seemed to me, concealed hostility even as they ingratiated themselves with him. The only time I saw Arindam get away from the constant handshaking, from the pleasantries and the promises, was when Doordarshan, the government television channel, interviewed him on the state of the economy, taking him to a small lobby and posing him in front of a painting of an Indian raja with a resplendent moustache and red robes.

There would presumably have been more glamorous television channels at the event if Arindam had been at the very top of the pecking order of wealth. Or was it that – as Sutanu had suggested – the largest media organizations were spurning him for his anti-elitism, for the crusading zeal of his magazines? They had certainly embraced him wholeheartedly when he first became a celebrity. At the IIPM campus in Satbari, I had picked up a brochure that featured a double-page spread of the articles that appeared when Arindam first made his mark as 'The Guru with a Ponytail'. The earliest pictures displayed a baby face; the designer glasses were not yet part of his appearance. Indistinguishable from press releases, these articles reproduced Arindam's thoughts on everything from 'how not to create more Osamas' (the solution, apparently, was 'wholesome education') to 'the MBA mafia' monopolizing management education in the country through the IIMs. But if Arindam was 'Guru Cool' in these articles, he was also combative (and the combative stance certainly enhanced the 'cool'), attacking the IIMs and pushing his 'Theory i Management' (the lower-case 'i' stood for 'india') to speak about a compassionate form of capitalism that took into account the overwhelming presence of poverty in the country. He talked about 'trickle-down economics' and 'survival of the weakest', and although it was never clear from these extracts how such concepts could actually be put into practice, they exhibited Arindam's desire to project himself as a thinker as well as an entrepreneur.

But Arindam's desire for greater influence also created a conflict with his closed style of running the company. Within Planman, he was surrounded by loyalists, people who subscribed to the cult of Arindam. Relatives became colleagues, while former students and classmates became employees and continued to refer to him in the nice, middle-class Indian way as 'Arindam sir'. The employees were so enamoured of Arindam that when I visited him at the IIPM campus or stood near him at the Power Brands Awards Night, some of them displayed a barely disguised hostility. Upset at the proximity I had stolen, sensing perhaps that I did not entirely share their faith in the guru, that I was not one of them, they seethed with the desire to protect Arindam from me.

Yet Arindam's business could not be contained entirely within the walls of Planman. It had a centrifugal force to it, spiralling outwards. In June 2005, nearly a decade after his first failed attempt at starting a magazine, Arindam began publishing a business magazine called *B&E*. This

led to the newsweekly *The Sunday Indian*, and to the marketing magazine *4Ps*. They were all printed on glossy paper, heavy on graphics and
syndicated material, thin on original content and, going by the mis-
spelled names appearing on *The Sunday Indian* covers ('Pamela
Andreson'), short of copy editors. In 2007, Arindam began bringing out
an Indian edition of *PC Magazine* under licence from Ziff Davis Media.
At the same time, he began discussions with *Foreign Affairs* in New York
to bring out an Indian edition of the magazine, and when that fell
through, he began negotiations with *Foreign Policy* in Washington, DC.

'In the school, I have an audience of only six thousand students,'
he had said to me. 'Now, every week, I reach one lakh people.'

The business schools also produced 'academic' journals with names
like *The Indian Economy Review*, *The Human Factor*, *Strategy Journal* and
*Need the Dough?* But the most significant arena of influence was occupied by films, turning Arindam almost into a household name.

In 2002, Arindam had entered the movie business. A few days
before his first Bollywood film was to be shot, Arindam said, the
director walked out on him. Arindam, naturally, decided to direct
the film himself. He admitted to me that he had perhaps not been
entirely qualified to do this. 'But I hope, some day, when I have more
experience, to make a truly revolutionary film.' Without the necessary experience, his first directorial venture turned out to be neither
revolutionary nor a blockbuster. With a plot that had been lifted
from the American comic strip *Archie*, it was a commercial flop and
panned by critics. Even the DVD stores in the Palika Bazaar underground market that specialized in cinema of all kinds, mostly in
pirated editions, were unable to procure a copy for me, and the only
interesting thing about the film seemed to be its title, *Rok Sako to Rok
Lo*, which translates into *Stop Me if You Can*.

4

A country that has seen a sudden infusion of wealth and a rapid dis-
engagement with its past tends to throw up people who are travelling
very quickly and seem to have no clear antecedents. A few days after

I attended the power brands ceremony, an email from a friend directed me to the annual world wealth report produced by the investment banking firm Merrill Lynch, which had ranked India, with 100,000 millionaires, as the world's second-fastest producer of millionaires, running just behind Singapore. It made me think of a factory producing millionaires at high speed, and when I surfed around on the Internet, checking out related articles from *Forbes* and *The Economist*, I felt as if I had been granted a slightly dizzying satellite vision of the country, one remarkably different from the view on the ground.

There were carefully produced graphics on these websites, with towers thrusting out from the flat map of India, their different heights announcing the amount and concentration of personal wealth in the country. Bombay, now known as Mumbai, had the tallest tower, which made sense. There, India's richest man Mukesh Ambani (who, in a piece of news concocted by the Indian media, had become the world's richest man in October 2007, ahead of Bill Gates and Warren Buffett) planned to build a skyscraper in the most expensive area of the city. Sixty storeys high, it would have just twenty-seven floors because of its vertiginously high ceilings. And the only residents in the building apart from the Ambani family would be their retinue of 600 servants.

A little over forty years ago, the *New Yorker* writer Ved Mehta visited the country of his birth and wrote a piece called 'The Richest Man in India'. This august personage, according to Mehta, was not an industrialist or a politician. He was the Nizam of Hyderabad, a southern ruler who had been stripped of his monarchy and much of his wealth by the Indian state in the years following independence in 1947. Although the Nizam was a political nonentity by the time Mehta wrote about him, he was still reputed to be the richest man in India and one of the richest in the world. Leafing through the pages of an official biography, Mehta found the Nizam described as 'a national asset of incalculable value', especially in a modernizing India whose 'most crying need is liquid investable capital'.

The passage of four decades has seen to it that India is awash in liquid investable capital, if only in select areas, and the Nizam appears even more of an oddity now than he did to Mehta at the time. A five-foot-three, ninety-pound waif who took his meals on a tin plate while squatting on a mat, the Nizam's relation to his personal wealth was royally idiosyncratic, supremely indifferent to portfolio diversification or conspicuous consumption.

Every age gets the rich people it deserves. In contemporary India, the new rich are the anti-Nizams. They are people in a hurry, expressing fevered modes of consumption, flaunting gargantuan appetites meant to astonish and dazzle the rest of us. They acquire things that are better, bigger and more exclusive, and while coolly expecting public admiration, they also attempt to carve out their own affluent nations, towers from the tops of which float prayers in a strange language, expressing desires that most of us can't comprehend. This is because there is a paradox at the heart of such affluence, where each rich individual, while being celebrated for his or her wealth, also expects to be something other than his or her wealth. People are the amount of money they make, but even in the world of the Indian rich, that is no longer enough.

This paradox of wealth became evident to me one evening at the Delhi Gymkhana Club, a formerly colonial establishment sited next to the prime minister's residence. I had been taken there by friends amused by my interest in India's new money. After we parked the car and walked past empty rooms with high ceilings, and long corridors featuring sepia tints of colonial clubgoers, we entered a crowded and noisy bar. From our corner table, chosen for its sweeping view, I watched the generously proportioned Delhi residents − businesspeople, civil servants and politicians − consume subsidized food and liquor, ringing little bells to call waiters to their overflowing tables. It was Thursday, a dance night at the club, and as the evening progressed, a sizeable contingent of the city's youth appeared on the scene, sending the middle-aged men in the crowd into a frenzied search for prospective partners among the young women in tight jeans.

The man who approached our table soon after the dancing began possessed a shock of white hair, a bushy moustache and two gold chains under his green polo shirt. My friends introduced us, but it was hard for me to make out what he did above the rendition of 'Hava Nagila' from the club band.

'I work for the world,' he said.

It seemed an especially unlikely claim in that setting, and I felt compelled to ask, 'Yes, but what exactly do you do for the world?'

'Ambassador,' he said. 'I am an ambassador for the world.'

He looked at my friends, looked at me and smiled at his private joke. Then he passed me his business card, which read:

> # THE WORLD
>
> ### Abhai Varma
>
> Ambassador
>
> *www.aboardtheworld.com*

*The World* was a cruise ship sailing across the globe, registered in the Bahamas and managed by a Miami-based company. Varma wanted to impress upon me just how exclusive this cruise ship was. People bought an *apartment* on the ship – *apartment* was the word he emphasized with some violence, just as he had emphasized *world* and *ambassador* before – for half a million dollars, at the very least. The money covered all expenses incurred on board, and the amount of money paid determined the number of votes residents had, who then, through the democratic exercise of their voting powers, determined the itinerary of the ship. When people went ashore, they partied, paying out of their own pockets for the pleasures of terra firma, but they tended to live more quietly on the ship, dabbling in refined pleasures like haute cuisine and art. Americans formed a large part of the contingent, but there were many Indians as well, and Varma's role was to match the right people from the Indian subcontinent to this floating signifier of his. *The World* was a cruise ship, its ambassador a salesman.

As for the clients, those who bought a piece of the world, Varma was both guarded about them and insistent about their *exclusivity*. He wouldn't give me the names of his clients, usually picked out from marketing lists compiled by companies like American Express, but he said that he had to see that people wouldn't board *The World* and start talking about the amount of money they had made.

I understood why Varma was concerned that people might talk about money on board the ship. India was full of people talking about money. Just half an hour earlier, in the men's room, I had passed a drunken group listening to a man who was saying, 'All the people I went to school with, they became doctors, engineers. I'm the one who became an ordinary garment exporter.' He waited a beat before delivering his punchline. 'I earn a hundred times more than them,' he said, producing a burst of appreciative, alcohol-fuelled laughter from his listeners.

To avoid such situations, Varma encouraged each prospective client to make a short trip on *The World* at a cost of $1,500 a day. 'That's the stage,' he said, 'when having dinner with other apartment owners, he'll learn not to flash his wealth. Everyone around him will be super rich, and they'll consider him crude if he talks about money. Either he'll learn to shut up, or he'll get off at the next port and not come back.'

Manish was used to rich people who talked about money. He was a pleasant young man, handsome in a generic way and with a veneer of softness that made him good at his business as a cigar dealer. He was one of India's two cigar importers, insinuating his products into hotels, bars and clubs, serving not only affluent metropolises like Delhi but also the second-tier cities that were full of people he described as 'aspirational'. Manish started laughing when he talked about these aspirational people, but he was accommodating in every way possible to the whims of his customers. For those in Delhi, he held monthly gatherings, usually sponsored by liquor companies, where men sat around on stuffed leather couches, learning the fine art of cigar smoking in relative privacy and connecting with each other through a dense haze of smoke. But Manish also delivered cigars to the homes of his clients, to business celebrations and wedding parties, ready with suggestions if people were uncertain about which cigars might make the greatest impression on their guests.

I had gone to see Manish in his shop, a glass-fronted store called 'Kastro's Cigars'. From the store, one looked out on to the winding walkways and upscale boutiques of the Santushti Shopping Complex, all of it built to a scale so small as to look like a shopping mall from Legoland. It could have been one of the more expensive retail complexes in America were it not for the fact that the land was owned by the Indian Air Force, and the cigars and designer handbags were being sold only a short walk from an airbase guarded by dour soldiers with thick moustaches and big rifles. The rents were subsidized, and the shops were offered only to senior defence personnel and their relatives, or to those with political contacts.

On the afternoon I visited Manish's store, we sat by ourselves in the front section. He had one employee, a Mizo woman from the north-eastern part of India dressed smartly in a Western suit. She brought us cappuccinos from a nearby Parsi restaurant and receded into the background, while we lounged on the armchairs, looking out at the shoppers trickling through the boutiques, at heavily jewelled women holding the hands of thickset men, and an ayah with a pushchair following a mother and her friend. Behind us, separated by a picture window and a door, was the temperature-controlled part of the shop where the cigars were kept on partitioned shelves running along one wall. On one side of the shelves were copies of *Cigar Aficionado*, while on the other end were lockers where customers kept their stock, each locker the distillation of a life.

Manish's best customer, the one whose locker held the most expensive cigars – Cohibas, a box of twenty-five selling in Manish's shop for 27,000 rupees – was someone who never smoked them. They were gifts for bureaucrats and politicians, people who were useful to his business. I could build a personality from that detail, and it was tempting to do so. I thought of the wheeling and dealing the nameless man was involved in: was it my imagination that Manish seemed slightly nervous, a little wary, when we talked about the owner of this particular locker? I thought of the self-control and possibly orthodox social and religious views that kept the man from smoking the cigars, as well as his ruthless ability to direct the gratifications of people useful to him. What vices would such a man have?

Manish couldn't, or wouldn't, tell me about the vices of this customer, but he had much to say about his other clients. His job, in many ways, was to assuage the insecurities of his rich customers, and he described them to me with anthropological pleasure. There were tycoons who would bargain furiously with him, asking for a 10 per cent discount; there were others who had temporary cash-flow problems and required credit; there were Sikhs who needed their cigars to be smuggled to them so that they would not be seen to be breaking a religious taboo; there were people who asked after their friends, also clients of Manish's, and then dismissed them as charlatans, dissemblers and criminals; there were men who talked about their marital and sexual problems; and there were those who wanted the handsome young Manish's approval of the hot mistress or prostitute they had acquired. Like a therapist at a private session, Manish listened to them all, taking care never to smoke cigars in public places so that his clients wouldn't feel he was competing with them.

'They're loud and brash because they don't know how much money they've made,' he said. 'They don't know who they are.' These were men whose self-control was a thin veneer, Manish said. 'You see such a man walk in aggressively and loudly, look flustered when he realizes that he has to go through a second door to reach the temperature-controlled section, and who closes the second door much too loudly when he finally goes in.'

A man in his late twenties came into the store, dressed American-style in wrap-around sunglasses, shorts and big white sneakers. Manish immediately became polite and deferential.

'I'll come back later,' the customer said, 'but can I take one of these matchboxes?'

'Of course, of course,' Manish said. 'Take a few,' he said, scooping them out of the tray and pressing them into the customer's hand.

'What's his background?' I asked after the customer had left.

'Family money,' Manish said with a touch of derision.

'How do you know?'

'Look at the clothes he was wearing. Too old to be in college but not smart enough to be in university. Doesn't need to go to work, so he can wander around in shorts on a weekday afternoon.'

Underneath Manish's smooth, solicitous manner, there was a resentment about the men he dealt with. He himself had struggled to get to where he was now, but he still had far less money than his clients. We stepped out of the shop and began walking through the complex as Manish told me the story of how he had entered the cigar business. He had wanted to be a pilot, and in order to pursue this objective he had enrolled in a flying school in Kansas. Like many Indians of his class and background, he had noticed almost nothing about America except its business opportunities and what had seemed to him to be an orderly and regulated public life. He had held numerous odd jobs, including at a nightclub, where he observed, with some perplexity, the popularity of cigars. When he came back to India with his pilot's licence, he apparently couldn't find a job. Manish's mother had a shop – this very one – selling imported artificial flowers, and Manish took it over. By his own account, he was drifting and unhappy. He was very close to his mother, with whom he still lived, but estranged from his father, who had been in the air force. Manish began thinking of selling cigars, and so he approached the man who was the only cigar importer in India. This man was much older than Manish and the cigars were simply a sideshow for him. His main business since the sixties had been as an arms dealer.

Manish entered into an uneasy partnership with the arms dealer, who agreed to supply him with cigars for a very high share of the profits. In 2000, Manish opened what he described as 'the first cigar lounge in India'. It was at the Park Royal in Nehru Place, the hotel that Arindam used for his company's events and to which I would return in a few days to attend a leadership session conducted by Arindam. But as Manish started doing well in the cigar business, his partner began demanding an even bigger share of the profits. When Manish tried to talk to him about this, he threatened to cut off the supply.

The problem with cigars, Manish said, was that they were a controlled luxury commodity. The arms dealer had moved into importing cigars because he was already importing weapons. 'There is a strong relation between the two,' Manish said, and in fact, when I met Manish again a couple of years later, he himself had expanded into the 'security' business. The fact that rich Indians could afford to smoke Cuban cigars, Manish said, depended on the political situation in Cuba. 'One hundred and sixty million cigars a year, that's it, that's all they produce,' he said. 'But there's been an El Tardes office in Florida for ten years, ready to swing into action when Castro dies.' When that happened, he said, Americans would move into the Cuban cigar market and that would be the end of smoking Cohibas for many people elsewhere in the world.

When Manish's relationship with the arms dealer broke down, he became desperate. He no longer had access to cigars and began calling exporters all over the world to arrange for a fresh source of supply. All the men he contacted refused to do business with him. They were already represented by the arms dealer in India and had no reason to enter into new arrangements with an unknown young man. Manish had very little money and just a couple more numbers to call, one of them belonging to a sheikh in Bahrain. He decided to meet directly with the man. He bought a ticket with the last of his money, flew to Bahrain and met with the sheikh. When the sheikh heard Manish's story, he was so amused that he agreed to supply him with cigars, even giving him credit at the beginning.

It was the kind of striving that Manish couldn't find among his customers. I got the sense that in his mind they were like the arms dealer, coasting along, building on a success that had been present in their lives from the very beginning. They were brash and vulgar on the surface, and cheap and insecure underneath.

'There is a certain kind of man who will walk in and say, "Show me the most expensive cigar you have,"' Manish said when we returned to his store. 'And what I will do right away is relieve the pressure that such a man obviously feels. I'll say, "Don't even go for this one." As soon as I say that and make it seem that the best cigar is not necessarily the most expensive one, he feels released from the need to spend as much money as possible in order to assert himself. I listen to this man and talk to him for a while and then he'll tell me what he really wants. "Forget it, *yaar*," he'll say. "I'm going to a party and I just want a long cigar that I can show everyone."'

'So what do you do when he says this?' I asked Manish.

'I tell him that he can buy a seven-inch cigar for fourteen hundred rupees, but he can also buy another seven-inch cigar for four hundred rupees. He'll happily take the cheaper one. Size is all that matters.'

## 5

One evening in September, I went back to the Royal Ballroom auditorium of the Park Royal Hotel to hear Arindam speak. I had heard him address a crowd before, but that had been a familiar audience, made up of graduating students herded into a hotel auditorium near the Satbari campus. The students had seemed awestruck but were also restless, their attention wandering whenever the talk veered away from the question of their future to trickle-down theory, no doubt because they were more concerned with trickle-up. Arindam hectored them a little, and he had been worried enough about this to send me a text message a few hours later, asking me to 'discount some of the harsh words i said to students'.

The event at the Royal Ballroom was different. It was the final performance in a day-long 'leadership' seminar for which people had paid 4,000 rupees each, the previous speakers having included Arindam's wife, A. Sandip and other IIPM professors and Planman employees. Over a hundred people, quite a few women among them, sat under the chandeliers as a laptop was set up on the stage. They looked aspirational rather than polished corporate types, the men with red sacred threads around their wrists, the women in saris and salwar kameezes, a gathering of middle-class, middle-rung, white-collar individuals whose interest in leadership skills had a rather dutiful air to it. After a number of children – it was unclear to whom they belonged – had clustered around Arindam to get copies of the all-time best-seller *Count Your Chickens Before They Hatch* signed, Arindam went up on to the stage. He was wearing a shiny black corduroy suit, the jacket displaying embroidery on the shoulders, and loafers that seemed to be made of snakeskin.

Arindam wasn't a natural speaker. In prolonged one-to-one conversations, he had the tendency to look away, not meeting the listener's gaze. This wasn't quite such a problem in a public gathering, but he also had a high-pitched voice and a tendency to fumble his lines at the beginning. He started that evening by asking people what leadership meant to them. As his listeners spewed out their answers, using phrases ('dream believer', 'reaching the objective', 'making decisions', 'simplifying things') that seemed to have been lifted from some ur-text of self-help and management, they seemed both eager and slightly combative, as if they were not entirely convinced of his ability to teach them about leadership. 'Here's the *great* Arindam Chaudhuri,' a man next to me muttered, using 'great' in the Indian way to mean someone fraudulent. Arindam seemed aware of the hostility. His responses were rather hesitant and his English sounded uncertain and pronouncedly Delhi middle class in its inflection.

As the session went on, however, it became evident that these qualities weren't drawbacks, not among the people he was addressing. The mannerisms gave Arindam an everyday appeal, and it was the juxtaposition of this homeliness with his wealth, success and glamour that created a hold over the leadership aspirants in the audience. By themselves, the Bentley Continental, the ponytail and the designer glasses, or the familiar way Arindam had of dropping names like Harvard, McKinsey and Lee Iacocca, would have made him much too remote. But the glamour was irresistible when combined with his middlebrow characteristics. He was one of the audience, even if he represented the final stage in the evolution of the petite bourgeoisie.

From the way Arindam played on the sensibilities of his audience throughout the evening, he was well aware of this. If he wasn't a natural speaker, he nevertheless had that ability of performers to gather strength the longer they stay up on the stage. His energy was unflagging, as I discovered in my first interview, which had gone on for five hours. And after about thirty minutes into the leadership session, as I began to be drawn into his patter, I felt that Arindam was telling the rising Indian middle class a story about itself, offering them an answer to the question of who they were. 'I am trying to be a mirror,' he said, a comment remarkably insightful in the way he represented a larger-than-life version of the people in the audience.

His listeners had come to the session with a rough sense of who they were supposed to be. They received feedback about this from the culture at large, from the proliferating media outlets that obsessed about them as members of 'India Shining' (the phrase coined by the BJP government in 2004 to describe the new India), and they were characterized in a similar manner by the West. They knew that as middle-class, well-to-do Indians, they were supposed to be modern and managerial. They were characterized as a people devoted to efficiency, given to the making of money and the enjoyment of consumer goods while retaining a touch of traditional spice, which meant that they did things like use the Internet to arrange marriages along caste and class lines.

Still, they needed reaffirmation of the role they were playing, and this is what Arindam provided, distilling down for them that cocktail of spurious tradition and manufactured modernity, and adding his signature flavour to the combination. He told his listeners stories about travelling to America, Europe and Japan. These, after all, were the nodes of the modern world, places that middle-class India was emulating and suddenly found within its reach. Yet the modern world was also remote; not many of the people in the audience had been there, and even if they had gone to these places, they would not have encountered them with any degree of intimacy. The very sites they were most drawn to – the business centres, the shopping plazas, the franchise restaurants, the tourist spots and the airports – would appear slightly illusory, never really experienced in spite of the photographs taken, the souvenirs bought and the money spent.

In the Royal Ballroom, though, these places were rendered anecdotally and brought down to the same plane as the India the audience knew – or the India they thought they knew. So there were jokes about national stereotypes, comments about the different strengths and weaknesses of the Americans, the Japanese, the French and the Indians. There were no individuals in these stories, merely nameless businessmen being met by Arindam in anonymous boardrooms, and the world itself seemed no more than a string of Royal Ballrooms, each dominated by a different ethnic group of capitalists.

After Arindam had given the audience this touch of the foreign, he came home to more familiar territory, turning to the established prejudices of his audience. He made fun of regional Indian identities, something done more easily in a largely Hindi-speaking, Delhi crowd that tended to see itself as national. He pandered to their middle-class prejudices, attacking the government as inefficient and corrupt, but he also satisfied their nationalism by praising the Indian Army as the most efficient and disciplined wing of the state.

As Arindam became more comfortable, he started slipping into Hindi, segueing into the story of the Mahabharata as a way of approaching his 'Theory i Management' concept of leadership. Like many contemporary Hindus who have tried to cut out of their sprawling range of beliefs the hard lines of a modern faith, Arindam wasn't interested in the complex ethical questions or sophisticated narrative strategies of the Mahabharata. Instead, his focus was on the Bhagavadgita, originally not much more than a long episode in the Mahabharata where Arjuna, wracked by doubt on the eve of going into battle against friends and family, is given a speech on duty by the god Krishna.

The Gita emerged as a foundational religious text only in modern times, when Hindu revivalists reeling from colonialism sought something more definitive than the amorphous set of practices and ideas that had characterized Vedic religion until then. It received a new life again in the early nineties when the Indian elites simultaneously embraced free-market economics and a hardened Hindu chauvinism. They discovered in the Gita an old, civilizational argument for maintaining the contemporary hierarchies of caste, wealth and power, while in the story of Arjuna throwing aside his moral dilemmas and entering wholeheartedly into the slaughter of the battlefield, they read an endorsement of a militant, aggressive Hinduism that did not shirk from violence, especially against minorities and the poor. Given this appeal of the book among the Indian middle and upper classes, Arindam's use of it was a canny choice. He was extending into the realm of management theory a story that his audiences would be both familiar with and respectful towards, so that to challenge Arindam's ideas would be tantamount to questioning a sacred text.

Arindam began the elaboration of his theories, naturally enough, by pulling a red Gita out of a pocket. A Planman photographer ran forward frantically to capture the moment and, for the first time in the session, the audience began scribbling notes. Arindam turned to the laptop as if he was going to boot Krishna and Arjuna into existence, but the laptop refused to cooperate. As one, two, three and then four people gathered around the laptop, trying unsuccessfully to get it to display slides, Arindam gave up, turned away from the computer, and faced the audience.

Recovering rapidly from the technological failure, he began a performance that was part television soap and part stand-up comedy, hamming the roles of housewives, husbands returned from work, fathers and babies, management trainees and their bosses, the audience bursting into laughter as each little cameo was played out. The laptop had been finally made to work, and on the screen floated a matrix of different character types Arindam had extracted from Hindu scriptures. There was the *tamas* or pleasure-loving type, who could be led only by domination; the *rajas*, ambitious but greedy, who needed a combination of encouragement and control; and the *satvic*, who was brilliant and talented and needed to be left alone. 'Leadership is about changing your colours like a chameleon to suit the situation,' Arindam said, citing Krishna, the androgynous, slippery god, as the role model for the ideal CEO. Labourers or blue-collar workers were *tamasic*, young management trainees *rajasic* and highly skilled professionals like research scientists were *satvic*. He had reinvented the caste system in two hours.

Arindam finished to all-round applause, and as he came down the stage, he was mobbed by his listeners. I went outside to the passageway, where *tamasic* workers in overalls were rapidly installing gates decorated with marigold garlands for a wedding reception that would take place later in the evening. I sat on one of the couches, next to a middle-aged, dishevelled-looking man in a suit who was holding a plastic shopping bag that said 'More Word Power'.

He had attended the entire day's session, and when I asked him what he had thought of it, he said that it had been interesting. Some of the earlier speakers had been good and he had been especially impressed by A. Sandip.

'And what did you think of Arindam Chaudhuri's talk?' I asked.

'Rubbish. It made no sense at all,' he said. He fell silent, avoiding my gaze, and when he looked at me again, it was with embarrassment. 'You are a friend? You work for the company?' He cheered up as soon as he found out that I was writing about Arindam. 'The man is a fraud,' he said, 'but a very successful one.'

He was a small publisher who churned out language education books. He would be releasing a management book during the World Book Fair in Delhi in February, a work written by a Canadian living in Beijing. 'It is mostly China-focused. You are aware that there is great interest in China these days? So I wanted to have an event like this for the Canadian during the book fair, and I decided to come and see this. You are writing about Arindam Chaudhuri?' He handed me his business card, leaned towards me, chuckled and said, 'You *must* find out how he makes his money.'

## 6

Arindam had told me a story about his childhood that involved a strike at his father's management school in Gurgaon. He described the strikers as 'rowdy elements', students who had failed their courses and objected to the academic discipline imposed on them. The strike climaxed in a telephone call late one night to his father. An anonymous man, speaking hurriedly, said that a student had been stabbed on campus. Arindam's father took a taxi, accompanied by one of his employees, a canteen manager. Around 200 metres from the campus, he saw a group of students, armed with iron rods, waiting for him. He asked the driver to turn around, came home and took his family to a hotel. The stabbing had been a ruse to bring him to the campus, and even the canteen manager accompanying him had been part of the conspiracy.

The strike continued for four months. When the Chaudhuri family eventually moved back from the hotel to their home, they were greeted by protesting students. 'They were carrying horrible placards calling us thieves and murderers,' Arindam said. 'The neighbours, who talked to the students, began calling my father "Bada Chor" ("Big Thief") and me "Chota Chor" ("Little Thief").' But what was most distressing about the incident, Arindam said, was that they eventually discovered that members of the faculty were behind the strike, inciting the students. 'All the people we trusted were involved, and I decided that I would not let this happen ever again.'

It was a touching story, a young boy seeing his father threatened by enemies and deciding to take them on. 'My father named me Arindam,' the grown-up man in front of me said. 'That means "destroyer of enemies".' Since he had been named a decade and a half before the incident, Arindam's father had either possessed a remarkably clear ability to foresee the future or a pronounced sense of enemies lurking everywhere. But the enemies, whether those drifting through Arindam's father's mind or the people I had been told about, were abstractions. The rowdy students, the traitorous canteen manager and the conspiratorial faculty members had no discernible motives in the story Arindam told me. They were there mostly to provide an opposition so that Arindam could have a motive for his success. They were also present to demonstrate a lesson about how people couldn't be trusted. It was as if Arindam was explaining to me why his business was so close-knit; why outsiders were viewed with suspicion by people in his organization; why his public relations person had demanded, unsuccessfully, that I show him everything I wrote; and why this same person refused to respond to the most elementary queries about the company's business practices or its revenues. There was more than the usual organizational secrecy at work here. Instead, a fundamental vision of life was involved, and underneath all the expansive theories of management with solutions for every problem in existence, below all the chatter of a world brought closer by corporate globalization, there was, ultimately, only this Manichean idea of people divided into the loyal and the disloyal, of Arindam at odds with the rest of the world.

This sense of tribalism had become especially pronounced after Arindam became successful. He had started, he said, by competing with the 'mafia' of management education in the country, but he provoked them beyond endurance by beginning a media division.

'The elite now saw that I was challenging them directly, in the realm of ideas.' He was no longer operating merely within the confines of business schools but in society as a whole, breaking down 'the establishment hold on thought'. Arindam's voice dropped low. 'That is the reason why I am hated by a lot of people.'

He had a specific incident in mind that involved a harsh piece about his institute by a woman who was an alumna of the elite IIM Ahmedabad business school. 'It was the world's most stupid article,' Arindam said, adding that he couldn't remember the name of the journalist. The article, which came out a couple of years earlier, was commented upon and linked to by a blogger, who was then sent a letter by Arindam's legal department, objecting to his characterization of the institute. 'We had no clue on what is the blogger world,' Arindam said. He found out soon enough, as other bloggers retaliated. Their attacks were picked up by the mainstream media, including a magazine called *Businessworld*. The war between Arindam and the establishment intellectuals was out in the open.

Because much of the skirmishing against Arindam took place on the Web, it is relatively easy, if somewhat overwhelming, to find out what the bloggers and other critics had to say. The journalist whose name Arindam couldn't remember was Rashmi Bansal. She had written the original offending article 'The Truth Behind IIPM's Tall Claims' in *JAM* (*Just Another Magazine*), a small periodical that she published herself and that was targeted at a youthful, English-speaking crowd. Her article said that IIPM's advertising was misleading: only the Delhi campus had the facilities prominently displayed in the pictures (from swimming pool to library), and the campuses in other cities were housed in crowded office buildings; the scholars from institutions like Wharton, NYU, Columbia and Harvard claimed as 'visiting faculty' were people who had just passed through, delivering one-off lectures; the degrees IIPM awarded were not recognized by the Indian government; the company fudged data from media surveys to claim top rankings; and contrary to its claims, it had not placed its students in multinational concerns like McKinsey.

These allegations led to a sudden scrutiny of IIPM. *Businessworld*, where Bansal was a columnist, reported that it had accepted Arindam's request to look fairly into the case for and against his institute, but was fobbed off with generalities about IIPM and its enemies when it asked for specific information. As a result, the article in *Businessworld* 'When the Chickens Come Home ...', while more moderate in tone than Bansal's piece, was sceptical of the claims made, especially the details about the placement of IIPM students and the consultancy work done by Planman. Most of the multinational corporations named in IIPM advertisements, when contacted by *Businessworld*, said that they had few, if any, dealings with Arindam's organization.

Planman struck back in curious ways. A reporter writing about the controversy in the news magazine *Outlook* noted that the IIPM website brandished supportive quotes from 'luminaries like Noam Chomsky, Sri Sri Ravi Shankar, and Microsoft CEO Steve Ballmer', but that 'these reactions vanished within days of being posted on the Web'. The students at IIPM threatened to make a bonfire out of the IBM laptops they used because Gaurav Sabnis, the blogger who had linked to the offending piece by Bansal, worked at IBM. Sabnis announced his resignation from IBM, claiming that he was doing so voluntarily, in order to spare his employers embarrassment. His fellow bloggers, however, felt that he and his company had been pressured by IIPM – which, after all, was an important client of IBM's. In the minds of the bloggers, Sabnis was a martyr to truth and freedom of expression, and so they went about the task of challenging IIPM's claims with even greater energy, discovering, among other things, that IIPM's campuses in Antwerp and Brussels had no more than a loose affiliation with a rather questionable institute that was not recognized by the Belgian government.

In sifting through the long, labyrinthine posts on the anti-Arindam blogs, it is hard to avoid the impression of a virtual world being hammered at by virtual tools. Most often, the claims made by IIPM and Planman had depended on no more than a careful selection of pictures, comments and data, and the creation of numerous websites. This approach had worked well because it was part of a larger narrative of corporate success in India. Most mainstream journalists were too lazy and untrained, and too enamoured of wealth, to subject these claims to the most basic scrutiny. But this was not true of the bloggers, who revealed an unflagging ability to probe the Web, sending out emails to people listed by IIPM as contacts, checking IP addresses, and conducting background research. The most interesting investigation the bloggers carried out involved IIPM's history, focusing not merely on the qualifications of Arindam and his faculty but also on the credentials of Arindam's father, the man who had started it all by beginning a management school in the then rural surroundings of Gurgaon.

In *The Great Gatsby*, there are two questions asked of the central character. Where did Gatsby get his money from? And where did he go to college? These are necessary questions in a Gilded Age, in a time when money is being made too fast and in too many ways for established social networks to keep track of all upwardly mobile individuals. For those on the move, this gap between old networks and the rapidly changing times can become an opportunity, and this is what Gatsby tries to cash in on. He hopes he can make good the promise of capitalism: that ambitious, driven people can have second acts to their lives. So when Gatsby tells people, in a voice inflected by British affectations ('old sport'), that he went to Oxford, he is trying to transform his new money, procured by questionable means, into old money. And because his assuming the persona of a blue-blooded heir leads naturally to questions about why he hasn't attended one of the Ivy League colleges where wealthy young men like Tom Buchanan are sent to receive a final polish, he comes up with Oxford as his alma mater, a place so far away that it is difficult for people to check up on him.

Arindam, unlike Gatsby, wasn't a working-class upstart from the interior of the country. He was a middle-class man who had grown up in Delhi, alert from the very beginning to the opportunities provided by the capital city, and who thus demonstrated that even the mobility provided by the new India is significantly more limited than what might have been possible in America at the turn of the new century. As for the degrees claimed by Arindam, they came not from some exotic overseas institution but from the business school set up by his father. But the question of pedigree, the bloggers realized, could be transferred back one generation, to Arindam's father, to 'Dr'

Malay Chaudhuri and his claim to have a doctorate from the Berlin School of Economics.

The bloggers discovered that it was hard to pinpoint any such school with certainty. Dr Chaudhuri had once contested elections to the Indian parliament – he received so few votes that he lost his deposit – and in his application to the Election Commission, he credited his doctorate to an institute in the other Berlin, in the former East Germany. What records could one possibly access when the country itself no longer existed? The bloggers concluded that there had never, in all likelihood, been a Berlin School of Economics and that Malay Chaudhuri's doctorate was simply the first of many fictitious degrees handed out by the Chaudhuri clan and their business.

I could see the rationale of the bloggers. In spite of the friendliness with which Arindam treated me, he gave the impression of being on guard when it came to certain details. There were all those unanswered questions about revenues and the size of the company, made even more interesting because I discovered that it was under investigation by the Indian tax authorities. Although Arindam's company had spent 31.6 crore rupees on advertising in 2006, it had paid no income tax that year or the previous year. There was also the company's social responsibility campaign, directed through its charitable Great Indian Dream Foundation. Arindam claimed that it was building schools in slums and villages, setting up a hospital in a rural area of West Bengal and giving 'experimental' seeds to farmers. 'We will have fifty-two schools in seven metros by the end of the year. Sixty thousand villages will be covered in the future. Eventually, I hope to fulfil my father's dream of doing something for the downtrodden in Africa.' Underneath the glittering capitalist, there was a closet radical, someone who admired Che Guevara so much that he had named his only son Che. But I found it impossible to verify any of these claims, and Arindam's promise to take me to a school for the poor in a Delhi slum never materialized.

There were other things that remained beyond my scrutiny. When I stopped to think about it, I had met Arindam only in hotels and at the main IIPM campus in Satbari, where he had talked, in expansive terms, of expanding to America. 'Let Harvard fume, "We are two hundred years old,"' Arindam had said, lopping a century and a half off Harvard's past. 'Eventually they will recognize how good we are.' It was astonishing, this idea of America, through Harvard, as the old, while the India he represented was the new – younger and more modern by far than America. And perhaps he was right. His institute was a fluid, virtual business school of the future, one that had done away with the arduous task of institution building.

The school's first campus had been in Gurgaon. Arindam had then moved it to the Qutab Institutional Area, on the southern fringe of Delhi, operating from a leased building that finally fell foul of the city's zoning laws. Now they were operating from Satbari, some-where between Gurgaon and Qutab, but even this building, its bright colours and abstract designs done to Arindam's specifications, its small gym and swimming pool throwing out a challenge to the well-funded IIMs, might not be the final stop. It was a leased space, and Arindam told me that negotiations were already in progress to set the campus up somewhere else.

If the school was mobile, Arindam was even more so. I had wanted to meet him in his office. 'I don't really operate from a fixed space,' he said. 'I am so much on the move.' One day in September, he sent me a text message at 7 a.m. 'Good morning!' it said. 'Totally totally for-got that day. However in the airport right now. And free. Can call. Do let me know if you've woken up! Sorry about this early morning missive!'

I called him back hurriedly, trying not to sound sleepy. Arindam was attending a film festival in Toronto, where one of his films, *The Last Lear*, was being screened. During the stopover in London, he would be joined on the plane by the stars of his film, the young actress Preity Zinta and the bearded superstar Amitabh Bachchan, who has gone from playing thin angry young men in the seventies to corporate patriarchs in the new millennium. After attending the festival in Toronto, Arindam would stop in at his London office for a couple of days.

I remembered reading an article in the *Financial Times* where he had said that he would be opening his London institute at Chancery Lane, and so I asked him, 'Where exactly is your London office?'

There was a pause. 'That's a good question,' he said. 'Where is it?'

He sounded boyish and vulnerable, and I found myself wanting to respond kindly, as if speaking to a child I didn't want to embarrass about an insignificant lie. 'It's hard for you to keep track of all the offices you have,' I suggested.

'That's right,' he said, apparently relieved that I had offered him a way out.

I had once asked Arindam about the criticism that his institute didn't really offer careers. It was undoubtedly successful in attracting students, but the students, on graduating, seemed to end up mostly in the very organization that had given them their expensive degrees, teaching at the institute and working for Planman as its managers. Arindam's response was that his organization was a 'family', one that offered a continuation of the camaraderie experienced by the students. He also pointed out that, unlike the IIMs, he was not using public money to produce a small number of MBAs who then received extravagant salaries from multinational corporations. 'They've cornered hundred-acre campuses in India. The six IIMs, taken together, teach a thousand students. And because they have so few students, the average pay package is eight to nine lakhs. That is aura! Wow!'

He was right in pointing out how higher education for the Indian elite, from the engineering colleges like the Indian Institutes of Technology to the IIM business schools, was being funded by the state, producing technocrats and corporate executives who then went on to attack the state for being inefficient and wasteful. 'Every American president should start by thanking the Indian taxpayer,' he said, noting that it was US multinationals that benefited most from the training given to IIT and IIM graduates. By contrast, Arindam said, he had privatized management education, applying to it the genuine rules of the marketplace. His graduates might get smaller starting salaries. They might be working, he said sarcastically, for distinctly unglamorous companies like 'Raju Underwear' and 'Relaxo Hawaii Chappals', but they were not coasting on the taxpayer's money. He was training many more MBAs, people who would work in Indian organizations that needed their skills. 'Our placements are improving. Foreign companies are also coming,' he added defensively.

The bulk of IIPM students still ended up working for Arindam. It was hard to get an answer to how much they were paid when they joined him, but I had a rough idea because Arindam had, in a different context, divided his organization's salary structure into three groups; those getting up to 25,000 rupees a month, those getting up to 75,000 rupees a month, and those making more than 75,000 rupees a month. It seemed reasonable to assume that a starting IIPM graduate was in the first category; at 25,000 rupees a month or 3 lakhs a year, they were pulling in a third of an IIM graduate, which doesn't seem bad. But this is also just double the amount a call centre worker with a basic – and cheap – college degree could earn, although the managerial work presumably offers more upward mobility and better hours than a call centre job.

Yet the problem with Arindam's approach lay deeper than the salaries his graduates made. Even in the world of closed Indian companies, Arindam's organization is unusual. It is not publicly traded, and it was incorporated only very recently. The success and failure of IIPM students depends largely upon what happens to Planman, and what happens to Planman depends on what happens to Arindam. As for what happens to Arindam, that depends on whether the students keep coming. If the business school produces the greater part of the company's revenues and employs most of the graduating students, this model can keep functioning only as long as there is a growing body of students willing to put up substantial sums of money for their degrees, at which point the whole thing starts looking like a pyramid scheme.

7

But even though the bloggers were right in much of their criticism, they seemed unable to comprehend that the questionable practices of IIPM and Planman were an expression of the times, and that Arindam wasn't so much a rogue management guru as a particularly blatant manifestation of the management principle of making money. For all of Arindam's tendency to evade questions about his business by referring to the elite IIM mafia, it was true that the initial criticism had been started by Bansal, an IIM Ahmedabad graduate and then picked up by Sabnis, who had studied at IIM Lucknow. It was equally true that there was a marked element of snobbery in the remarks of the bloggers. Along with the more substantive criticism of IIPM and Planman, there were many comments on the way Arindam and his acolytes dressed and spoke, with an element of resentment and surprise that such pretenders could claim to belong to the corporate world that most of the bloggers came from.

None of the bloggers seemed willing to consider that the corporate practices they cherished necessarily spawned imitators. IIPM had the same relationship to IIM as knock-off goods do to branded products, which is to say that there is always a market for the knock-off version among the aspirational crowds. In other ways too, the cult represented by Arindam – and the bloggers were puzzled by the vehemence by which IIPM students, the people apparently being defrauded, defended him – was only part of the larger cult that was India Shining.

Arindam's management factory produced something less tangible but more resonant than durables or consumer products. It took people who aspired and had a fair bit of money but little cultural or intellectual capital and promised to turn them into fully fledged partners of the corporate globalized world. The students at IIPM were not from impoverished backgrounds. They couldn't have been, since the courses were expensive. Many came from provincial towns, from small business families that had accumulated wealth and were canny traders and now felt the need to upgrade themselves so that they could compete in the realm of globalization. Arindam gave youth from these backgrounds a chance to tap away at IBM laptops, wear shiny suits and polished shoes, and go on foreign trips to Geneva or New York. All this involved a considerable degree of play-acting, and the students spent the most impressionable years of their lives in what was in essence a toy management school – mini golf course, mini gym, mini library – but play-acting was what most of the Indian middle and upper classes were doing anyway, wandering about the malls checking out Tommy Hilfiger and Louis Vuitton.

There was an occasion when I saw the overlap between the pretenders and the legitimate management schools on proud display. One morning, I dropped in at Taj Palace Hotel, walking past the smiling women at the front desk to the venue where the Indian Chamber of Commerce was holding a marketing conference. I was there to hear a talk on 'luxury brands' in India by Vijay Mallya, a liquor baron, an airline owner and one of the wealthiest individuals in the world. Mallya was also a nominated member of parliament, and when he arrived at the Taj Palace Hotel, he came with gun-toting government bodyguards in tow. A crowd of photographers and cameramen followed him, trying desperately to record every facial crease and every sparkle of his diamond earrings as he walked to the stage.

Mallya had a pale, fleshy face with a salt-and-pepper goatee, and his hair was rakishly long at the back. He was a portly man, handsome in a grizzled lion sort of way, keenly aware that his status in that gathering was something close to royalty. When a panellist asked him to share his 'wisdom' with the crowd, he began a rambling speech that contained words shouted out very loudly, which, when I looked at my notebook later that day, seemed to come to this:

VODKA – WINE – YOUTH – ROCKING – DEMANDS – DRIVES – SMIRNOFF – ROMANOFF – SURVIVE – WHITE MISCHIEF – CAMPAIGN – EVE TEASING – FUN – MISCHIEVOUS – BORE – OLD-FASHIONED – POISON – YOUNG – DARING – CONTROVERSIAL – POISON *LAO*.

After the speech was over, Mallya offered more nuggets of his philosophy in response to questions from the floor. When he was flattered by the questioners, as was often the case, he was pleased but slightly bored. When he really liked a question, he sounded kingly as he responded, 'There is merit in your comments.' He remained prickly and nervous throughout the questions, however, his left leg furiously working an invisible foot pedal, and he became flushed like a watermelon when a female member of the audience asked him why his companies objectified women with their pin-up calendars and risqué advertisements.

As the questions went on, however, I realized that the corporate individuals among the questioners were heavily outnumbered by management students and faculty members, each of whom turned to the audience to announce the institute with which he or she was affiliated before asking the question. Here were the aspirers again, rubbing shoulders with wealth and power, their hopes visible in the style of asking the questions, which involved blurting out the question and turning away from Mallya before quite finishing, looking sideways at a companion with a smile of triumph, and then sitting down and disappearing from the scene as if they had never even been born to trouble the world with their dreams.

There were no IIPM students in the crowd, and yet it was the same phenomenon at work, of young men and women raised to believe that somewhere up there in the hallowed corporate corridors existed all the wisdom and fruits of modern life. Arindam offered his students proximity to this world by his own style and the take-them-on attitude he breathed. Joining IIPM, for which not much was required other than a high school degree and the ability to pay steep fees, they were suddenly up to par with the nobility of the globalized world. IIM, Harvard, McKinsey: these were the names Arindam shouted out with familiarity the day he strode up and down the aisle while addressing a class of graduating students. And because the students, in spite of the money spent and the Executive Communication classes taken, still sported bad haircuts and wore awkward clothes, they appreciated the adversarial air projected by their honorary dean. They formed an army of Gatsbys, wanting not to overturn the social order but only to belong to the upper crust, which is why they felt compelled to defend Arindam and IIPM against the bloggers.

8

Arindam, I had been told at the very beginning of my encounter with him, was a man of the times. His flamboyance, his ambition, his moneymaking: if his lightning-rod persona made these aspects visible, it did so because these qualities already existed as charged elements in the atmosphere of contemporary India. As I came to know him, though, I felt that there was another crucial aspect in which he was a representative of the times. His fortune, ultimately, was built on the aspiration and ressentiment of the Indian middle class. Without the aspirers looking up, emulating, admiring and parting with their cash, moguls like Arindam would not exist. He had made a business out of their aspirations, calibrating the brashness and insecurity that had come to them on the wings of the market economy and its political partner, right-wing Hinduism. Arindam understood well how these aspirers had been given a language of assertion by the times they lived in, and how they had also been handed a vocabulary of rage that is quite disproportionate to their perceived provocations. It is one of the triumphs of our age that aspirers can be made to feel both empowered and excluded, and that all over the world, one sees a new lumpenbourgeoisie quick to express a sense of victimization, voicing their anger about being excluded from the elite while being callously indifferent to the truly impoverished.

I had begun feeling some of this aspiration myself. I remember one particular afternoon when I had lunch with a former IIPM student who was also one of Arindam's prized employees. His name was Siddharth Nambiar, but apart from the common first name, there was nothing about him that suggested he was a doppelgänger come to reveal my secret life to me. Wearing a suit and designer sunglasses, his head shaven, he appeared in front of me with long strides, car keys dangling from his right hand. He was late because he had rammed his car into the back of a bus, but he was unfazed by this 'fender bender', as he put it.

We were meeting at a shopping plaza just across the street from where I lived at the time, an odd mix of multinational franchises and run-down shops that was especially popular with young people who worked at call centres. Nambiar led me up the stairs to an Italian restaurant called Azzuro. It was quite empty: the call centre workers preferred the kathi roll stand around the corner or the T.G.I. Friday's outlet across the square, and it was too early for the Western expats and upper-class Indians who liked the place.

Nambiar was a regular at Azzuro. The waiters knew him, as did the woman who ran the restaurant. He took off his sunglasses, ordered with a flourish and began telling me about his career with Planman. He had been a student at IIPM Delhi, joined the company on graduating and been put in charge of the media division almost immediately. He was twenty-three years old. Sutanu, whom I had met at the very beginning of my involvement with Arindam, was junior to him in the hierarchy of the company.

Arindam had put considerable thought into sending Nambiar to meet me. If his primary business was churning out management graduates, he had sent me his finest product, glistening and confident, someone who could compete effortlessly with the MBAs from IIM. Nambiar's shaven head shone in the bright afternoon light coming in through the windows as he spoke about how he had negotiated with *Foreign Affairs* about bringing out an Indian edition (and although the effort had been unsuccessful, he had apparently impressed *Foreign Affairs* with his presentation, according to a friend who worked there). He didn't know much about the content of the publication and didn't think journalism was very interesting, but he liked marketing. He had travelled around the world with Arindam, and in a few weeks he would be leaving for Oxford, where he would do an MBA. When he returned, he expected to work at Planman again.

I asked him about Arindam's conspicuous consumption, and he was delighted to give me the details. 'The car?' he said. 'It's a Bentley Continental four-door. Actually, he got it because of me. We were in London, near Lincoln's Inn Fields, and I saw a Bentley parked outside this restaurant where I was having lunch with friends. I had one of them take a picture of me leaning on the hood of the Bentley with a glass of champagne in my hand.' He laughed, waiting for the image to be fully processed in my brain. 'It looked so cool, you know? Then I went to see Arindam at the Ritz, where he was staying. I was showing someone else the picture on my laptop, and he grabbed the laptop from me, looked at the picture, and said, "What kind of car is that? I'm going to get one."'

Arindam had another Bentley in Bombay, as well as a Jaguar

Sovereign. His wife, Rajita, drove a Porsche. Arindam's mobile phone, a birthday gift from his wife, was a Vertu.

'You don't know what a Vertu is? Look it up on the Web,' Nambiar said encouragingly.

I asked him if he could describe Arindam's office for me.

'Let me think,' he said. 'I'd say it has a nightclub in the daytime look.'

We laughed at this. Nambiar's laughter had a double edge to it, containing the knowledge that he himself was too sophisticated to make such a mistake but also revealing his admiration for a man who had the money to flaunt his taste, no matter how questionable. He described for me the main chamber that had a fluorescent red leather couch curving around the wall, the shelves filled with management books and magazines. There was an anteroom to one side, containing a treadmill, a television and a pull-out sofa where Arindam's son, Che, sometimes slept in the afternoon. The office floor had blue granite tiling, and the building itself had tinted blue glass. From the windows of Arindam's office, Nambiar said, it was possible to see the Ernst & Young building on the left.

It sounded quite recognizably like Arindam's office, and very much like his house, which had been written up in the pages of the *Hindustan Times* a few weeks earlier:

No wonder, then, that from wall colours to concealed lights and from artefacts to Swarovski crystals, everything is blue in the Chaudhuri residence. While Renaissance paintings adorn the walls, a sparkly floor stone in dark blue is quite a novelty ... The Chaudhuri residence may not have 132 rooms like the White House, but within its own confines, it is a reflection of identities both homely and attractive, modern and trendy.

What gave Nambiar's description a touch of virtual reality was the fact that Arindam's office no longer existed. It had been closed down for violating zoning laws and survived only in the images created so expertly by Nambiar.

When I asked for the bill, the waiter said that it had already been taken care of by the manager.

'She's my girlfriend's mother,' Nambiar said.

'That's really too bad, because I was hoping to treat you.'

I told the waiter to bring me the bill, insisting that I would pay for lunch.

The waiter smiled and disappeared, while Nambiar looked surprised. I said something about journalistic ethics, but I could see that this made no sense to him. I was beginning to lose my temper, and I wondered why I was losing my temper. Who would really care if I let Nambiar's girlfriend's mother pay for lunch? Who would think that my honesty as a writer had been compromised because of this? Yet as I cornered the waiter again and forced him to bring the bill, I felt that I was beginning to lose my own self in this world of appearances and aspirations and that paying the bill was the only way I could return to steady ground.

After Nambiar had left, I walked around the shopping complex for a while. I came often enough to the shopping complex, sometimes with my two-year-old son. There was a group of street children who hung out near the fountain choked with rubbish, one of them a girl of ten or eleven with a baby in her arms. There were other forms of life surviving in the cracks of the marketplace, like the puppies that lived with their mother between the fountain and the cigarette shop and were given scraps of food by the vendors and security guards. My son was especially fond of the puppies, and a vendor asked me why I didn't just take one home. 'It'll make your son happy,' he said. 'And at least one of these dogs will get a good life.'

But I didn't think of any of this then. I thought instead of Nambiar's confidence, and looked at myself in a shop window. I wondered why I didn't have a suit, designer sunglasses and car keys. I wondered why I wasn't making money at this time in India when moneymaking opportunities seemed to be everywhere for the asking. I was an aspirer, finally, oblivious to anything but my own inchoate desires, filled with a sense of victimization as well as a trembling awareness of opportunities that it was perhaps not too late to capitalize on. 'I don't like an image of me that isn't me,' Arindam had told me early on, anxious to clarify his essential self. And here was I, not liking the image of me that was me.

These thoughts stayed with me as I walked back home, but eventually they gave way to other considerations. I often wondered, in the years that followed, if the papers would some day carry the news that Arindam's empire had collapsed. Until that moment came, though – if it ever did – the advertisements would keep appearing, offering a background rhythm as I made my way into other lives and other stories. When I saw those advertisements, I would peer closely at Arindam's face, as opaque and unfathomable as ever, and I would wonder whether I had ever known the man at all.

# Ghosts in the Machine: The Engineer's Burden

*An earlier incarnation – supplying happiness – low context and high context – Special Economic Zones – the million-dollar house – the Nanopoet – the Gandhi computer – what the Master said – a fascist salute – caste in America – the stolen iPhone*

1

A society does not usually change direction with a sudden jolt. It alters course in incremental amounts, running small, secret simulations of experiments that achieve their full-scale elaboration only much later. Its project of transformation contains repeats and echoes, and it is always possible to trace earlier versions of an organization, a phenomenon, or even a person. That is what I began to think after my encounter with Arindam, when a niggling feeling of déjà vu started to take over, as if I had met an earlier version of him somewhere, and whose source I finally traced back to my first job, in the early nineties, in Calcutta.

The position had come to me after some hard years in the city, when unsuccessful job applications and humiliating interviews were punctuated with one-off ventures that paid little or no money. In a city that still contained the black-and-white corridors and alleyways tunnelling through the films of Satyajit Ray, I had been a black-and-white protagonist sweating rage, obsessively counting the change in my pocket to figure out just how far I could travel on a bus, or cursing the man who had called me for an interview and then cancelled the appointment without explanation. It was a relief to leave all that behind when, soon after my university examinations, I found work that involved travelling across the eastern flank of the city, past the tanneries of Chinatown and the mountainous Dhapa landfill, where sections of garbage set on fire sent up volcanic plumes of smoke, to a two-storey house in south Calcutta.

Not too long after starting my new job, I entered the house one day to find my boss doing push-ups on the floor. He had taken his tie off and rolled up his sleeves, and as he dipped and rose on the concrete floor, the employees stood around in a circle, counting off loudly. I had come in late, and he finished soon after I entered, sweating slightly from the Calcutta humidity and the exertion of a hundred push-ups, but otherwise none the worse for wear. As he buttoned and knotted himself back to his usual suave state, he challenged those gathered around to do better than him. He was rewarded with embarrassed laughter, which is probably what he wanted. The people in the room were computer instructors, shallow-chested geeks who couldn't have bettered his effort and would never have dreamed of competing with the man who employed them. They were grateful for their jobs, which involved giving lessons in data entry and computer programming to young people who weren't very well educated and didn't have much money. When the instructors weren't in the classroom, they were usually brandishing thick manuals at each other, muttering arcane phrases like 'Foxpro' and 'C++' that signalled their involvement with a mysterious, incomprehensible world.

Because the company still exists, its advertisements prominently visible in Calcutta, I am not going to name it or the man who owned it. But even with a fictitious name, I can picture Indranil very clearly, a well-built, light-skinned megalomaniac who combined business management flair with a hustling instinct. He had worked as a marketing man for a large multinational, and you could see the corporate touch in the ties he wore and the crisp English he spoke on the phone. But he also had the street-smart ways of a neighbourhood tough, and this had helped him muscle his way into the computer education business.

This was the early nineties, still some way from India's technology boom, but there were already dozens of private institutes offering computer courses for people who had failed to get into engineering colleges. Indranil had carved out his niche in this competitive business by targeting people who couldn't afford the fees charged by other institutes. Like Arindam Chaudhuri, he too was cashing in on aspiration, but unlike the guru with a ponytail, he had to make his courses really affordable. This might have been one of the reasons why Indranil's computer centres always had an even more makeshift air than the IIPM campus, as if they were the outposts of some mildly disreputable business that could be dismantled at the slightest whiff of trouble.

The computer schools were located inside nondescript houses in mostly residential neighbourhoods. They had none of the neon lighting, soft carpeting and attractive female receptionists to be seen in the upscale institutes around Park Street, but that did not bother the young people who showed up for the computer classes. Their shabby clothes crumpled from long rides in crowded buses and trains, the heels of their slippers worn unevenly from pounding the city streets, they would have been ill at ease at the more expensive institutes. Many of them lived in the run-down suburban settlements scattered around Calcutta, or in the polluted township of Howrah, just across the Hooghly river from Calcutta, and it was apparent that they struggled to put together even the fairly modest fees charged by Indranil. Yet they had received just enough education to make them unfit for work as maidservants or bus conductors. In a few years' time, they might well descend to that level, but as they wandered around clutching notebooks and photocopied sections of computer manuals, they were still aspirers, dreaming of office jobs that would give them a semblance of middle-class life.

The instructors hired by Indranil weren't that much more secure, although perhaps a notch or two above the students on the class ladder. They were people whose certificates from the more reputable computer institutes had cost them a lot of money, and they were now trying desperately to earn back that money. Since there weren't too many jobs as yet for people with computer skills, many of these graduates inevitably found themselves regurgitating their knowledge back to others, often for very long hours and rather poor pay.

The combination of underprivileged students and insecure instructors meant that although Indranil had a flourishing business, few of his students found work after finishing their courses, which is where I came into the picture. Indranil had decided, in one of the sudden insights he was prone to, that the students performed badly at job interviews because they couldn't speak English. Their computer skills were sound, he said when I first met him. The problem was, metaphorically speaking, that they hadn't learned to zip up their trousers after taking a piss. I had been hired to redress this problem by creating a 'module' that would teach the students 'spoken English'.

I didn't know what a module was or how one might teach people to zip up their trousers. But I needed money and the 2,000 rupees Indranil paid me every month seemed like a lot, even if the 'part-time' position he had spoken of when offering me the job evolved into sitting around waiting for him from eight in the morning till eight at night, writing the occasional advertising copy for his company, and putting up with odd rituals like Indranil's practice of having lunch in the staff office with the female instructors while all the male employees wandered around the streets like disbanded soldiers.

It was in the course of all this that I got my first exposure to computers. Although Indranil himself didn't know how to use one, he had asked an instructor to give me lessons to make me a better fit with the culture of his company. One afternoon, a chubby-faced instructor took me into an empty classroom, his usual smile giving way to suitable gravitas as he scribbled:

8 bits = 1 byte
1,024 bytes = 1 kilobyte

I wrote this down dutifully, but when he began drawing a computer on the blackboard, I suggested that it might be more useful to go and look at an actual computer. 'What if you press the wrong button?' he said, and between his refusal to diminish the mystery of computers and my reluctance to play along, the lesson came to a swift end. Instead, I borrowed a *DOS for Dummies* ('1,024 bytes = 1 kilobyte') from another instructor and began trying my luck on the machines in the computer lab. Eventually, I abandoned DOS machines altogether and started dabbling on a black-and-white 386 that ran Windows, where I spent most of my time drawing grinning skulls that created some perplexity among students and instructors engaged in more worthwhile tasks.

It occurred to me that I was behaving badly, but I didn't know what else to do. There was little I could talk about with my faux-engineer colleagues. They were decent people, generous to help when I crashed the computer, hard-working and deferential towards authority, intelligent and socially awkward. I found them a little sad, with their twelve-hour shifts and their submissiveness towards Indranil. I have no doubt they found me sadder still, especially when I left the company after a couple of months.

Their time would come soon enough, though, when the West got caught up in a growing panic about the Y2K bug, which was expected to create mayhem when the new millennium began. The panic created jobs for people with computer skills and, from the mid-nineties onwards, the United States began issuing tens of thousands of H1B visas to Indian engineers, even as American companies started setting up offices in India where people worked late into the night to stay in sync with US time. The Y2K bug failed to have any discernible effect, but it was followed by a dot.com boom that also required people with computer skills. When that petered out, there came the back office jobs being 'Bangalored', or outsourced, to India.

These phases had transformed the sort of people I worked with at Indranil's company, turning them into the globally recognizable figure of the Indian engineer, a mobile professional who is at home in cubicles everywhere, from the back offices of India to the body shops in the West. The instructors I had known were insecure figures, anxious to hold on to their jobs and in awe of Indranil; even though he had no knowledge of computers, he was the boss running the show. In the years since then, engineers have become bosses. They have become a new breed of capitalists, creating ventures like Hotmail (which Sabeer Bhatia sold off to Microsoft in 1997 for $400 million), or building vast Indian companies like Infosys (one of whose founders, Nandan Nilekani, was elevated into sainthood by Thomas Friedman in *The World Is Flat*) and Satyam (whose founder, Ramalinga Raju, created a huge empire of software, construction and real estate in Hyderabad). These companies were so successful that by 2006, the information technology sector in India was earning about $25 billion annually, much of that from exports.

In the West, in spite of provoking the occasional backlash from people unhappy about their jobs being outsourced, Indian engineers are perceived as model minority citizens. Clustered into the suburban ghettos of places like Edison, New Jersey, and invisible for the most part in the social landscape, they are considered safe people, productive at work, conservative in values and unlikely ever to raise difficult questions about race or inequality.

But if they are invisible in the West outside the office, Indian engineers have become particularly prominent at home, especially those who began returning from the West during the boom years of outsourcing. As they recolonized sections of their own nation in the image of the suburban West they had experienced, they became oracles of the future: 'Honey, the world is flat.'

Success, or even the appearance of success, is a hard thing, especially in a country so populous and so unequal as India. For the engineer, it has meant being elevated to the role of world-builder, capable of solving all the problems of the country from poverty, caste and illiteracy to sloth and corruption, even if the ways in which the engineer will solve these problems remains unclear.

Most of the engineers I know are very likeable people, but what I know of them as individuals clashes with what I see of them in the aggregate. The engineer celebrated for being clean-cut and decent in public, especially in the West, is often also the one lurking on websites, filling cyberspace with a viral chatter that is sectarian, sexist and racist, convinced always of his own meritoriousness and ready to pour invective on those who disagree with him. If there is a schizoid personality at work here, that seems to be furthered by the fact that the engineer is both a public persona and a rather enigmatic figure. There are few books or films, even in India, that have successfully depicted what it might be like to live the life of an engineer, to be a person whose experience ranges from the productive, efficient work carried out in cubicles to the hate speech left, like scent marks on a lamppost, on the comments section of news-sites like Rediff.com (India). Years after my stint at Indranil's company, I wondered what people working in information technology were really like. While most of the current rhetoric about the engineer was about how skilfully he worked with computers, prized for being a sort of computer producing efficiency and profit, I wanted to find out more about the inner life of the engineer. I wanted to know if there was a ghost in the machine.

2

I had felt the dissonance of the place from the moment I arrived. The airport at Bangalore was new, its floors and conveyor belts gleaming brightly, its uniformed staff politely attentive. The turquoise-green taxi I took from the airport was air-conditioned and comfortable, and the fare was six times the amount charged by the battered cabs of Delhi and Calcutta. Then I got to Benson Town, the neighbourhood where I was staying, and I began to see landmarks of the colonial city built by the British as a cantonment area around and over an older Indian settlement. A short walk from the apartment was the Masjid-e-Khadria, glimmering white and gold in the night; across from it stood the Bishop's House, its grey stone walls laced with ivy; a little further down, there was the Jayamahal Palace, a folly of an English mansion whose grounds were disproportionately large for the building and which functioned these days as a heritage hotel.

When morning came, these sights were hidden by streams of traffic. They meant nothing, anyway, to the young professionals arriving every day in Bangalore from the far-flung corners of India. Even the people I was staying with were outsiders, although they were journalists and not engineers. Samrat, whose flat it was, came from Shillong, while his room-mate, Akshay, was a photographer from Bombay. When the three of us talked in the evening, closing the windows of the living room so that we could hear each other above the sound of the cars, it seemed as if we were shutting out not just the traffic but Bangalore itself. There might be professional opportunity in Bangalore, created by the technology hubs, and there might be an older city, genteel and spacious, but the two did not come together as a unified experience.

If this posed a problem for Samrat and Akshay, sociable individuals whose work depended on interacting with other people, it created a far more difficult situation for the tens of thousands of people who had been recruited off college campuses or from other companies to work in the cubicles of Bangalore's technology concerns. They were far from their homes, disliked so much by the local people for driving up prices, crowding the city and supposedly bringing in a rootless, Westernized lifestyle that a few months earlier *Outlook* magazine had carried a cover story called 'Why Bangalore Hates the IT Culture'. And yet, in some ways, the IT culture was as much about loneliness and a sense of displacement as it was about high salaries and a consumer lifestyle. The engineers arriving in Bangalore were dedicated to the virtues of work, productivity and upward mobility, but even engineers cannot fill up their lives with just these things, which is why technocratic Bangalore had come up with a technocratic solution – a company that supplied happiness.

The offices of A Fuller Life were in the neighbourhood of Austin Town, the location evoking the uneasy juxtaposition of old and new that is so characteristic of contemporary Bangalore. The directions I had been given on the phone involved getting off near the Lifestyle Mall, where Western men in khakis accompanied their Indian co-workers on a hesitant sampling of the food court version of native cuisine. The office itself was inside a residential neighbourhood near the mall, approached through twisting alleyways where people lingered in front of small storefronts, while above them, on rooftops crammed closely together, housewives vigorously shook out their washing before hanging the clothes up to dry. It was a setting that made the idea of supplying happiness seem absurd, but there was money to be made from such absurdity, as Arvind Krishnan made clear.

Arvind was the owner of A Fuller Life or, in his own words, 'the founder and CEO'. He was a short man with a firm handshake, a shaven head and snappy phrases ('Warren Buffett is God') that he threw out at me with a slight degree of impatience. A former engineer with a degree in business management, he had worked his way through a series of corporate jobs before beginning his company in 2001. It had started, he said, as a service for people who had just moved to Bangalore and wanted to take guitar or painting lessons. Arvind found them the classes they wanted and made his money by charging the instructors a commission. Two years later, he bagged his first corporate client, a software company that hired him for a 'ninety-minute session on graphology that was attended by a hundred and fifty people'. From there, Arvind's company had expanded into providing services for companies at four kinds of 'sites': 'external', or outside the office, with the activities mostly involving sports; at office cafeterias, where they held competitions 'usually involving song or dance'; on the workfloor, where people were given puzzles to do; and on the computer itself, in the form of quizzes and games.

'It sounds like an extension of college,' I said.

'It is,' Arvind said tetchily, 'and that's a very good thing. Many of these people are straight out of college.'

We were sitting near the kitchen and had to move aside briefly when two young men showed up from an external site to stack the cricket gear they had just used, grunting with effort as they lifted each bag. Chatura Padaki, one of Arvind's employees, had joined us. She was a soft-spoken woman who had worked with Arvind before at a dot.com. Unlike Arvind, whose focus was always on the peaks achieved by his company (it had a 'market capitalization' of 5 crore rupees and intended to increase that to 100 crores in twenty years), Chatura was more reflective, less programmed to respond with packaged phrases. Where Arvind had skimmed impatiently past the details of his work life, Chatura talked about the fact that they had both been laid off by the dot.com where they had worked together. She was also more willing to let me see how A Fuller Life worked, suggesting that I accompany some of the employees on a client visit.

'That won't be possible,' Arvind cut in quickly. 'They've refused such requests in the past, and by the way, don't name any names in your piece.'

It was in the same reflective vein that Chatura talked about why their clients needed the services they provided. 'These companies hire thousands of people from different parts of India, youngsters who are new to the city and whose work day runs from eight thirty in the morning to eight thirty in the evening. They eat most of their meals at work, they spend much of their time at their workplace, and they depend completely on their company for recreation possibilities. These people can't explore Bangalore even if they want to, because the companies have set up their offices on the fringes of the city.'

'It's a sticky workplace model,' Arvind said. 'It's more efficient for the companies to retain their workforce by providing engagement.'

Chatura brought me two pieces of paper to give me an idea of the activities they used to get people involved. The first was a crossword puzzle with the heading 'Health'; it was something employees would find on their desks when they came into work. The other was a hand-out showing a man doing the 'Japanese sport Nanjatsu [sic]', which would be distributed by workers from A Fuller Life.

'They'll go on to the office floor with the company's HR people and say, "Stop everything you're doing for ten minutes,"' Chatura said. 'Then one of our employees will show everyone how to do the exercises.'

'These are meant for different kinds of workers,' Arvind said. 'The Nanjatsu one would be right for the call centre crowd, but not for IT workers. The crossword puzzle is the one meant for IT workers.'

I asked him to explain the difference between call centre workers and IT workers.

'The call centre people display a tighter distribution in terms of age,' Arvind said. 'The IT people reveal a tighter distribution in terms of homogeneity.'

He meant that the call centre workers were all young, recent college graduates in their twenties. The IT workers were more likely to have engineering degrees, come from similar middle-class backgrounds, be older than the call centre workers and therefore less receptive to things like ninjutsu. But it would also be wasteful, Arvind said, for a company to use up the work hours of engineers with activities like 'Nanjatsu', because they brought in more money per hour than the call centre crowd. The higher qualifications and greater productivity of engineers meant that their lives were less full even when it came to play.

### 3

It was Chak who gave me a sense of what an engineer's life might look like from the inside, even if he was in most ways far removed from the people staring at quizzes sent to their computers. He was in his fifties, with a senior position at a well-known American semi-conductor company that he asked me not to identify. It was with the same candour that he asked me to call him Chak rather than Chakravarthy Prasad, which was his actual name. With his curly, dishevelled hair, greying moustache and rimless glasses, Chak had an almost professorial air about him. The rest of him, however, consisted of a corporate man in a hurry, from the BlackBerry winking against his small paunch to the giant Ford SUV in which he came bursting out of his office complex when I first went to meet him.

I was late for that meeting, the result of finding an auto-rickshaw driver enthusiastic about the fare but ill-informed about the corporate topography of Bangalore. We had been driving for an hour through the fringes of the city, past farming plots and wetlands that were periodically broken up by a sudden eruption of office towers. Finally, I reached the company where Chak worked, one of a string of outsourcing and software complexes situated along the Outer Ring Road, their cool, gleaming exteriors shimmering like mirages amid the rubble and scrubland of an area where city and village met in an uneasy convergence.

I called Chak from the gates of his office and he came out to meet me. He drove us a few hundred yards down to an adjoining business complex, parking in front of the Accenture building. Two uniformed attendants approached Chak as he climbed out.

'Sir, do you work for Accenture?' one man asked.

'No,' Chak said brusquely.

'Sir, parking only for company people.'

'It doesn't say that anywhere,' Chak said. 'This must be visitor parking.' He walked off, gesturing at me to follow.

The attendants gaped at us as we crossed over to the food court on the other side. We walked past lone, overweight managers in company polo shirts crouched over late lunches of rice and dal.

'The first thing they say in India is "No",' Chak said as we entered a Café Coffee Day. 'It's a reflex position, and so you learn to throw your weight around.'

Chak had come to this understanding of India gradually, over decades of living in India and in the United States. He had grown up in a middle-class Tamil Brahmin family in Madras (now called Chennai), very focused on his education.

'India is a highly tiered society,' he said, 'where you go the range from the labourer to the CEO. Education is an important vehicle of mobility in such a system, and that is what explains the appeal of engineering in India.' He looked at me and added politely, 'And writing too.'

Chak, in spite of being a good student, had at first been unable to move up the tiered system. He'd failed to gain admission to an engineering college and had settled for studying mathematics at a local college. After finishing college, however, he entered the graduate programme in mathematics at the Birla Institute of Technology and Science in Pilani, Rajasthan. It was one of India's top engineering institutions, and after two years there, Chak switched from mathematics to computer science.

It was at this point that Chakravarthy Prasad began becoming Chak, and the machines he worked with played a significant role in the transformation. At Pilani, Chak and all the other students used an IBM 1130 mainframe computer.

'It had a typewriter keyboard, a kiosk, and punch cards on which we wrote the programs,' Chak said, describing the computer rapidly and efficiently. 'There was always a long queue for the programs created by different people – they were written on punch cards in those days – and we gave our punch cards to the attendant and came back later for the printouts with the results.'

In 1983, he completed his degree and returned to Madras, joining a small company run by another BITS Pilani graduate. There, Chak worked with an Osborne PC.

'It had a green LCD display,' he said. 'Looked something like a present-day logic analyser. Eight-inch monitor. Floppy drive. We did a project for Fairchild Semiconductors, working on a simulator for a 64-bit processor. We did another project for IBM on their PC. In 1984, we bought our first Mac, which was a class act even at that time.'

After a couple of years, though, the projects dried up, and in 1986, Chak left for America. He travelled to Rockford, Illinois, where he lived in an apartment building that housed seven other Indians, all of them working for the Barber-Colman company. Rockford is the third-largest city in Illinois, a slice of Middle America whose prosperity was built on factories making industrial machinery and furniture. But, like other manufacturing centres in America, Rockford eventually saw many of its factories close down, their production moved to countries like Mexico and China where workers could be paid less. By the time Chak arrived in Rockford, it had already entered a trajectory of decline.

Chak didn't know that Rockford had declined. To him, it was a 'picture perfect' place, although it was also 'middle of nowhere', 'bitterly cold' and 'a small town'. Above all, it was a place where he had to learn to negotiate America and understand that it was 'a low-context society'.

'India is a high-context society,' he explained. 'It is a place where people interact with each other in many different ways. But in America, people work on the basis of interest groups. People are together for a reason, like work, and the interaction focuses on the reason for being together. It doesn't get deeper than that. So, for example, we used a maid service in the US, but we learned that it's not like in India where the maid would expect my wife and me to sit and chat with her. The American maid would think me transparent if I did that. But I also felt uncomfortable having another person in the house without interacting with her, so eventually I learned to put my Walkman on when she came in to clean.'

In the beginning, Chak had found all this difficult. 'Every Indian

wants to return in the first year or two,' he said, 'but it doesn ι
out that way.' Eventually, when he began coming back to India on
business trips, he found that its high-context nature bothered him.
He felt awkward about the sheer number of people paying attention
to him at hotels and restaurants when he wanted nothing more than
to be left alone. At some point, however, Chak began to sense a
change in India. He decided to return, hoping to contribute to the
change because he'd 'been there', at the heart of the low-context society that was leading the world.

Even within the realm of technology, though, he found cultural
differences. In India, people were quick to take on engineering careers
because it was a way of moving up a highly tiered society, but they
began to stagnate after ten years. They were also more likely to have
'irrational expectations' at the beginning of their careers. 'They're
knowledge workers, but they don't have it right,' Chak said. 'Engineers here want more money, more money, more money. Everybody
wants more.'

Chak's world could seem utterly self-contained, and nowhere more
so than in the physical environment he functioned in. The company
where he worked stood behind high walls and a guard booth, encased
in silence and reserve, its bright blue logo when seen from the road
suggesting some imperial palace glimpsed by a lone traveller. This
feeling was enhanced by the court protocol of going inside to meet
Chak, as I did a few days after our first encounter.

I stopped at the security booth, complying with the tiresome
requirement of filling out name, address and contact numbers in a
register. The guard called Chak to confirm that I was expected, then
handed me a visitor's pass. 'Follow the yellow line,' he said, and so I
did, obeying its zigs and zags past an empty tennis court and a
crowded parking lot. Outside the complex, a dust storm billowed on
the horizon, blocking out a yellow construction crane poised over a
half-built tower. As I reached the main building, low and wide, the
rain began falling, thick drops that splattered on the dust and sent up
the sweet, heady smell of wet dirt.

Once I entered the granite-floored lobby, I could no longer smell

leather armchairs were distributed along the
otted palms to break up the pattern of man-made
were people reading newspapers or tapping at lap-
me gave me a glance when I sat down to wait for Chak
out some notes. It was a low-context society inside the
complex, just like America, and no one would bother me as
long as I had gone through the proper security procedures and stayed
within my designated space.

I remembered how when we had gone to the neighbouring office
park during our first meeting, Chak had stopped on the way back to
the car, seemingly transfixed by what he saw. We were standing on a
central reservation, a mild breeze blowing at the tufts of palm trees.
Neat grids of concrete lay all around us, holding up the buildings of
steel and glass, and not many people were visible. 'This could be anywhere,' Chak said. 'It could be Arizona, where I worked in an office
park that looked just like this. That's the world standard we've
brought to India.'

Unlike Arizona, the low-context technology hubs of Bangalore
existed in conflict with the high-context society all around. Chak
was conscious of this. He lived, in his own words, in a 'gated community'. The same was true for his office, self-contained with its
cafeteria and recreation facilities. If he wanted a change while having
a coffee or a meal, he went to one of the franchise outlets in the business park next door. The only time he interacted with high-context
India was when he travelled between his two nodes of work and
home, jostling through traffic that was, in his mind, heedless of all
rules other than the one of every man for himself.

I got to see both high-context and low-context India every time
I went to meet Chak. I travelled southwards through Bangalore, a
journey of over an hour that took me across stretches of the city that
existed in discrete historical segments. I began in the close-packed,
colonial neighbourhood of Benson Town in the north, where small
grocery stores slept on the corners once the rush-hour traffic died
down. A third of the way on my route, I went past the cricket sta-
dium of Cubbon Park and entered central Bangalore, where the
coffee houses and bookstores suggested an older, cultured urbanism.

Then the city got taken over by long stretches of walls and forbidding gates that belonged to HAL. This was military-industrial Bangalore, where the state-owned Hindustan Aeronautics Limited manufactured – independently and in collaboration with Americans, Israelis and Russians – combat aircraft, attack helicopters and unmanned drones. From the road, nothing of HAL's facilities was visible apart from the name, which tolled in my head and brought to my mind the computer HAL created by the scientist Dr Chandra in Arthur C. Clarke's novel *2001: A Space Odyssey*, a computer that eventually goes mad because of the conflicts created by human greed. It seemed it would be only a matter of time before my experience of Bangalore became a story about a mad computer and a Dr Chandra.

As I came closer to Chak's office on the Outer Ring Road, I passed the area around Bellandur Lake, where fishermen and villagers were in retreat before the technology companies. The road ran straight, past air-conditioned franchises mixed in with smaller, local establishments ('Mangalorean Food Veg and Nonveg', 'Andhra Style Cooking'). Everywhere there seemed to be construction and ruin, hard to distinguish from each other, one pile of stone and brick being rubble while another represented raw material for new buildings. The sun reflected now not just off the water of the wetlands, but off glass that appeared in shades of blue and grey, held together by aluminium latticework and encased in blocks of concrete and marble. There were brick walls embroidered with iron posts, some of them surrounding the finished sheen of a software park but also often encircling what was still field and scrubland.

The enclosed spaces, seemingly so neutral, exemplified the essential conflict between high-context and low-context society. The conflict wasn't about technology. Instead, it was over land – that necessary, rudimentary, unsophisticated and finite thing on which the organized rationality of the office parks and their modern features ('high-end OFC connectivity', '24/7 100% back-up power', 'high-security arrangement') were being built.

This struggle over land in Bangalore has received little attention, except from a few journalists like Sugata Srinivasaraju in *Outlook*.

Srinivasaraju had written about the area of Bellandur, and how farmers there rioted in 2002 over attempts by Infosys, Bangalore's best-known technology company, to acquire their land at rates well below the market price. The anger of the farmers had been partly over the fact that Infosys wasn't buying directly from them but through the government, which had determined the prices at which the plots should be sold. But their agitation was also about how there would be no role for them in the technology parks even if they received suitable compensation for their land.

This kind of collusion between the state and private companies has been exacerbated since 2000 by the government's policy of setting up Special Economic Zones, or SEZs. Hoping to emulate China's success in creating export-friendly manufacturing zones in Shenzhen, the Indian government had by 2006 approved 200 such SEZs throughout the country, offering tax breaks and exemptions from labour laws in areas that were effectively defined as foreign territories. Even as I was in Bangalore, farmers in Nandigram, West Bengal were protesting against the attempt to establish an SEZ on their fields – they eventually succeeded in stopping the project – and there were similar protests happening elsewhere in the country.

The argument in favour of the SEZs and technology parks (which also received tax exemptions) was that they would generate employment through their factories and outsourcing offices. The displaced farmers would be converted into industrial workers, which was a necessary part of the process of becoming fully modern, especially since agriculture is nowhere as good at generating profits as factories and technology companies. While the software industry in India had produced, in 2006, $25 billion while employing just over a million people, the agricultural sector employing 400 million people had produced just $150 billion. This contrast makes quite clear which sector is better at generating wealth, but there is always the question of what is to be done with the 400 million who cannot become software engineers.

This superseding of the traditional by the modern was visible everywhere as I walked around the Outer Ring Road, taking in the straight lines of the technology parks and the perfect circles of satellite dishes networking the companies with offices in the West. There was a stretch of land right next to Chak's office complex, protected by a security barrier and guards, with a small sign that declared it to be an SEZ in development. Beyond that was the village of Bellandur, its huts hardened into crooked concrete structures ranged along a narrow alley. This was where the construction labourers congregated, gathering around a tea stall that stocked the basic necessities, from batteries to cigarettes, and where the bench was made of a plank balanced on bricks, perhaps one of the most common sights in India. Sometimes, if I was early for an appointment with Chak, I sat at the stall to drink tea. The working-class women who passed by, looking tired but still possessing graceful little touches like the strings of jasmine flowers wrapped around their hair, seemed like relics from the past, as did the little girl who appeared one day to ask for money and then vanished into the recesses of the village.

## 4

One evening, Chak took me to see his new house. We drove out of his office complex and turned into the SEZ next door, riding along a dirt track that stretched out towards a vast expanse of rock and green scrub. There was a large pit to our right, the foundation for a building, while on our left there was a row of grey towers, surrounded by reversing trucks and loaders dumping sand. Groups of small but sturdy-looking teenage workers came off their shifts, dressed in mud-splattered clothes and walking past a sign that proudly proclaimed 'Child Labour Not Permitted'.

There was no way to tell what the buildings were for, except for one that had a sign for Honeywell, a US company that was setting up a 'research, development and engineering unit' in Bangalore, apparently with the purpose of producing engines for Indian Air Force strike aircraft. I pointed at the largest building I could see and asked Chak if he knew what it was for. It was going to be a five-star hotel, he said, part of the Shangri-La hotel chain. The hotel was owned by the Adarsh Group, an Indian company, but it would be managed by a

Hong Kong-based concern owned by a reclusive Malaysian-Chinese billionaire called Robert Kuok. When complete, I found out later, Hotel Shangri-La would include 469 rooms, 276 service apartments, and 'a separate spa village complex designed as a sanctuary within the hotel', which meant that a fake village would replace the real village that had existed here. As we left the hotel behind and Chak pointed out a row of five towers that would be apartment buildings, I began to wonder why so much of the SEZ was taken up by housing and hotels rather than factories, and why the government was giving tax breaks for what was essentially private property for the affluent classes.

We reached a section at the end, cordoned off by walls of corrugated tin. There was another guard here, a man in a grey raincoat and black rainboots hurrying to open the gates. Chak drove in, shut off the engine and got out. I followed him and found myself standing in the middle of an American suburb.

The road was straight and geometrical, stitching together houses fronted by perfectly aligned lawns and garages with roll-down shutters. Black wrought-iron lamps had been planted at regular intervals along the pavement, accompanied by palm trees that had not yet grown to their normal height. The double-storey houses, their sloping roofs topped with red tiles, were mostly unfinished and unoccupied, although a man working for a biochemical company had moved into the house next to Chak's. The developer, Chak said enthusiastically, enforced a uniformity to the houses so that the property values could be maintained. All the houses were required to have sloping roofs and red tiles. The lawns in the front couldn't be fenced off, although an owner could put shrubbery around the back lawn for privacy.

Chak's house had not yet been painted. There were slabs lying around it, pieces of yellow granite from which workers had been cutting out small bricks to create a finish for the walls – a touch of individuality specified by Chak, and approved of by the developer. Chak unlocked the front door and took me to the high-ceilinged lobby.

'What do you think?' he said.

I made appreciative noises. Even in its unfinished state, the house stood for something. It suggested a completeness of existence, ranged around comfort and modernity, and I could connect it easily with the American suburbs I had seen and that Chak had lived in.

His vocabulary too reflected the domesticity of those no-longer-distant suburbs. There, to the right, was the 'master bedroom'. That was a 'walk-in closet'. He led me to the back of the house and stopped in the middle of an open space, with windows looking out to the lawn and the biochemist's house. 'This is the kitchen.'

There was a marble-top counter in the middle, with burners. Above it was a strange contraption bolted to the ceiling. I stared at it for a while until some hidden nugget of memory made me say, 'That's for the exhaust.'

'Yeah,' Chak said. 'The stuff for the kitchen was imported from Italy. Everything from the marble down to the smallest fittings. You can't get things of this quality in India.' He took me towards an L-shaped counter with a row of brown cabinets running above and below. 'See how this works,' Chak said, grabbing one of the cabinet doors. 'It doesn't slam if you push it back.'

He demonstrated its working for me, giving it a hard push, watching the mechanism slowing the door down until it closed with a soft, sucking sound. I began trying out the drawers under the counter, pulling them out and giving them varying pushes, sometimes soft and sometimes hard. It was satisfying to see how they all closed at the same pace, and how snugly, no matter how much or how little force I applied. Chak and I started laughing, slightly hysterical in our appreciation of the Italian material.

'You can't get this quality, even in America,' he said.

We went up the stairs, along a passageway where Chak planned to create a library. There were three bedrooms on this floor, each with their own bathroom. The rooms were for his two daughters and his son. 'If he ever comes back,' he added.

'Is there a question about that?' I said.

Chak laughed, but he didn't answer the question.

We went downstairs again, crossing the lobby and standing to the right of the main entrance, where the sitting room would be. He had bought the plot three years earlier, and in two more years his house would be complete. 'Things take time in India,' Chak said, 'but they get done. The value of the house, when it's completed, will be at least one point five million dollars. It's worth one point three million dollars now.'

'Really?' I said.

'Easily,' Chak said. 'There's this other guy whose house is unfinished and is smaller than mine. He sold his for six crore rupees, which is one point three million dollars, so I can get at least that much.' He beamed at me. 'I couldn't imagine that even when I was living in America. India is where it's all happening.'

I could see how real the $1.3 million house was for Chak. It stood for more than just the value it represented, the intelligent investing it exemplified, or even – as I would come to think more than a year after I stood in that house with Chak – the way in which it was part of the struggle over land, of gated communities for the elite and a global speculative frenzy over housing. Later, I would see places that were half-finished, where the money had run out, but I didn't know this at the time. As I stood in Chak's house, I could only see the energy that had gone into creating the turmoil visible through the rain-splattered windows: the rubble, the skeletal hulks of buildings and the mounds of earth on which workers clambered like yellow-helmeted ants. The floor we were standing on was uneven, coated in a lumpy plaster of Paris that had been laid down to protect the marble surface, a discarded newspaper at our feet. But to Chak and to others like him, the house was the beginning of a process that was unstoppable, that was even, in some ways, natural. It was a taming and ordering of the landscape by laying low context over the high. It would be possible, in some years – or maybe it already was possible – to put the Walkman on in India and ignore the maid coming in to do the cleaning. The newspaper flapped under my feet. When I looked down, I saw Arindam Chaudhuri's face, round and glossy, staring up at me.

5

There were other forms of shutting oneself off from the world. A few days after seeing Chak's house, I met up with another engineer who worked for an American technology company. His name was S. S. Prasad, and I had been introduced to him by a friend who said that Prasad was a poet as well as an engineer. I would find him interesting, she said, as long as I could convince him to talk to me.

S. S. seemed willing enough to talk when I called him. I got the sense that his ambition as a poet was involved in this decision and that he was perhaps thinking, in a modest way, of some sort of publicity for his work. We met up one afternoon at a Barista café on Church Street in central Bangalore. Dressed plainly, telling me right away that he usually never went to cafés like Barista because that seemed like a waste of money, S.S. came across as a measured and earnest 28-year-old. Although he was slightly built, he seemed very solid to me, finished in a way that made me think that S.S. at eighty-two would not be remarkably different from S.S. at twenty-eight.

Like Chak, S.S. was a Tamil Brahmin who had grown up in Madras. His had been a similar middle-class upbringing, and his journey towards becoming an engineer seemed to partly have been a matter of eliminating things he cared about, from cricket and television shows to Carnatic classical music. He had moved to Bangalore a few years earlier, and he was quite settled, married, with an apartment and a car. The same habit of thrift that made him avoid expensive cafés also determined that he used his car very sparingly, so that even though he had to come a long way to meet me, he had taken a bus.

S.S. had got married two years earlier. His bride had been selected for him by his parents, who had looked among relatives for a suitable match, comparing horoscopes. S.S. didn't think this was unusual in any way. 'The temple has always been in my ambience,' he explained, and an arranged marriage was part of that ambience. It was part of his Hindu cultural inheritance, as were the sacred texts of the Vedas, in which he found both scientific rationality and an advanced aesthetic sensibility.

S.S. had attempted a similar synthesis in his own writing, although when he started writing poetry, he was mostly just trying to capture his ambience, including that of the temple. He had chosen to write in English, for which he'd trained himself by methodically reading

other Indian poets also writing in English. He had attended a poetry
workshop, and his poems had begun to appear in small Indian literary journals. S.S. later emailed me some of these poems, and when I
read them, I liked them for the snapshots they provided of his world,
with some sharply observed details.

Yet these poems of S.S.'s, important though they were for him,
took second place to the form of poetry he claimed to have invented.
These consisted of 'nanopoems' that brought together the realms of
engineering and poetry. S.S. wrote the nanopoems in a binary language of zeros and ones, and what made them special was that he
inscribed them into the computer chips he designed at work. The
chip design was part of his job, the nanopoems were not, but his
employers were aware of what he did and were quite encouraging
about it.

'There's a lot of space left on a chip after you put in the circuitry,'
S.S. said. 'I fill in some of that emptiness with a nanopoem.'

In writing poems in the binary language of mathematics, S.S. was
echoing – unconsciously or consciously? I never had a chance to ask
him – the efforts of an Indian writer from 200 BC called Pingala, who
had created the first known description of a binary numeral system in
an attempt to describe prosody. The nanopoems S.S. wrote were,
however, singular in that they were invisible to the naked eye. When
I asked S.S. who he imagined his reader to be, he replied, 'An engineer at the other end.' Somewhere in the United States, an unknown
engineer would be checking the chip design when one of S.S.'s poems
would appear suddenly under the microscope, a part of the chip that
had nothing to do with the efficient, functional circuitry that made
the chip work. The testing engineer could decide whether to let the
poem remain, and if he did, the design would be sent back to Asia, to
a manufacturing facility in Taiwan. It would then get replicated in
every single chip with that particular design, a poem with a print run
of millions that would be read by no one other than the solitary,
anonymous engineer.

S.S. and I met up again a few days later to talk about the nanopoems. Although I had suggested we go to one of the cheaper coffee
houses he frequented, S.S. insisted on the Barista outlet. He preferred

to interact with me on neutral ground, where he would perhaps not have to reveal too much of himself. We sat on a small outdoor deck and looked out at the shoppers parading down Church Street, an occasional working-class man stopping at the liquor store across from us to have a quick shot of Old Monk rum from its pavement counter.

S.S. had brought me a book, a slim yellow volume with the magnified image of a computer chip on the cover. It was self-published and had the modest title *100 Poems*. All the poems included in it were nanopoems, which suggested that at some level S.S. did want readers other than just one engineer at the midpoint of the production cycle. The nanopoems consisted largely of sequences of ones and zeros, although S.S. occasionally used other mathematical signs or letters from the alphabet. They had conventional titles ('Sunflowers', 'In the School Auditorium', 'Shooting' and 'Binary Porn') and from the photograph in the book of a nanopoem on a microchip ('Game'), it seemed that S.S. used similar short titles in his chips.

Once the novelty of the approach wore off, there was a certain monotony to the binary sequences. Sometimes, they went on and on, as in 'Fireflies', which spread across two pages like a virus, and sometimes they were quite short, like 'Common Centroid Sheep', which read:

ABAABAABA

BABBABBAB

BABBABBAB

ABAABAABA

S.S. said that the numbers in his poems carried a special significance, as did the title *100 Poems*. When I said I didn't understand, he scribbled down the following sequence in my notebook.

1980

$2 + 0 + 0 + 8 = 1$

$2 + 8 = 1$

$40 + 0 = 1$

$\$10 = 1$

Rs 100 = 1

100 Poems

It made no sense to me, but the pattern had some kind of numerological significance for S.S. He began to talk about how proud he was of inventing the nanopoem, and that a short piece on this had appeared in *The American Scholar*. He had been inspired, he said, by a Chilean poet called Raúl Zurita who had written poems in the sky with the help of an aeroplane. S.S. had gone in the other direction from Zurita, choosing to focus on the minute, on what could be read only by an engineer's cyborgian eye, part human orb and part microscope. The near invisibility of the poems did not mean that S.S. was deliberately seeking anonymity.

'You know how they find pottery shards in archaeological digs?' he said. 'The inscription on such a shard might be all we know about an ancient civilization. I sometimes think that the same could happen with one of my chips. Chips get thrown away after they are used. Millions of them. They don't disintegrate. It is possible that a chip might be all that is left of us, to be discovered by some other civilization that would then find one of my nanopoems on the chip.'

S.S. had struck me as remarkably polished when I first met him. As he spoke of civilizations and immortality, I felt the same about his world view, running smoothly from ancient Hindu texts through the present to a future where all that was left of human civilization was a chip containing one of his nanopoems. I wondered if there were any edges at all in the plane of his existence, if there was something that would shake up his unsmiling, intelligent and always composed face.

I asked him if he talked about poetry with his colleagues, or of the world that he tried to capture in his poetry.

'We don't talk about other things at work,' he said. 'We work.'

I asked him how he felt as an Indian and as a Hindu about the inequalities evident in the country, especially about the hierarchies of caste.

'I don't disturb the environment,' he said calmly, 'and I don't want it to disturb me.'

Our session was nearly over and S.S. was getting ready to leave. I lingered on the word 'environment', and somehow the image that came to my mind was of millions of chips sitting in the earth some-where. I didn't know if chips ever disintegrated, but according to S.S., they didn't, and so I asked him, 'What do you think about global warming? Climate change?'

S.S.'s face finally began to exhibit something like tension and unhappiness. 'I don't know what global warming is,' he said tersely. He listened carefully to my rambling explanation. Then he replied, 'I haven't heard of global warming until now and so I do not have an opinion on it.'

Later that evening, I got a phone call from S.S. He said he would prefer it if I didn't write about him. I asked him why, feeling certain that he was upset about the questions I had asked him about inequal-ity and global warming. He was indeed perturbed by this. But what worried him even more was the possibility that I wouldn't give him credit for inventing the nanopoem.

'I don't want you to write that some person has invented the nano-poem,' he said, sounding increasingly anguished. 'I want it to be made clear that I invented the nanopoem. Otherwise, I would prefer it if you didn't write about me.'

A few days later, S.S. sent me a long email. It was polite and thoughtful, grappling quite sincerely with the question of the rela-tionship between his poetry and the larger world. He spoke admiringly of Raúl Zurita, the sky-writing poet who had a back-ground in engineering and mathematics and who had identified with the Chilean people oppressed by the dictatorship of Augusto Pino-chet. But he also referred to Indian women poets who had written about widowhood and about not wanting to have children, and maintained that these were 'purely personal choices of individual selves and if it has to be applied to a larger mass of people, it needs to be time tested'. I got the sense, from the email and from our phone conversations, that S.S. was saying his 'immediate surroundings' were more peaceful than Zurita's Chile and that he didn't have to take an immediate position on social questions. In some ways, he was right. He lived in a democracy, in the relatively peaceful surround-ings of Bangalore. If there was turbulence here, it wouldn't be easily visible to someone like him.

Yet there was turbulence even in S.S.'s placid life, and that was clear from the rest of the email.

> If you want to portray me as an engineer who writes poetry anonymously, I'm not game for it. Not many engineers in India write poetry and none of them have even attempted to merge one field with another ... 'Nanopoems' are what I arrived at on my own. There is no second thought or looking back and forth the book about it! When Jerry Pinto wrote an e-novel, he advertised it everywhere with a note that it was India's first-first 'e-mail' novel. My book is not a gimmick and in case you want to discuss anything about my poetry and engineering together in your work, I must be fully credited for it.

I had asked S.S. why he thought personal credit was so important, given his admiration for the Vedas, whose authors were, after all, anonymous. He had been rather annoyed by this sophistry on my part. He didn't think the anonymous authorship of the Vedas was relevant to his concerns. Perhaps it wasn't, but the stridency of his tone in talking about inventing the nanopoem offered a sharp contrast to how measured he was in all other ways. I had struck a nerve somewhere, and if at the beginning of our interaction S.S. had hoped for some publicity, he ended it with the fear that I would indulge in intellectual property theft.

6

S.S.'s interests had led him to the chip even when he was being a poet. His was the song of the engineer, communicating not with just any human listener, but with another engineer. His poems appeared in a realm beyond the human eye, hidden, for the most part, inside a computer, and visible, briefly, under a microscope. They were written to function in a dimension beyond human time, speaking to future civilizations.

I wondered if there were engineers who went in the other direction, towards the human sphere, into the world rather than away from it. There has long been a rhetoric of social change around the IT industry in Bangalore, promoted heavily in the media and in countless best-selling books that assure the reader that a new technological approach is putting an end to old social inequities. One day, I met up with Sugata Srinivasaraju, the *Outlook* journalist who covered the IT industry quite extensively, and often in relation to the larger society in which the industry functioned. Srinivasaraju's take on the issue was far more critical. He spoke of the engineer's perspective on Bangalore as a combination of the traditional and the modern, as 'technofeudal', viewing the city and its environments as a neutral and apolitical space. He said that the IT industry in Bangalore and in India had never acknowledged that its success was built on the infrastructure created by the old Nehruvian state – the engineering colleges with their subsidized fees, the state industries like HAL that created a manufacturing and technical base – and instead indulged in anti-government rhetoric while continuing to depend heavily on the government.

Srinivasaraju also spoke about how engineering had become a Brahmin occupation. The liberalization of the Indian economy in the early nineties had come directly after affirmative-action policies promised quotas in state jobs for traditionally oppressed castes and tribes. When the upper castes began to fear that they would be shut out of their traditional dominance in the civil services, they began to move en masse to jobs in the private sector, especially in technology. Srinivasaraju's perception of the upper-caste dominance in the IT industry is supported in studies made by social scientists like Carol Upadhya. She has written, for instance, that the perception of IT jobs as being dependent solely on 'merit' is not borne out in empirical surveys. She discovered instead that engineers were 'largely urban, middle class, and high or middle caste'. As Arvind of A Fuller Life had put it, they possessed a tighter distribution in terms of homogeneity.

There is also something Brahminical in the very way engineers perceive their work around computers, if by Brahminical one means the idea of exclusive access to knowledge that cannot be shared with commoners. There is no glamour in India, for instance, associated with being a civil engineer, and in this it differs remarkably from countries in the West, where, through the nineteenth and a great part of the twentieth century, the civil engineer has been celebrated for his rugged masculinity, especially in the way he dominates nature by building dams and bridges.

Today's Indian middle class, in contrast, celebrates the engineer-entrepreneur who makes money or the engineer-functionary who sits at a workstation. The cubicle is clean, air-conditioned and unpolluted, while the factory is dirty and physical. The cubicle is Brahminical, the factory is Sudra, the realm of the low-caste craftsperson. Seen from this perspective, S.S.'s nanopoems could easily come across as Brahminical, part of a techno-millennial Hinduism where a secret, and sacred, text is passed on from computer engineer to computer engineer.

Even as Bangalore confirmed this sense of engineering and computers as a Brahminical, inward-looking profession, I kept hearing about one project that had attempted to go in the other direction. It was about a special computer that had aimed to connect the esoteric knowledge of the engineer with the India that existed outside the technology parks, that had attempted to build a bridge between low context and high context. The computer was called the Simputer, or 'Simple Computer', and it was a device meant to be cheap, easy to use, and available to every villager. When it was first announced, in 2001, it had been considered one of the best inventions of the year by the *New York Times*, which spoke of the Simputer as 'computing as it would have looked if Gandhi had invented it'. The engineer who had tried to make the Gandhi computer was Vijay Chandru, or Dr Chandru.

I went to see Chandru one evening, taking an auto-rickshaw to the Sadashiva Nagar area at the western end of the city. Chandru's house was across from the Sankey Tank, a large artificial lake built in the nineteenth century by a British Army official and that now featured prosperous-looking Indians in white sneakers going on their evening walks, each walker followed by a long shadow created by the halogen lamps planted around the perimeter of the lake. The house was separated from the road by a small garden. Chandru wasn't in when I arrived and his wife, Uma, chatted with me until he came in an hour later from the biotech company he ran.

Chandru looked tired as he walked in, his grey hair rumpled, his right arm a source of obvious discomfort to him. The stiff arm was the result of a shoot-out in 2005 when a man opened fire on a gathering at the Indian Institute of Science, where Chandru was a professor at the time. The assailant, who escaped after the shooting, was said to be Abu Hamza, a member of Lashkar-e-Taiba, an Islamist outfit based in Pakistan, and a man who is said to have trained the ten gunmen who carried out an assault in Mumbai in December 2008. One professor was killed in the Bangalore shooting and three people injured, among them Chandru, who was shot in the arm.

He had become a professor at the IIS in 1992, after spending a decade teaching at Purdue University in the United States. He had completed his PhD in 1982 at MIT, where he had been interested in the intersection of science, technology and the needs of poor people. Among those Chandru had admired while at MIT were Ivan Illich, a European thinker critical of Western modernity who had done much of his work in Puerto Rico and Mexico, and an Indian scientist called Amulya Reddy who had attempted to harness technology for rural Indians, especially in promoting *gobar* — cow dung — gas as a cheap source of natural energy. Uma, sitting in on our conversation as Chandru offered these details, said that the MIT group had been 'a Marxist think tank', but Chandru politely demurred.

Chandru became increasingly interested in how technology, especially computers, could be made to contribute to the well-being of the poor, illiterate majority in India. In 1998, around the time Bangalore's technology industry was booming, he took part in an international seminar on bridging the 'digital divide'. The seminar had been called, in the usual hyperbole of the times, the 'Global Village', but it was out of this seminar that the Simputer project emerged. It was imagined as a device that would be 'simple, inexpensive and multilingual', a 'people's computer' that would make access to digital information much more egalitarian. As Chandru put it in a paper he wrote later, it was 'technology with a social conscience'. Three years later, when the first Simputer prototype was made public, it was received especially enthusiastically by the media in India and the West. The Gandhi computer was on its way.

It is easy, now that the hype has vanished, to look back and see how the Simputer was part of a broader phenomenon that can be called the 'technofix'. At any given moment in the past twenty years, there has always been some device or technology on the verge of saving the world: the personal computer, email, the Internet, Wi-Fi, the mobile phone, the netbook. But the Simputer belonged to a particularly interesting category, that of the low-cost computer, something attempted – and eventually abandoned – by Intel corporation as well as the non-profit venture One Laptop Per Child initiated by Nicholas Negroponte of MIT. These devices, which specifically addressed cost, were trying to solve the baffling contemporary paradox whereby incredible innovation in technology seems to go hand in hand with an equally incredible inequality.

If the Simputer was significantly different from all other technofixes, it was in the fact that it hadn't been thought up in the West, to be engineered there, manufactured in China and shipped to children in Mongolia. It had been birthed in India, a country whose upper layers demonstrated great technological ability but who were presumably closer than a Westerner to the social and economic conditions producing poverty. If there ever was any substance to the claim made time and time again by India's new techno elite that it could uplift the masses, the Simputer was the device that should have made the claim good.

The minds behind the Simputer, representing a convergence of academe, business and government, were brilliant. Its development was a joint effort by the Indian Institute of Science, a government institution, and Encore, a software company based in Bangalore. Together, the developers created a non-profit Simputer Trust that consisted of, in Chandru's words, 'four people from the academic world and three from the corporate world'. The trust was meant to hold the licence for the Simputer's design and software, which it would offer to different manufacturers who might want to put the Simputer into mass production. The manufacturers could modify the design but were required to 'pool back the changes to the trust' after a one-year head start. The trust also created a sliding scale for the licence fee, charging a one-time amount of $25,000 for companies in developing countries and $250,000 for firms in developed countries. The money from licensing would be put back into research and development.

The operating system of the Simputer was based on the open source GNU/Linux platform, but application development for it could be done on any platform: 'Linux, Windows, Solaris, Mac OS.' In this, Chandru said, he was inspired by Richard Stallman of the Free Software Foundation, who had addressed a conference in Bangalore in 1993 on open source software. 'If you really think about what launched computer science,' Chandru said, 'it was UNIX, written in C. What we called Berkeley UNIX became the de facto standard in engineering colleges. If we in India found an entry into computer programming in the West, it was because of our skill in UNIX.'

There were a number of ways in which the Simputer was remarkably advanced and innovative. It had a touch-sensitive screen. It also included text-to-speech features in different Indian languages in order to allow non-literate users to operate the system. The device itself was expected to cost just $200, but since even this amount would place it beyond the buying capabilities of most villagers, the developers imagined that people would own just a cheap smart card rather than a Simputer. The smart card would contain the personal data and people would be able to use it on a communally owned Simputer, one for each village. Finally, because electricity is unreliable in rural areas, the Simputer was designed to run both on electric power and on rechargeable AAA batteries. 'We wanted something small, hand-held and not too imposing,' Chandru told me. 'Villagers in India were already familiar with the transistor radio.' The Simputer was envisaged as something similar, a transistor radio for the twenty-first century. 'This was the first time a computer was built in India from scratch,' Chandru said. 'It even had an indigenous motherboard.'

There was a packet waiting for Chandru. He opened it as he talked to me. 'It's my Simputer,' he said. 'I sent it back to be recalibrated.'

He gave me the Simputer to take a look at. It was a grey device, around the size of a smartphone. 'It was ahead of its time in so many ways,' Chandru said. 'You know how everyone's talking about the Apple iPhone and the motion sensors in it that switch the picture from portrait to landscape view when you tilt the phone?' I nodded. 'We developed that for the Simputer. Here, I'll show you.' He pulled up a game on the Simputer screen, the kind where you try to guide a series of small balls through a maze into the centre. He gave the Simputer back to me and watched as I played the game, tilting the device to make the balls roll in the right direction. 'There's something even more cool you can do with this,' Chandru said. 'You can set the sensor to work in an anti-gravity mode. Which means that you change the sensor to pretend that gravity is upwards, not downwards. Now try the game.' I did, and although I was holding the Simputer the right way up, the balls moved as if they were upside down – gravitational force directed towards the ceiling, as it were. It was fun, and Chandru was pleased that I liked his device.

Chandru and his colleagues had taken on the engineering challenges with gusto, working in the IIS labs from five in the evening till midnight, with graduate students helping them. At the beginning, they had not tried to raise money from outside sources because they were worried that venture capital would restrict the innovations they wanted to try out. Some of the initial funds came from Encore, some from the money provided by the IIS. The developers built the first ten prototypes in April 2001, which was when the media showed up and showered its superlatives on the project.

When the prototypes were well received, Chandru said, the seven trustees planned to form a company to manufacture the Simputer, although they also hoped that other companies would buy the licence and manufacture other models of the Simputer. 'But something awkward happened along the way,' Chandru said. Encore, the private software partner in the project, had undergone a merger with another company. Then, the merged company went public. The people in Encore who had supported the Simputer no longer had much flexibility in the new company. Chandru, with a few of the trustees, formed a company called PicoPeta to produce the device anyway, but the drift between the original initiators of the Simputer had already started. Then, when PicoPeta went looking for venture capital to produce the Simputer, they failed to get anyone interested.

It wasn't incompetence on their part that prevented them from raising funds. Chandru's biotech firm, which he started in 2000, had no problem getting money, especially from the Indian diaspora in Silicon Valley. But the same diaspora techies weren't interested in the Simputer. For all the media hype, for all the rhetoric about bridging the digital divide and creating a global village, it wasn't an appealing project to them.

'There was no history in India of a device built to scale,' Chandru said, ruminating over the failure. 'The cellphone was also beginning to take off, and it had so much more value as a retail device.'

'Do you mean people could make profits out of the cellphone but not out of the Simputer?' I asked. 'Was that what stopped the venture capitalists from giving money to the Simputer?'

'Yes,' Chandru said. 'As engineers, we kind of didn't guess right. We didn't guess that cellular technology would take off in India, which, in 2001, had the highest long-distance rates in the world. Maybe we should have anticipated that, maybe we should have packaged the Simputer into a cellphone. We could have, but we ran out of money.'

PicoPeta tied up with Bharat Electronics, a public sector company, to manufacture the device. The Simputer they turned out could have been much sleeker, Chandru said, but there was no money to be spent on design. Meanwhile, Encore, which also owned the licence on the Simputer, got $200,000 from the Singapore government and manufactured their own Simputer. Between the two companies, fewer than 10,000 units were built.

By this time, according to Chandru, he had become more interested in his biotech company. The Simputer still remained, in two versions, one being produced by Encore and the other by Amida, a spin-off of PicoPeta, but its applications turned out to be for HAL, so to speak, and for big business. One version of the Simputer is now used by the Indian Army, primarily for its battle tanks. The other version is being refined to be a hand-held credit card reader that can be used in malls and restaurants, for the India on the right side of the digital divide. The Gandhi computer never made it to the villages.

7

One afternoon, I went to Chak's office to talk to him over lunch. It was quiet inside the office complex, the only sound coming from gardeners pruning the hedges outside. The cafeteria was large, with marble floors and a food counter in one corner. It was two in the afternoon and the regular meals of rice and curry were finished, so Chak got vegetable sandwiches and coffee for us. 'There's this whole other part of my life we haven't talked about yet,' he said as we sat down, 'the spiritual side of things.' Chak was part of a 'meditation group' called the Sahaj Marg. 'It's meditation of the heart,' he said. 'We do it together every Sunday morning. You can look it up at sahajmarg.org, the Shri Ram Chandra Mission.'

When Chak was studying computers at Pilani, he had been an atheist. He had remained one through his early years in the United States, unaffected by the religiosity he saw around him. Then, in 1988, the man who founded Sahaj Marg passed through Illinois. A relative of Chak's had married the founder's son, and the founder had taken advantage of the social occasion to hold a spiritual session in Rockford. Chak was derisive about it and did not attend, but his wife went. She was given a booklet about Sahaj Marg with a contact number in New Jersey. It was called 'The Fruit of the Tree'.

Shortly after, Chak had to go to New Jersey on work, and he took the booklet with him. It was a long drive, beginning in Rockford, Illinois, with an overnight stop in Pittsburgh and ending in Edison, New Jersey – almost a pilgrimage of industrial America, much of it already declining into the rust belt. When Chak read the booklet during the trip, he found himself laughing at the things it said. Nevertheless, he decided to 'give it a shot' when he reached New Jersey, where he called the contact number.

That was how Chak had found his guru, whom he referred to as 'the Master', the word 'master' being pronounced with a sharp American accent. 'You should never read spirituality, but dive into it,' Chak explained to me in the empty canteen. 'It took six months to work for me, but once you start fiddling with the transmission, it starts making sense. Then, as we progress in our spirituality, life becomes finer and finer. It's like starting with crude oil, moving on to becoming kerosene, diesel and petrol, until at the most refined stage, you become aircraft fuel.'

Chak became increasingly devoted to the teachings of the Master even as things changed around him. He switched jobs, became an American citizen in 2002 and returned to India. When the 9/11 attacks happened, he was in America and disturbed enough to call the Master in India to ask him for his advice. '"Governments have to do what they have to do, individuals have to follow their core values," he told me.'

When I said that this could be interpreted to mean that the American government had to do what it had to do and that the individuals within Al Qaeda should follow their core values, Chak hastened to assure me that the Master unequivocally supported the American government. In the spiritual scheme of things, however, neither terror nor the war on terror mattered. 'The only thing you can do is towards yourself. You can't change the world. You can change yourself.'

I wondered how spirituality could be reconciled with a profession or with possessions like a $1.5 million house. 'A job or a profession is a purely transactional thing,' Chak responded. 'If you have money, if you want a Mercedes car, the Master says, "Go ahead and buy it, but don't fuss about it. Don't complicate it."' He explained this further with an anecdote that he told me as we strolled back to the leather armchairs in the lobby. 'There is a pious king and a pious poor man. God keeps giving the king more and more riches. The poor man has one cow but God makes the cow die. How can this be justified? The poor man is dejected. See, the cow is all that stands between the poor man and God. The king, however, has all these possessions between him and God. He has much further to travel.'

I wasn't quite convinced by this, so Chak told me another story to reinforce the point. He had recently sent his two daughters on a trip to the United States. They had wanted to travel on their own, and he was supportive of the idea of their becoming independent. 'It was one of the things where there was a difference of opinion between me and the Master. "They're going on their own?" he said when I told him about the plan. He's slightly conservative in these matters, you see. I thought it was fine, but then they ran into problems. First, they were stuck at the Chicago airport for twelve hours because of a missed connection. Finally, they reached my brother-in-law and his family in Oklahoma. They were sitting on the lawn there, watching fireworks for a Fourth of July celebration, when an insect bit my younger daughter. She went into seizure. She was having a severe allergic reaction and they had to call 911, and an ambulance came and took her.' Chak paused and held up two fingers. 'She was this much away from ...'

His daughter was fine now, he reassured me. She had been put on steroids, and she had recovered. I found the story interesting, especially how this conversation about Indian spirituality had become a tour of contemporary America: Rockford, Pittsburgh, New Jersey, 9/11, the Bush government, Al Qaeda, Oklahoma and the Fourth of July. Was the spirituality emanating from these nodes the significant phenomenon, or was it the nodes themselves? Because there was some way in which I didn't understand the point of Chak's story, unless it was that anyone could be subject to the vicissitudes of fate. It was, to my mind, the old religious justification, stretching from the Eastern idea of karma to the Western concept of the postlapsarian individual, employed always to argue that people, especially poor people, suffered as a result of past actions, and that they always got what they deserved.

Chak had been speaking in a relaxed, even tone throughout. When he saw that I was dissatisfied, he leaned forward and gave me the point of the story, closing it like a perfectly solved problem. 'The trip, you see, wouldn't have been possible without money. Without money, there would have been no insect in Oklahoma, no seizure, no chance of death. So the Master was right to have his doubts about the trip. The Master was right when he said that it's people who have the most money who have the most trouble. The Master was right about everything.'

Chak's certainty in his spiritual world view was of a piece with the certainties in his life. He had been with the semiconductor company for years, and unless something dramatic happened, he didn't anticipate changing jobs. His $1.5-million house was around the corner, and he was looking forward to being closer to work when he finally moved in. 'The company has an open, mature culture that I like very much. That's another area where I have a disconnect with the Master. He thinks I like the office too much and his attitude is, "You don't yet get it."' Chak sighed and leaned back. 'He's right, you know,' he said. 'This is not everything.'

When Chak socialized with colleagues, it was at events organized by the company, either on campus or at a hotel. People didn't visit each other at home, nor did they socialize on their own initiative. 'People don't do much of the Western thing here, go and get a drink in a nearby pub,' Chak said, sounding slightly regretful. 'Everyone commutes in from a different area. As for the weekends, those are completely taken up with my meditation. See, instead of friends, what you get from the satsang is brotherhood. The difference between friendship and brotherhood is like the difference between religion and spirituality. Friendship is a social thing, and it's exclusive because you choose your friends. You don't choose your relatives and similarly in the brotherhood of spirituality, you accept everyone. There is no formality, it's inclusive, you don't judge them, and you do things for them. If you can.'

On weekends, apart from meditating, Chak sometimes travelled to give meditation 'sittings' for newcomers. He had graduated to being an 'abhyasi' – literally meaning a practitioner, but Chak translated it as 'preceptor', bringing a little hierarchy into the more neutral Sanskrit word. 'I will take a train to a small place in northern Karnataka where I don't know anyone but where someone wants a sitting. I don't even know the language, so we communicate with gestures.'

'What kind of people?' I asked.

'All kinds of people. Teachers, workers,' he said a little vaguely.

'What if the people tell you about problems they have?'

'They sometimes do,' he said. 'You listen. You help if you can.'

'Are there other people in your company who belong to the brotherhood?'

'Yes, there are some.'

'Do you talk about spirituality at work?'

'If it happens naturally in the course of the conversation. I don't bring it up of myself. There was a woman from Admin·who found out I did this. I arranged for her and her husband to·come for a session. Now they're part of the brotherhood too.' Chak looked around at the lobby and smiled. 'It's like the movie *Men in Black*. From the outside, the place looks very normal, just an IT firm.' He started chuckling. 'In secret, we do other things. We're all members of the brotherhood here.'

## 8

Chak's brotherhood was, in itself, relatively benign. It was no doubt self-involved – navel-gazing, unwilling to look too deep into questions of justice and inequality, but it was clear that its circle was limited. It was one of the many cults in modern India claiming a separation from both low context and high context while depending on the structure and economy of the low context. But there were other gurus who were far more global and powerful than the Master.

Just outside of Bangalore was the Art of Living Foundation, run by a man called Sri Sri Ravi Shankar. He had been a disciple of the sixties guru Maharishi Mahesh Yogi, who had attracted the Beatles, among others (until that relationship went sour and resulted in the song 'Sexy Sadie'), but Shankar was a corporate guru, perfectly attuned to the millennium and therefore possessing no hint of the counterculture. He was equally popular among Bangalore's engineers and among Manhattan socialites, a man who gave lectures to the poor to be happy with their fate, presumably because this kept them closer to God. He was also, in spite of his combination of New Age mumbo-jumbo and management speak, close to militant right-wing Hindu groups that have less interest in spirituality and more interest in violence against minorities, especially Muslims. These right-wing brotherhoods include the Bajrang Dal, the Vishwa Hindu Parishad (VHP), and the oldest and most notorious of them all, the Rashtriya Swayamsevak Sangh (RSS), whose origins go back to colonial times, when it modelled itself on Mussolini's Blackshirts and the Nazis. It was the RSS that sent an assassin who killed Gandhi in 1948, for which it was banned by the government for one year. The fortunes of the RSS improved vastly from the late eighties, when the organization and its allied groups saw their political wing, the Bharatiya Janata Party (BJP) becoming increasingly popular among the Indian upper classes and running a national government from 1998 to 2004.

Bangalore, for all its talk of cosmopolitanism and modernity, was part of that loop of right-wing Hinduism. The BJP had emerged as the largest party in the state of Karnataka (of which Bangalore was the capital) in the 2004 state elections. By the time I was there, it would form an unwieldy government in coalition with other parties, and in another year, in 2008, it would win the elections in Karnataka to form a government on its own. There were other Hindu formations in this software city, as evident in the red tilaks smeared on the foreheads of some auto-rickshaw drivers, but my brush with right-wing Hinduism happened, in a particularly Bangalore way, because of the Internet.

At the beginning of my stay in the city, I had got in touch with many people about engineers they might know. One of them, an acquaintance in Delhi, posted a request about this on an online discussion group. He had told me, in passing, that it was a 'libertarian' discussion group, but this was a detail I didn't give much attention to except to note, in passing, the sheer absurdity of being a libertarian in India. I had forgotten about this posting when, some weeks later, I received an email from a man called Kartik. He had an engineering degree and although he had never worked as an engineer, he would be happy to meet me. 'I have seen enough of s/w engineers and would be willing to supply dope about them,' he wrote in the email.

When I called him, he sounded neither very interesting nor particularly coherent. Yet he seemed so eager to talk that I asked him if

he would come and see me at Koshy's, a restaurant in central Bangalore, where I was meeting Akshay, my photographer room-mate.
Kartik showed up soon after I got there, looking hesitant as he made
his way towards our table. He was dark and stocky, his face gleaming
with sweat, and I began to lose interest in him as he talked. He was
alternately opinionated and nervous, making random statements that
seemed to have no point to them. When I asked him to clarify a comment he had made, he would run his palm through his hair and say, 'I
will have to think about that. I am not good at expressing my
thoughts.'

I put my notebook away and ordered dinner, asking Kartik to join
us. I didn't like him, but I felt bad for him. He seemed lonely, a little
confused, and I made it clear that dinner was on me. But even though
he didn't want to leave, he refused to eat. He ordered a coffee and
sipped at it while continuing to make rambling comments. There
were things about him that didn't quite add up, I thought. He had
grown up in Bangalore, but he had never been to Koshy's. He looked
around at the other customers uneasily, a middle-class gathering of
men and women, some of them poets and journalists, whose conversation rang in an easy, animated tone, interrupted by their banter
with the uniformed waiters. Then there was the fact that Kartik was
in many ways a member of the elite. He was a Brahmin, someone
who had done engineering at an IIT and studied management at an
IIM, both elite institutions. Yet there was no polish on him, and he
didn't have a job. When I asked him why, he mumbled, 'I am still
looking for the right thing.'

He grew slightly animated when I asked him about the online
group through which he had been put in touch with me. 'What does
it mean to be libertarian?' I asked.

'We believe in free-market economics, the kind that has made
America so successful,' he said.

I had assumed that civil liberties would be no part of this Indian-
style libertarianism, and I was right. Kartik began to talk about a
column he had read in the *Financial Times* in which, he claimed, the
writer had commented harshly on the unproductive, welfare-seeking
mentality of black people in America.

'Is that right?' Akshay asked me. 'You live in America.'

I said I didn't agree, but Kartik grew increasingly vehement that the *Financial Times* columnist was right. He began to speak disparagingly of black people, although he admitted he had never met any. He also spoke dismissively of what he said was my tolerance, comparing it to the similar attitude of his parents.

'What's wrong with your parents?' I said. 'They sound like decent people to me.'

'They're old-fashioned,' he said. Then he added, 'My father is an atheist.'

'And your mother?' I asked.

'She's religious,' he said. 'But she's just like my father. They're too easy-going when it comes to other kinds of people.'

'Do you mean people from other religions?' I said.

He refused to answer and instead stared at me, sweaty and nervous, playing with his empty coffee cup.

'So what about your religious beliefs?' I said.

'I believe in Hindutva,' he said, using the name coined by right-wing organizations to mean an assertive Hindu identity.

'Do you belong to any organization?' I asked.

A sudden change galvanized the man in front of me. He sat erect and puffed out his chest. Then he gave me a fascist salute, right arm swivelling to meet his chest, palm pointing down. 'I belong to the RSS,' he said.

Akshay stopped eating and stared at him with shock. I stopped eating too, feeling both angry and interested. From then on, Kartik did most of the speaking, in a long rant that was perfectly articulate in flow if incoherent in thought. He had turned his attention from blacks in distant America to Muslims and lower castes in India and to their backwardness. He who a little while ago had been scratching his head and had talked about not being good at expressing his thoughts spoke clearly and disdainfully now about the Muslim and lower-caste students he had seen at the IIT and IIM. 'They had no academic standards, no social standards, they couldn't think. They have such poor communication skills. They didn't deserve to be there.'

We had finished dinner. Kartik made a fumbling attempt to pay, but I stopped him. He lived with his parents, quite far from central Bangalore, and would take a bus back. He had once again become a polite, diffident man, and I wondered what his story was. He had gone to an IIT and an IIM, but they had not given him polish and confidence. He possessed what were extremely desirable qualifications in India yet did not have a job. He had been in the RSS, but although he admired its quasi-military discipline, he found it hard to immerse himself fully in the organization. The only thing he truly felt he belonged to was the online libertarian forum that had the same hate objects as the RSS but that had modernized it further with inputs from Ayn Rand and Western right-wing columnists.

Kartik wasn't a whole, just bits of conflicting impulses swirling around a self, and it was hard not to wonder if the anger at the seeming backwardness of minorities, of those socially and economically disadvantaged, was a disguised anger at himself. He looked troubled as he left our table, as if he too was puzzled by these bits of himself. He halted at the door and turned to stare at us, as if he was disappointed that we hadn't liked him, as if he wanted to meet with us again but knew that there was no place for him among us, and that we had rejected him as firmly and unequivocally as he had rejected his shadow selves among people from different backgrounds.

9

A few days later, I ran into Chak at Koshy's. I was there to meet a journalist, but she was running late and I was sitting on my own when I saw Chak come in, accompanied by his son and nephew. He'd brought them to the neighbourhood for shopping, but he also had a lunch meeting at Koshy's with alumni from BITS Pilani. Chak had earlier told me that he avoided alumni gatherings. Sometimes, he visited their online discussion group because he could read 'nice and curious and interesting' things, but he himself didn't post. 'It's too much of a nostalgia trip sometimes and there are some blabbermouths going on about who met who,' he'd said.

It was the first time Chak had been to Koshy's, and in spite of all that he had told me about keeping his distance from fellow alumni, his face lit up when he saw the group sitting at the back, their beer bottles and cigarette packs creating a happy picture of male cama- raderie. 'I'll go and hang out with those guys,' Chak said. 'You two can sit here.' Chak's son, pudgy, bespectacled and possessing a Mid- western twang, looked at me with embarrassment. He and his cousin sat down with me, but then the journalist I was meeting arrived, and there wasn't room at the table for everyone.

Chak's son looked despairingly at his father, but Chak was busy with his friends, looking happier than I had ever seen him. 'You know what,' Chak's son said, 'we'll just hang around outside till Dad's done.' They must have done so for a long time. When I left, Chak was still deep in conversation with his friends.

I was thinking about the son when I went back to Chak's office next week. I remembered how Chak had pointed to his son's bedroom while showing me around the new house and said, 'If he ever comes back.' When I met Chak in his office lobby, I asked him about his fam- ily. He began by talking about his parents. His mother died when he'd just finished high school, he said. He didn't see much of his father dur- ing the years he spent in Pilani. When he got married, Chak said, the traditional thing would have been for his father to move in with him and his wife. But that was also the time Chak left for America, and it was the elder of his two sisters who took the father in.

'At heart, men are more independent,' Chak said. 'Women are more attached to the family. So the old paradigm where parents stay with the son is changing. These days it's the daughters who keep the parents.' It sounded rather convenient, but I wondered if he was thinking of his own children. He seemed closer to his daughters than to his son, who was studying engineering in the United States. Chak said that there was a distance between him and all his children, but especially with his son. 'We like to believe that we're closer to our children,' he said. 'I like Western music. I grew up with the Beatles, Pink Floyd, that sort of thing. I listen to rap, even when it's vulgar. It's not the lyrics that appeal to me but the rhythm, the music. But when I listen to music my children like, they see this as something artificial on my part, something I am doing either to get closer to them or to spite them. My youngest daughter is forgiving, but the elder daughter, who's fifteen, and the son, who's nineteen, they'll turn off the television or leave if I sit down to listen to a song with them on VH1.'

'What kind of song?' I asked.

'Something like "Delilah",' he said, laughing with embarrassment. 'They want me to act my age, whereas I think I would have preferred my parents to be slightly closer to me.' But Chak also thought that things were harder for his children than they had been for him. They had more opportunities, but that meant that they had to take many more decisions. 'They have a stronger sense of privacy, they need to maintain a greater distance.'

I thought that his account of what happened when 'Delilah' played on television showed some interaction within the family. At least they weren't each watching television in his or her own room.

'It's getting like that here too,' Chak said. 'But their machine is not the television. It's the laptop, portable, always connected to the Internet. They don't want a desktop because it's too restrictive and doesn't offer enough privacy. With a laptop, when I walk into their room, my son or daughter can turn the screen away so that I can't see what they're doing.'

'Will your son come back to India?' I asked.

Chak smiled but didn't answer.

'What does he want to do?'

'He's not interested in a career,' Chak said. 'He's pretty open about the fact that what he wants is to make easy money.'

'Is that different from your outlook?'

'Well, I guess I went to the US to make money too.'

The conversation about family had made Chak mellow, even more reflective than usual. He looked around at the lobby, at the people walking purposefully past the electronic ID machine, the men wearing jeans and the women in baggy salwar kameezes. 'Will the priority of my spiritual life demand more time?' he said abruptly. 'That is what I am waiting for. I could do more for the mission then. In the company there is no retirement age. You keep going on, like the Energizer bunny.'

I let him talk, and he began assessing his life, including the two decades he had spent in the United States. 'In America, there was no free time, you know. The home environment is demanding everywhere, but here it's a tiered society that allows you to have quality time. In the US, when it was Fall, you had to rake the leaves, in December you had to winterize the sprinkler system, and when it was February, you had to use the weedkiller. Mowing the lawn, washing the cars, I don't have to do any of that here. The bulk of the US is caught in this mediocrity. You're really a machine, an automaton. It's a programmed society that is trained not to allow weeds on its front yard. If you do let weeds grow on your lawn, you get a note, you get ostracized because you're not maintaining the property value. Lots of Indians struggle with this. There I was the Home Depot king. You're told it's good to know how to do these things yourself. That's bullshit. Nobody wants to be a jack of all trades and master of none. Sure, there's discipline and improvement in America, but it comes at a huge cost. Sometimes, I wonder, "Did I really enjoy it?" Then I think, "Did I have a choice?"'

I was surprised at this sudden criticism of America, especially since he had spoken of it admiringly at the beginning of our interaction. I asked Chak whether it was fair that India was so tiered, even if that worked better for him in that it allowed him more free time and let him be less of an automaton.

'It's always going to be a tiered society here,' he said, 'and actually it's not wrong. Just because I have a driver doesn't mean I am a slave-driver.' He laughed at his play on words. 'I'm supporting his family and he's doing the best he can in his stratum. And besides, you really think the US isn't a tiered society?' He sounded both energized and sorrowful, as if he was delivering a final, complicated lesson to me. 'We in India think it's a free society,' he said. 'It's a lie. The reality is that America is hugely regimented. It's just a different caste system in the US, an economic caste system. It's an unfair system. The rich protect their interests and keep away from the poor. The bulk of the people are in between the rich and the poor, without much of an idea of what's going on.

'Have you ever been to a downtown in an American city?' he asked suddenly. I was confused, but then it became clear he was talking about inner-city areas. 'What about those Americans who are born in poor neighbourhoods? They are born poor, they stay poor. They won't get access to proper schools because schooling depends on the tax base. It's not like in India where you can have a five-star hotel next to a slum. We embrace each other.'

## 10

Bangalore did not seem like a good example of five-star hotels sitting next to slums, or of people from different tiers embracing each other. That might have been possible in the old India, but the new India was all about gated communities, like the SEZ next to Chak's office, where Hotel Shangri-La would sit near the million-dollar houses whose uniformity and property values would be maintained in the very spirit of American regimentation that, Chak said, had made him a machine. In such a landscape, the poor – all those left behind by the creation of a low-context society – were like ghosts. If they appeared at all, they did so without warning.

I was in the flat one evening, sitting in the bedroom, when I heard Akshay come in. I could hear him speaking on the phone. When I came out, he cried out, 'You missed me getting extorted. These guys want five thousand rupees.'

It took me a while to figure out what was going on. Akshay had an iPhone, an unlocked one because Apple hadn't released the phone in India at the time. When he got home, he found that the phone wasn't in his pocket. Akshay thought that he had dropped it while getting out of the auto-rickshaw. He had a second phone, which he used to call his iPhone. The man who answered did not identify himself. 'It was the auto-rickshaw driver!' Akshay said. 'I recognized his voice.' Then he looked thoughtful and said, 'But, man, how did he know how to use an iPhone? I mean, come on, it's not easy to figure out that you have to swipe the screen to open it.'

Not only had the man known how to use an iPhone, he had also known its value. He asked Akshay to come to the Majestic cinema hall with 5,000 rupees in cash. The area around the Majestic was desolate, so Akshay had suggested meeting near the Indian Express office, but the man had refused to do so.

'So what did you agree on?'

'He's coming here.'

'Here? Now?'

'Right now. He'll call me when he gets here.'

For a second, I thought we should just grab the man when he showed up. Then I realized that he wouldn't be stupid enough to come alone. Akshay's old phone rang. They were waiting outside, across the street, which, in spite of the traffic streaming through, was deserted in the sense that there were no pedestrians. 'The bastard is using my iPhone to call me,' Akshay said.

We went out of the flat, crossing the street to where a lonely auto-rickshaw sputtered in the darkness, right in front of the State Bank of Mysore. The driver, who stepped out, hadn't come alone. There were two other men with him. The driver and one of the other men were still wearing their khaki uniforms. They also had red tilaks on their foreheads, which declared that they were Hindus, and that they belonged to the Karnataka Rakshana Vedike or Karnataka Protection Society, an organization that was Hindu and nativist in its politics, modelling itself on the fascist Shiv Sena organization in Bombay and equally ill disposed towards those they considered outsiders in Bangalore.

The driver who had found the iPhone stayed quiet. It was the third man, the one not in a uniform, who did the talking. He was in his early twenties. His face projected the hardness of a street tough and the tiredness of a man who lives by physical labour. His grey T-shirt and pants were smeared with grease, as if he had come straight from work on fixing an auto-rickshaw, and that seemed to give him a sort of moral superiority over us, especially over Akshay, who kept pleading that he was poor and incapable of coming up with such a large sum, but who looked much too plump and well-off for this plea to carry much force.

The three men listened silently, staring at us with contempt from behind their thick moustaches. I asked them to bring down their asking price a couple of times, and they finally said they would take 4,000 rupees, a 20 per cent discount. Akshay kept bargaining, but they wouldn't budge, and he eventually went into the State Bank of Mysore to get cash from the ATM. The rest of us loitered around, not talking, as if we had all taken a liking to this one unremarkable spot in Benson Town, as if we were just hanging around rather than taking part in a process that was either extortion or redistribution of wealth, or possibly both.

The men looked utterly confident as they stood around their auto-rickshaw, displaying no worry that a police van might come by. I thought I would take the number of the auto-rickshaw when they left. Then, if Akshay wanted to, the Indian Express could make a fuss to the police. If enough pressure was put on the police, they would find the men. Akshay came back and made one last bargaining effort, which failed. Finally, he handed over 4,000 rupees and received his iPhone. The auto started an uproar and made a sharp, squealing U-turn. Akshay and I waited for the licence plate to be visible and glimpsed it as the auto began to speed away. The law in Bangalore was that licence numbers had to be in English as well as in Kannada, but these men hadn't bothered with the law. We looked stupidly at the squiggles on the licence plate, at the Kannada numbers neither of us could read, and we kept staring until all that was visible was a red tail light blinking in the distance. A few days later, Akshay lost his iPhone again. This time, when he called the number, no one answered.

# Red Sorghum: Farmers in the Free Market

*The dying countryside – the navel of India – the chemical village – McKinsey and Vision 2020 – Victory to Telangana – the farmers' market – Prabhakar and the overground Maoists – Dubai and debt – the dealers – 'Ain't No Sunshine When She's Gone'*

1

From the cities in which I had been spending so much of my time, the Indian countryside felt like an afterthought, the remnant of an ancient rural world finally being absorbed into modernity. It didn't seem to matter where I was – in Delhi, Calcutta, Bangalore or Hyderabad – everywhere the metropolis was expanding, thrusting out the spokes of its highways and throwing up office parks, apartment complexes and SEZs on what until recently had been wetlands or agricultural plots. In places like Gurgaon, the transformation was complete. In other areas, many of the buildings were still shells, altars being prayed over by vast yellow construction cranes, but the process was nevertheless under way.

The emphasis on such urban expansion conceals what might be happening to Indian farmers, who are utterly absent from mainstream accounts of progress. There are some solitary efforts to write about what is happening to them, as in the work of the journalist P. Sainath – who first documented the devastation of rural India in 1996 in his book *Everybody Loves a Good Drought* and who continues to report on this in the *Hindu* newspaper – or in the bleak roll of names put up by activists on a blog on farmer suicides. The list of names goes on and on, giving a hint of the individual suffering involved in what can otherwise seem like an utterly abstract process. Yet the numbers themselves are significant. From 1995 to 2006, in the very years that the urban economy was expanding, nearly 200,000 farmers killed themselves in different parts of India. These are official figures, based only on cases accepted by police officials as unambiguous instances of suicide, and depending on the fact that the police count as farmers only male heads of households who have agricultural land registered in their names. The suicide figures do not include women, nor do they include the tens of millions who farm on land owned by other people. Yet even these conservative official figures show something of the distress in rural India, where the most common method of killing oneself is by ingesting pesticide, a substance that is easily available to the farmer even when he or she has nothing else.

This crisis, barely noticed by the promoters of the new India, affects the majority of people in the country. About 400 million people depend on farming for their livelihood, as compared with the approximately one million people employed by the software and outsourcing industry. Many of the farmers, according to surveys conducted by the government and by independent organizations, do not see agriculture as a viable occupation. Even without the debts that force some of them into committing suicide, farmers see no future in what they do, and if they nevertheless continue to work in the fields, it is less because of some apparently traditional inertia and more because the alternative is perhaps worse. It involves joining the growing ranks of migrant workers who shuttle between the countryside and urban areas, working at jobs that pay little, offer no mobility and are usually temporary in nature.

The southern state of Andhra Pradesh is one of the places affected especially badly by the distress of farmers. It is among the top five states in India in the number of farmer suicides, and when one looks at a map of India, it forms a continuous zone with the other four states in that group – Karnataka, Maharashtra, Madhya Pradesh and Chhattisgarh. Taken together, this is a vast area of 942,940 square kilometres, stretching from the west coast of India to the east coast, running from the far south up to the centre of the country, comprising poor states like Chhattisgarh and Madhya Pradesh and those that are considered developed and contain three of the most prosperous urban economies in India, including Mumbai in Maharashtra, Bangalore in Karnataka and Hyderabad, the capital of Andhra Pradesh.

The overnight train journey I made from Bangalore to Hyderabad in the summer of 2008, travelling nearly 500 kilometres north up the Deccan Plateau, was therefore a journey across two worlds superimposed on one another. The first was from the flat world of Bangalore to the equally flat world of Hyderabad. The city of Hyderabad possesses a large concentration of IT and outsourcing companies, including the behemoth Satyam, most of them located in a northwestern strip that has been given the futuristic name of Cyberabad. Like Bangalore, Hyderabad contains an agglomeration of shopping malls, franchise outlets and condominiums as well as a new airport forty kilometres out of the city, in Mahabubnagar district, that is indistinguishable from the new airport in Bangalore. But even as I moved through this flat world, I was traversing a jagged zone where desperate farmers were killing themselves, where millions of men and women were leaving their homes to work as migrant labourers in faraway cities in India or in the Gulf States of the Middle East, and where forest squads of Maoist-inspired guerrillas were busy fighting police forces associated with the oppression of government and big business.

It didn't take me long after I arrived in Andhra Pradesh to see how these different aspects overlapped, although the manner in which I acquired the knowledge was strange, more affected by random events than at any other point in my journey through the new India. It was a contingency that affected the entire duration of my stay in Andhra Pradesh, seizing my attempts to depict the life of the farmer and twisting it in different directions, making my narrative more driven by plot than at any other point in this book, transforming my objective of sketching the portrait of an individual farmer into a more collective account. In fact, as I look back at the time chasing this plot not of my own making, it occurs to me that the main character in this chapter may be not a person but a thing, a crop called 'red sorghum'.

2

It was the red sorghum that brought me to Armoor. I had taken a bus from Hyderabad early in the morning, watching as the malls and the condos of the city gave way to clusters of engineering colleges. Then came the countryside, where rows of women harvested green stalks of rice, humped bulls ploughed deep furrows into the land, a borewell gushed water on to a field and a farmer sprayed pesticide from a canister on his back. The rest of the land, uncultivated, was gently undulating, filled with palm trees, cactus plants and rocks all the way to Armoor, in the north-western district of Nizamabad.

The dust lay thick on the flat landscape, coated especially heavily on the two-lane road that was the main street of the town and that created a spine for what was otherwise a shapeless settlement. On the map, Armoor was the navel of India, exactly equidistant from the two coasts and bisected by National Highway 16. When seen from the ground, it was no more than a cluster of ramshackle houses and shops set up on scrubland, appearing at random in the sea of rice and maize of Nizamabad district.

Prabhakar and Devaram had promised to meet me at the bus station, but there was no one there as I got off the bus from Hyderabad. I tried calling Prabhakar a number of times but he refused to answer, and when I finally got through to Devaram, he sounded distracted and irritated. 'Come to the municipal office,' he said and hung up. I found my way to the municipal office, a concrete building sitting in a field of dust just behind the highway. Devaram was busy inside, sitting at a table where government officials were gathered around thick ledgers, writing out cheques for farmers. I sat on a plastic chair on the verandah, waiting for Devaram to finish and feeling anxious. I had come to Armoor to capture something of the travails of Indian farmers, but the men I saw converging towards the municipal office seemed utterly alien to me.

They were dark and wiry, with greying hair and wrinkled skin, dressed in dhotis, their feet bare. One man limped up to the verandah with a stick. His right leg was shorter than the left, and he hopped past me along the uneven stone floor, past the pockmarked walls, ducking when he came to a stretch where the ceiling had been festooned with paper flags of India. Finally, when I spotted two men who looked younger and more modern than the rest because they were wearing trousers and carrying mobile phones, I tried to talk to them. But neither of them spoke Hindi, and nor did any of the other men gathered around the municipal office. I hadn't expected to run into such a problem. Although Telugu is the main language in Andhra Pradesh, I had been told that most people in Nizamabad spoke some Hindi. I looked to Devaram for help, but he seemed too busy.

After two hours, I gave up and walked out. Dripping with sweat in the August heat, I wandered down the main street of Armoor, past shops selling agricultural implements, fertilizer, buckets and motor parts. I kept trying to contact Prabhakar and, when I failed to reach him, I called every single friend I could think of in Hyderabad who might know someone in the Armoor area. It was around one, and there were few people other than me wandering around the streets. There wasn't a single cloud in the sky and almost everyone was trying to stay indoors.

Eventually, desperate to be out of the sun and to find a place where I could sit and think, I made my way to Mamatha Lodge, the only hotel in town. It was squeezed in between two restaurants, down a long alleyway where a group of three ranged around a tiny desk heard my request for a room. They represented the three ages of man: a young boy in shorts, a man with thick wavy hair and big moustache who swivelled his ledger around to face me, and an old man in a red tunic like a railway porter's. I filled out the ledger, the frequent appearance of 'Mr and Mrs' on its pages indicating that Mamatha Lodge served as a love hotel of sorts. The young boy was deputed to lead me to my room, but as we left, the old man winked at me, moving his shrivelled hand up towards a toothless mouth, indicating that he would appreciate a tip. The gesture – so servile and so unselfconscious, without the theatricality that accompanies an urban beggar making a similar motion – took me aback. It was a reminder of what I had thought of the old India, where desperation was displayed openly rather than hidden, and it was one more indication of how different Armoor was from the big cities.

Up the stairs we went, through a dark hallway where a group of men crouched, furiously beating at a pile of old, stained mattresses. Room 202 was tiny, with a single bed and a portable television placed on a corner stand. The squat toilet in the bathroom was badly stained

with shit and when I took a bath, the water ran under the bathroom
door, across the length of the room and into the corridor towards the
pile of mattresses. There was a mirror on the wall, broken. I could
only see half of my reflection, my face cut off at the top, and it seemed
to depict accurately how I felt, and how uncertain I was of what I
was doing in Armoor. There was a rooftop of corrugated tin sheets
visible through the single window in the room. The sheets had been
arranged so as to leave a large gap at one spot, and I could see down
through the hole into the kitchen of the Geeta Udipi Vegetarian Restaurant, where bare-torsoed men displaying rolls of fat were stirring
large vats and pans, sending smoke up through the gap. I looked at
this for a while and then went out again, past the men beating the
mattresses and the old man repeating his servile gesture, to choose
my lunch option from 'Geeta Udipi Restaurant', 'Captain's Biryani
Hotel' and 'House Restaurant Veg and Nonveg'.

After lunch, I walked down the main street, a solitary pedestrian
among the men on two-wheelers and villagers crammed into auto-
rickshaws. I hadn't gone far from the restaurant when I came across
the skeleton of a jeep, stripped down to its metal chassis and sinking
into the ground. There were two other such jeeps further down the
road, on the other side, and Devaram caught up with me as I was
looking at them. He wore thick glasses and a big, unkempt beard, and
his face glistened with sweat from the midday heat. He was a small
but aggressive man, abrasive in a manner that at first struck me as off-
putting but that made more sense as he told me about his life.

Devaram had grown up in a nearby village. He was a Dalit, or an
'untouchable' in the taxonomy of the caste system. He remembered
his childhood as a time of deprivation and humiliation, of not having
a pair of slippers and being banned from drinking tea from the regular glasses at the village stall. Then, as a ten-year-old, in the early
seventies, he had gone to a meeting held by an organizer from the
Andhra Pradesh Revolutionary Communist Party. By this time, he
had already dropped out of school and started working in the fields
as a labourer. He became a dedicated member of the party. He and
the other labourers were made to work from four in the morning till
ten at night in the fields, their wages amounting to 1,000 rupees in a

year. Devaram and other workers from the party went on strike for fifteen days, their agitation spreading to nearly fifty villages. Their pay was increased and they were given, for the first time in their lives, lunch, a torch for working at night and a pair of rubber slippers.

In the mid-seventies, Devaram left for Hyderabad when the police started going after party members. People got 'encountered', Devaram said, shaping his right hand into an imaginary pistol and shooting me in the chest to illustrate the process. Sometime in the eighties, he migrated to Abu Dhabi to work as a construction labourer. 'I caused trouble there too,' he said, chuckling. 'They treated us like animals and so I organized a strike. They deported me when I did that.'

As we walked around the town, Devaram told me the story of the red sorghum and the turmoil it had caused in Armoor. The farmers in the area, he said, depended heavily on middlemen known as seed dealers. The dealers bought produce from the farmers and sold it to buyers from other parts of India, determining what crops farmers should grow in a particular season. The process of agriculture was therefore decided in reverse, beginning with the demand for particular crops from distant buyers, a demand that was then communicated, through the seed dealers, to the farmers. The dealers had also replaced functions carried out in the past by state agencies, giving out seeds, fertilizers and even cash loans to farmers as advances against payment for the final produce.

A few months earlier, around 25,000 farmers in the villages surrounding Armoor had chosen to grow a crop called red sorghum or 'lal jowar'. They had contracted their produce to the biggest of the local seed dealers, a man called Mahipal Reddy, who had offered them an exceptionally high price for red sorghum. When the farmers finished harvesting, however, Mahipal reneged on the deal and refused to take delivery of the red sorghum or to pay them. The farmers found themselves sitting on stocks of unsold red sorghum. The autumn planting season, the most important one in the year, was around the corner, but they didn't have money to buy the ingredients needed for the autumn planting.

The farmers began to agitate, with men coming in from the villages to demonstrate in Armoor as well as in Nizamabad town, the headquarters of Nizamabad district. They gathered outside the district collector's office there, but as their agitation dragged on without any discernible result, they converged in Armoor early one morning in June for an all-out demonstration. Devaram, whose party had been instrumental in organizing the protests, enjoyed telling me about the chaos that had ensued that June day, starting with thousands of farmers bussing into Armoor at the beginning of dawn to gather outside the municipal office.

Around eight in the morning, nearly 10,000 farmers marched down the main road. There was a small contingent of police to monitor the situation, but they abandoned their jeep as the farmers converged on it. The men set fire to the police jeep and to two vehicles belonging to the Revenue Department. Then a group of people turned right off the main road, up a side street containing scattered houses, and stopped in front of the building that belonged to Mahipal, the seed dealer.

Mahipal did not live in his Armoor house. The farmers surrounded the house, and after allowing Mahipal's tenants to leave, ransacked the place and set it on fire. At this point, the police tried to intervene. They were pelted with stones and bricks and took shelter behind a neighbouring house from where they fired at the crowd. One man got a bullet in his ribs, while three others were slightly injured. The mayhem continued. Some men advanced in a different direction from the main road, up a street to the other side of the town, where they set fire to a house belonging to a different seed dealer, a man called Anand Reddy. Then the farmers gathered at the edge of the town, where Highway 7 meets Highway 16, and sat down on the road to hold up traffic for the rest of the day.

Devaram had led me up to Mahipal's house as we talked. It wasn't a house but a mansion, standing three storeys high, with fluted pillars, marble floors, a sweeping staircase and numerous balconies. It was a Venetian merchant's palazzo that had travelled to Armoor by way of suburban Florida, although Mahipal had apparently been inspired in the specific design by a mansion he had seen in a well-known Telugu film. The white walls were now blackened by fire, and where the doors and windows had once been, there were only gaping frames. The steel gate that had protected the house was gone, carted away by angry men to be sold as scrap metal. The police had put up iron sheets around the mansion to protect it, securing the sheets with chains and locks.

It wasn't just the gutted state of the mansion, with debris strewn everywhere, that made its aspirations so incongruous. The mansion seemed to have been airlifted on to the terrain, placed in the middle of nowhere. There were a few other houses nearby, smaller concrete structures that were scaled-down versions of Mahipal's aspiring vision, but they were all islands of individual mobility floating in a sea of scrub and rock. There were no streets, no lights, no parks – and no town that was not simply a rough-and-ready, hardscrabble settlement emerging from the countryside.

The same was true, I saw, when we went to the other side of the road to Anand Reddy's house. Its gates were still intact, and in the circular driveway of the house stood a black Ford Ikon car. The roof of the house was sloping, topped with red tiles, but here too the white of the walls was darkened by fire, the windows and doors gone. The only inhabitant of the mansion was an old, bearded man on the second-floor balcony, furiously dusting as if this was the best way to restore the gutted house.

The scale of aspiration in the houses of Mahipal and Anand made it easy to see the scale of the destruction. But there were, as always, smaller dreams also being destroyed. Devaram took me to a nearby tea shack, no more than a bench, a kerosene stove and a bag of supplies set amid the rubble of brick. The owner was a Dalit, who pumped his stove and conversationally said that he had had a proper shed until recently, when it was demolished by thugs hired by a man who owned a large building nearby.

'He's going to construct flats on the upper floors and shops on the ground floor, and he didn't like the fact that my tea stall was so near to his building.'

I asked him who owned the land on which the tea stall was located. 'It's government land,' he said. 'But I have a permit from the government to have a stall here.' His manner was calm and unsurprised, used to such arbitrary blows from the powerful. He wouldn't take any money for the tea.

'He's my brother,' Devaram said, by which he meant a brother in Dalit identity and in class struggle. 'How can he take money from you?'

## 3

Soon after I arrived in Hyderabad, and before I knew anything about Armoor and red sorghum, I had met Vijay, a lecturer in economics at Hyderabad University. One Sunday, Vijay took me on a drive to a village called Qazipally. We travelled northwards out of Hyderabad, moving along a highway lined with restaurants and shops. Eventually, the urban sprawl gave way to a more ambiguous space where open stretches of land alternated with the walled and manicured complexes of pharmaceutical laboratories – segregated plots that consisted of little more than a brick wall, an iron gate and a security guard – and large construction sites where cement mixers and ashen-grey workers laboured to fill in the skeletal outlines of apartment buildings. Vijay's small, battered Maruti car bounced furiously as we went uphill along a dirt track and then descended into a valley with clusters of huts lining the road, the land opening out behind the huts to rise towards a low hill.

The farmer Vijay was looking for was not at home, but Vijay knew his way around and led me behind the houses to a stretch of uneven, rocky land. He stopped when we came to a stream, a shallow strip of fluorescent green water. This had been a canal carrying fresh water, Vijay said, just as the land scattered with weeds and rocks had once been farming land. There was a shepherd grazing goats nearby, and he came closer when he heard Vijay. He had grown rice here, he said, until the land stopped being fertile and he had to resort to rearing goats. We walked parallel to the stream towards the hill I had seen earlier. The stench hit me when I climbed to the top. My nose and eyes started to burn. There was a lake of sorts below us, bubbling and brown, its surface indented with rocks, and although we were well away from the lake, the fumes coming from it were so strong that it was like standing over a vat of sulphuric acid. Vijay pointed to the horizon on the other side of the lake, where the factories releasing the effluents were located.

Afterwards, Vijay and I stood on the road talking to the villagers, who converged on foot and on motorcycles. They were very fond of Vijay because he had been with them from the beginning of their struggle, when they had tried to resist being encircled by the factories. The villagers had taken the polluting companies to court and had lost. They had held protests and been beaten up by hired thugs. They had seized trucks coming to the area to dump pollutants and had been arrested by the police while the truckers were released. They had asked the government to stop the pollution, but the state pollution control board had said that the land was clean. They had come together – across religion, caste and varying levels of affluence – to present a united front, but their village chief had been bought off by the companies and subsequently murdered by a rival. In fifteen years, the men around me had gone from growing rice to not being able to grow anything. Some had taken to grazing livestock, while others had sold portions of their land and built concrete houses on the remainder of their holdings, where they sat and waited for the city to expand and for tenants to show up.

But most of the men gathered there did not want to become land-lords or move somewhere else to continue farming. Their families had been in Qazipally for nearly five centuries, and the polluted lake, called Qazi Talab, was 400 years old. It had once occupied forty acres. There were still the ruins of a hunting cabin near the lake where the feudal lords of the kingdom of Hyderabad had come to hunt deer. Blasts rippled through the air as the villagers spoke, shaking the ground we were standing on. They originated from stone quarries that had been set up five or six years earlier, unlicensed operations working with impunity on government land. From time to time, yellow trucks loaded with the quarried stone passed us, teenage boys covered with dust sitting next to the drivers.

As dusk came down on the land, Vijay and I left the chemical village of Qazipally behind and began making our way back along the unlit, unpaved roads. There was a bus coming towards us, empty apart from the driver. I read the logo on the bus as it passed us. It said: 'Maytas Hill County SEZ'. The name seemed familiar, and when we reached Hyderabad, I saw it plastered on a series of billboards offering luxury housing: 'Maytas Hill County SEZ: Less concrete, more chlorophyll'.

Qazipally offered a picture of the changes that have been wrought in Andhra Pradesh since the nineties. That was the time when a certain kind of urban growth, centred around Hyderabad, began to be promoted even as rural Andhra Pradesh was subjected to new approaches to agriculture. Both came from the brain of Chandrababu Naidu, the investor-friendly chief minister who held office from 1995 to 2004, and who was much loved throughout his tenure by the press and by officials at the World Bank, the International Monetary Fund and Britain's Department for International Development. Naidu was the consummate technocrat politician, periodically announcing various 'e-governance' schemes, so futuristic in his approach that he hired the American consulting firm McKinsey to prepare a report called 'Andhra Vision 2020'.

The McKinsey report, which cited the structural reforms carried out in Chile under the dictatorship of Augusto Pinochet as a model for Andhra Pradesh, recommended a smaller role for the government and generous incentives for private businesses. It strongly recommended the winding down of support services for farmers, including the agricultural offices dispensing advice and seeds, the loans given through public banks and the programme of buying back produce at a minimum guaranteed price through the state-owned Andhra Pradesh Seed Development Corporation. The McKinsey report suggested that the state let market forces take over, even as it focused on encouraging service-oriented business in Hyderabad – an approach that would guarantee that, by the year 2020, 'poverty will have been eradicated and current inequalities will have disappeared'.

The success of the McKinsey method can be measured both by the resounding defeat of Naidu's party in the state elections in 2004 and by the fact that the report, once easily available on the Internet, has since disappeared from cyberspace (although McKinsey continues to do business as usual, last year producing a report for Nasscom, an Indian consortium of software and outsourcing companies, that was titled 'Perspective 2020'). The Congress government that succeeded

Naidu has been careful not to mouth the free-market rhetoric quite so openly. Yet while portraying itself as a friend of the farmers and posting signs on the backs of rural buses with a helpline number for farmers feeling suicidal, the new government hasn't substantially changed any of Naidu's policies.

The rural crisis was continuing unabated when I arrived in Andhra Pradesh. It was concentrated especially strongly in a region that is known as Telangana, and that includes the city of Hyderabad as well as the districts of Warangal, Adilabad, Khammam, Mahabubnagar, Nalgonda, Ranga Reddy, Karimnagar, Medak and Nizamabad. Spread over an area of some 155,400 square kilometres, Telangana is an arid region, dominated by gneiss rocks that are billions of years old. It possesses an identity distinct from the rest of Andhra Pradesh, in part because it belonged to an area ruled by the Nizam of Hyderabad until the formation of independent India, and in part because it is impoverished, with all its districts, apart from Hyderabad, classified by the Indian government as 'backward' or extremely poor.

Telangana is also a region known for peasant revolts, the most famous of these being the Communist rebellion from 1946 to 1951, an uprising that began as a movement against the Nizam – the very person Ved Mehta had profiled as the richest man in India – and that continued against the independent Indian state that seized the Nizam's territories in 1948. From the seventies onwards, Telangana was home to a number of left-wing armed groups referred to as Naxalites or Maoists, which by 2004 had combined into one political party known as the Communist Party of India (Maoist). The McKinsey-Naidu government alternated between initiating talks and carrying out paramilitary operations against the Maoists, and as the police carried out a series of encounter killings, the Maoists began moving into neighbouring states like Chhattisgarh and Orissa. The leadership of the Maoists continued, however, to consist of people from Telangana, and its chief, Mupalla Laxman Rao or Comrade Ganapathy, comes from Karimnagar district, where he had worked in the seventies as a schoolteacher.

The Maoists were still around in Telangana, but they had toned down their operations in the region. The discontent of the area had been channelled instead into the demand for a separate Telangana state, and one afternoon I travelled to Nizamabad district, just outside Armoor, to attend a meeting in favour of statehood. It was taking place at the 'Garden City Function Hall', across from a stretch of empty fields, the vegetation everywhere blasted dull yellow by months without rain. As waiters dressed in jeans, waistcoats and shoes without socks circulated with glasses of water, a man with a splendidly oiled moustache and long, curly hair climbed on to a stage and began singing, his right hand theatrically pressed to his heart at times, and at times swept out to raise the audience from their midday torpor. A chorus line of young boys, bare-chested and in white dhotis, danced behind the singer, breaking out periodically in a sheepish refrain of 'Jai Telangana', or 'Victory to Telangana'.

They didn't sound very convincing, and the gathering itself seemed unfocused except in its air of Sunday leisure. Behind the hall where the singer was performing, a large tent had been put up over a lawn crowded with plastic chairs. The entire complex was enclosed by walls and palm trees, with swans in a small enclosure in one corner. It represented someone's idea of a resort, and the people milling around looked like they were taking the day off. There were a few farmers, distinguishable by their hardened hands and feet and simple clothes, but the gathering otherwise spanned a middle class ranging from minor clerks to lawyers holding video cameras. Children played around the chairs and smoke billowed up from the kitchen where giants pots of rice were being made for the free lunch that would highlight the day's events.

It was in this gathering that I was introduced to Prabhakar and Devaram, men who brought a coiled energy into the holiday atmosphere. They worked for a small left-wing party with a big name. It was called the Communist Party of India Marxist-Leninist New Democracy (CPIML-ND), a group that had been one of the numerous Naxalite underground factions but since the nineties had surfaced to work through more traditional methods of organizing and electoral politics while also maintaining a few armed squads.

Prabhakar, who was in charge of the agricultural workers' union of the party in Nizamabad district, was a burly man. His hands were large and callused, and only his eyes, small pinpricks of brightness, seemed out of proportion to his body. He was carrying a yellow notepad that said 'Infosys', and when I pointed at the incongruity of a Maoist union organizer carrying a notepad branded with the name of one of India's biggest IT corporations, he guffawed loudly. His daughter worked for the company, he said, and she had given him the notepad as a gift.

As I talked with Prabhakar and Devaram, it became apparent that while they had some sympathy for those struggling for a separate Telangana state, they didn't feel too strongly about the issue. Their own activities, which they had been engaged in for the past three decades, were unlikely to change even in a new state. They tried to 'redistribute' land and check atrocities by upper-caste people in the rural areas, for which purpose they maintained an armed squad. 'We have to protect ourselves,' Prabhakar said. 'Otherwise, the thugs of the upper-caste landlords will finish us off.' They organized women who rolled the handmade Indian cigarettes known as 'beedis' and tried to protect farmers who got trapped in debt after taking loans from private moneylenders. 'These moneylenders are typically in the gold and jewellery business,' Prabhakar said. 'If you borrow one thousand rupees, you have to pay back two thousand to them after twelve months. We try to negotiate that interest rate. Sometimes we are successful, sometimes not.'

They were polite and confident, although obviously playing up the strength of their party. Prabhakar asked me to come to Armoor if I wanted to see how farmers were faring these days. When the government stopped the lending programmes of the public banks, the moneylenders had moved in, while the disbanding of the state agricultural offices had led to the rise of middlemen seed dealers. The state-run seed development corporation, which in the past had given farmers reasonable prices for their produce, had become virtually defunct, its warehouses abandoned and its offices empty.

4

After Devaram had shown me around Armoor, we went to the neighbouring village of Padgal to meet Sekhar, the 25-year-old farmer who had been shot during the rampage around Mahipal Reddy's house. The village appeared sleepy in the afternoon heat, smelling sharply of cow dung, while Devaram hammered insistently on a wooden door set into a stone wall. We were let into the courtyard of the house. Three women gathered around Devaram – Sekhar's grandmother, mother and wife – speaking in hushed voices and looking worried. Sekhar was in a Hyderabad hospital and it would be a couple of weeks before he was well enough to come home.

We went back up National Highway 16, cutting through Armoor and emerging on the other side of the town. There was a massive heap of black rocks on the edge of the town, old volcanic formations. 'It's called Navnath,' Devaram said. There was a temple on top of the rocks, but as a Dalit and as a Maoist, he felt no particular attachment to the temple. We left Navnath behind, the road opening on to fields of green. It was a pastoral scene, picturesque and hard to connect with the strife of red sorghum or the distress of farmer suicides. Poultry farms began to appear amid the agricultural plots, low-slung buildings with netting in place of walls, and then came the warehouses belonging to the seed dealers, at least twenty of them spread along a three-kilometre stretch. The warehouses were flat-roofed structures protected by high boundary walls. Most of them had the word 'Ganga' worked into their names, perhaps in part to evoke the protection granted by that faraway sacred river and perhaps partly out of a herd mentality. The warehouses were new, painted in pleasant shades of orange and green, unusual in a region where houses and buildings had not much more than a coat of whitewash, and the paint made the warehouses seem alien structures, seemingly disconnected from the land.

I asked Devaram if there was a way to meet Mahipal Reddy.

'Of course. His warehouse is just a little bit further on,' he said.

I wondered if Mahipal's men would recognize him.

'Only too well,' he said, speaking belligerently. 'I gave them a lot of trouble during the red sorghum agitation. How could they forget me?'

I said that it might not be a good idea for me to try and see Mahipal in his company – perhaps the seed dealer would speak more freely if I went with someone else.

Devaram became even more aggressive. 'Let's just go. Let's see how they stop us from meeting him, or how he doesn't talk to us,' he said.

It was with difficulty that I convinced him to hold off from visiting Mahipal and instead give me just a drive-by of the warehouse.

Devaram slowed his scooter down as we passed Mahipal's den. There was little I could see at first because of the canopy of trees and the boundary wall surrounding the warehouse. His business was called Godavari Seeds Company, and I found it interesting that he had chosen a local river for the name of his business instead of using 'Ganga', as most dealers in the area seemed to have done. There was a touch of confidence in this display of individualism, a sign of the brashness that had led him to become the biggest seed dealer in the area, and it made me even more curious about him. Devaram stopped in front of the gate, caught between the temptation to go in and start a fight and his promise to me that he wouldn't create any trouble. I could make out the long, horizontal shape of the main warehouse, with a couple of tarpaulin-covered trucks parked in front. To the right, there was a house, a white, two-storey concrete building that was as functional as the Armoor mansion had been ostentatious. There were a few people inside, but the atmosphere was low-key, with no indication that all this belonged to the biggest seed dealer in the area. According to people I spoke to later, Mahipal had offered farmers 15.4 rupees for a kilo of red sorghum when the market rate had been only 9 rupees a kilo. In fact, he had actually paid some of the farmers, I discovered later, clearing 34 crore rupees of the outstanding amount, although he owed an even greater sum of 44 crore rupees to the remaining farmers.

We drove back down the highway and stopped at a farmers' market in a village called Ankapur. There were vegetables and cobs of maize being weighed on large scales in an open shed, while bagged produce, the green leaves sticking out of the loosely tied sacks, was being loaded into tractors and trucks. On one side of the road, stunted, sunburned women with cropped hair (they had probably consecrated their hair to a local deity) sold roasted maize to people driving by, swishing bamboo hand fans over piles of coal and dabbing lime juice and salt on the cobs.

The Ankapur farmers looked nothing like the wiry, dusty men I had seen earlier that morning around the municipal office. They were sitting on plastic chairs drinking tea, their white clothes spotless, their wrists gleaming with gold watches. Devaram had told me that Ankapur was a prosperous, upper-caste village where farmers owned fifteen to twenty acres of land when the average landholding of an Indian farmer tends to be five acres or less. Devaram introduced me to the farmers, but he didn't join me as I sat down. He seemed to dislike them for their upper-caste prosperity, and if the farmers weren't openly hostile towards him, that was probably because of Devaram's ability to create trouble.

The farmers called for more tea and began talking in Hindi. Rajamma, a former sarpanch or village council chief, even spoke English. He was a slim, good-looking man in his early sixties, dressed in crisply pressed white clothes. He seemed quite interested in me, asking me to sit next to him. He wanted to talk about America. His son was an engineer there, he said, and so were the sons of many of the farmers gathered around. There were sharp nods, and as Rajamma asked the men to tell me where their sons were settled, the foreign names rang out in the marketplace, accompanied by the background noise of the maize sellers shouting out their prices to slowing vehicles and the grunts of migrant workers loading sacks of vegetables on to trucks. 'America', 'Germany', 'Australia', 'Scotland', the men cried out, as if these were the names of the crops they grew. Then they settled down, listening quietly as Rajamma talked about his visit to the United States.

He had gone to see a farm in Michigan with his son, Rajamma said. He had been astonished that a 125-acre plot could be farmed by just three men. The other farmers laughed, more with wonder than envy. They looked rather well rested, and I remembered that Devaram had said that few of them worked on the land any more, depending on hired labourers to do the farming. When I asked Rajamma if he had workers cultivating his land, he grew sanctimonious, saying that it was his social obligation to give jobs to people.

Later, I would find out that most of the workers were migrants, and almost none from the Telangana region.

But when I asked Rajamma who would run the farm after him, his smile faded into a wry look. His son would not return to the village life. Even his grandchildren, when they visited from America, grew restless after the initial few days of excitement. The other farmers nodded their heads in agreement. They had all done well enough to educate their children and send them to the West, but now there was no one to carry on the farming after them.

It was almost dusk when Devaram and I headed back towards Armoor, where I planned to stay the night at the Mamatha Lodge. Around seven, just as I was getting off Devaram's scooter, I got a call from Prabhakar. He wanted me to check out of the hotel and take a bus to Nizamabad town. 'You will stay the night here,' he said. 'I've arranged for you to meet several people. You can go back to Armoor later.' I had no idea where I would be staying, but ever since the morning I had been possessed by the feeling that nothing was under my control. So I succumbed to Prabhakar's request, feeling a little as if I had been recruited into the lower ranks of his organization as what they called a 'courier'.

I took my bag from Mamatha Lodge, giving the old man a tip on the way out, and went to the bus station. It had been stifling all day long, but now, as the bus began to make its way to Nizamabad, past the black rocks of Navnath, the warehouses, the empty market of Ankapur and Mahipal's headquarters, the skies opened up with rain.

## 5

As the bus rattled and rolled its way through the darkness, the rain began to pour in through holes in the roof, drenching people and forcing them to move aside. In an hour, the seats were mostly empty, while the aisle, somehow less leak-prone, was packed with crouching passengers. The young man next to me, an electrical worker who had been playing loud and bad Hindi film music from his mobile phone, looked at the people in the aisle with self-satisfaction. We were on the one seat that would not get wet, he declared. He had boarded the bus well before Armoor and had had time to observe the topography of the leaks. The bus entered the outskirts of Nizamabad town, the shops and houses appearing as a blaze of blurry lights through the rain-smeared windows, and water cascaded down over the electrician. He cursed, stood up, squeezed himself into the crowded aisle and did not look at me again.

Prabhakar was waiting for me at the bus station, smiling happily through the rain. He led me through the people gathered at the bus station, past shops selling cheap household items and eating places where pakoras were being fried in bubbling oil. The brands and consumerism of urban India had disappeared, and although I felt an acute sense of displacement, I was also oddly comforted by the rough utilitarianism of the place, which reminded me of the India I had grown up in. Here, there would be no escape from the self in objects or in technology. There were no cafés where I could hide my loneliness behind a cup of coffee and an open laptop, no shopping aisles where I could wander, picking out items that momentarily created an image of a better life. There was no escape here except through human relationships, and for that I was utterly dependent on Prabhakar speeding through the rain on his motorcycle.

He had planned everything out for me. I would meet his colleagues, including a senior comrade who had spent much time in jail. Then, at nine in the morning, I would go with Prabhakar to the office of the district collector, the highest government official in Nizamabad, where I could ask him questions about farmers and the red sorghum agitation. After that, I would visit a village far less prosperous than Ankapur, with a greater concentration of lower-caste farmers, many of whom had taken part in the agitation in Armoor. As for the night, I could sleep in Prabhakar's house, although he had reserved a room at a hotel near the bus station just in case I felt more comfortable that way. 'You're a city person, right?' he said, chuckling. 'Maybe you will not feel relaxed in my house.'

Prabhakar's house was packed with people who seemed to be a blur of names to me in my state of disorientation and tiredness. They were all members of the party, an assortment of shopkeepers, lawyers, waiters and mothers who seemed to have an extra edge imparted to their functional identities by their political activism. I met Prabhakar's wife, Godavari, a dark, good-looking woman with a slight limp who worked as a schoolteacher as well as for the party. Then, after we had tea and I dried myself off, I was taken to a house a short distance away to meet K. Yadhagri, a senior comrade who was the district secretary of the party.

Yadhagri was an idealist, one who had placed his faith in an unsuccessful movement. He had not become a big politician or even a junior functionary in a powerful party. He talked to me about how he had been influenced by Marxist literature − 'literature' was the word he used − as a young man in the late sixties. He had held a modest government job which he left in 1975, when the then prime minister Indira Gandhi suspended civil liberties throughout the country and imposed an 'Emergency' that gave complete autocratic powers to herself and to a small coterie of advisers. Yadhagri had gone underground, as had many others. The man who had been his political mentor was 'encountered' that year, by which he meant that the police had killed him and declared it as an encounter where both parties were armed. From 1978, Yadhagri had participated in both the armed movement of the party and in its non-violent protests, although his recent activities had largely been overground in nature.

I hadn't been particularly interested in the meeting with Yadhagri when Prabhakar had first mentioned it. I thought of it as something I had to go through in exchange for the help he was giving me. As I sat in Yadhagri's house, the rain cascading outside on empty, dark streets, I understood that I had been brought there because no journalist from the city would have any interest in interviewing Yadhagri. The overground Maoists were irrelevant in India, neither a potent political force on the national scale where what counts is money or identity politics nor as threatening as the underground Maoists with their liberated zones. But although it was 11 p.m. and I was tired and hungry, I gradually became interested in Yadhagri's story in spite of myself, especially given the setting in which I was listening to him. He was professorial in manner, simply dressed, the walls of his tiny house lined with leftist books and portraits of Marx and Lenin. But, along with his comrades, there were sons and daughters coming in and out of the sitting room, including a granddaughter who came and lay down on his lap, staying there quietly as he spoke to me of a deferred revolutionary struggle and the importance of the 'mass line' approach, which involved working at rousing the masses before the revolution could be launched. The simplicity of the surroundings as well as the idealism it evoked seemed intensely familiar, until it brought to me, in a sudden, unbearable wave of nostalgia, my child-hood and a time in India when many middle-class households had been like this, animated by literature, art and politics, and where people still lived in a community and believed in social justice.

When we went back to Prabhakar's house for dinner, I took a closer look at the neighbourhood. There was a white bust in the mid-dle of the street, recognizable by its hat, its pencil-line moustache and its fine, aquiline features as a representation of Bhagat Singh, the Indian socialist hanged by the British for killing a police officer. On the other side of the street from Prabhakar's house was a union office for workers who made beedis. The office was closed now, at mid-night. The neighbourhood was dark and quiet except for bits of light spilling out from the windows and the sound of rain dripping off leaves. I was surprised by how clean and tree-lined the neighbour-hood was, even though the people who lived there were mostly party activists and well below the middle class.

When I mentioned this to Prabhakar, he looked thoughtful. 'It was a dump, this land. It belonged to the government. We seized the land because all the comrades needed a place to stay. We were work-ing for the party and none of us had much money. There were police beatings, we held protests, but eventually the government allowed us to stay on. We made it what it is now.'

It was a story of social mobility, but a rather unexpected one. Prabhakar had grown up in the Khammam district of Telangana. His father, a shopkeeper, had been a Communist and participated in the Telangana peasant uprising from the late forties to the early fifties. Prabhakar, in turn, had dropped out of school after the seventh grade. He had become a Maoist and gone underground in the early seventies. While he belonged to a middle caste, he had married outside it. Godavari, his wife, was a Dalit. But their children were entering middle-class professions, with the daughter an IT worker and the son finishing a journalism degree.

'What do they think of your work?' I asked.

'They're proud of me, of us,' Prabhakar said. 'My daughter might work in Infosys, but she doesn't look down on what I do.'

We were late getting to the collector's office in the morning. I had stayed the night at the hotel, and although I called Prabhakar a number of times, he showed up only around nine thirty. The appointment had been made for ten, and we reached the collector's office half an hour late. We sat in the clerk's room. A man wearing a white uniform decorated with a black sash and a big brass badge that said 'Attender' walked into the collector's room carrying a tube of toothpaste. He returned a little while later carrying an empty bowl. It appeared that the collector was brushing his teeth: had he been in the office all night? I suddenly overheard Prabhakar explaining to the clerk why we were late. Even though I didn't know Telugu, I could understand perfectly well from Prabhakar's slight shake of the head towards me that he was saying that I had overslept. I felt momentarily indignant, but then I thought it was funny that even a Maoist comrade needed to save face. Later, I would find out that Prabhakar had been at a hospital all night, taking care of a fellow activist's son who had broken an arm in an accident.

The collector was holding a video conference with the head office in Hyderabad at eleven, and our only chance to see him would be after the conference. We decided to take a tea break and sat outside at a stall chatting with a couple of local reporters. A man without feet or arms made his way towards us, pulling himself painfully through the dust, sandals strapped to all four of his stumps. When he had left, the reporters told me that he was a leper who wanted to complain to the collector about the bad quality of the footwear issued to lepers by the government. It was an absurd yet poignant detail, making Nizamabad town feel suddenly like a magical-realist setting, a feeling that was enhanced as we walked back to the collector's office and saw nearly 100 children appear from nowhere, gathering in the courtyard and shouting slogans.

The children were very small, perhaps between eight and ten, looking colourful in spite of their shabby clothes as they fluttered around the office like butterflies holding a demonstration. A group of policemen came running into the courtyard, holding sticks and automatic weapons, their expressions turning foolish and confused when they realized that their adversaries were children. A dozen adults were visibly directing the children, whom they asked to squat in the courtyard while holding their placards and keeping up their chants. Prabhakar spoke to the men and found out that they were members of a village committee who had brought the children here because the government hadn't filled vacant positions at the local school. But the collector remained on his conference call and refused to meet the children. Instead, in keeping with the refinement of Indian bureaucracy, the collector's deputy, who had the designation of 'joint collector', dispatched her 'camp clerk' to take their 'petition'. The children left after presenting their case, and so did the collector, surrounded by a flurry of attendants and officials as he disappeared into a white Toyota Innova with an official red light revolving on top. Prabhakar turned to me with an embarrassed look on his face and suggested that we try again another day.

## 6

The village of Hasakothur was about sixty kilometres from Nizamabad town, a small cluster of houses and huts separated from National Highway 16 by fields of soy, maize and turmeric. In the late afternoon, when I arrived there, it seemed peaceful and slow, caught in the winding down of a work day that had begun just before dawn. It was a village of 5,000 residents, with the plots closer to the average size owned by Indian farmers – four to five acres rather than the twenty or so owned by the rich men of Ankapur.

Gopeti Rajeshwar was one of the farmers who worked on his own land. He had short, cropped hair and a moustache and was wearing a green lungi and a white vest that showed his powerful arms and sturdy build. He also possessed the calm, pragmatic air that seemed to be characteristic of farmers. Although he was more vocal than the other men who gathered around us, it took a while to get information out of him. He talked at a slow, steady pace, and even when he was discussing the suicides and the difficulties faced by farmers, he did so calmly, with only the occasional twitch of his lips to indicate emotion.

We sat on a bench outside the house of a man known as Dr Satyanarayana, a member of Prabhakar's party. Dr Satyanarayana wasn't really a doctor. He had been trained as a compounder and used the skill to provide much-needed medical services to the villagers. He was a small, friendly man, urging the farmers to talk to me but also content to leave Gopeti and me alone.

Like everybody else in the village, Gopeti had decided to supply red sorghum to Mahipal because the price offered had been very good. It was also relatively easy to grow red sorghum, he said, largely because it didn't need as much water as other crops. Once he had agreed to grow red sorghum, Mahipal's workers brought the seeds to the village, leaving them in the building that served as an office for the farmers' association. The seeds were in sacks of six kilos, each sack sold to a farmer for 300 rupees.

Gopeti took three sacks, which cost him 900 rupees. He spent another 1,800 rupees on a pesticide called Protex and on urea for fertilizer. The rest depended on his labour and skill. He had taken the seeds in November and expected the crop to be ready in four months. According to his calculations, three sacks would produce 3,600 kilos of seeds. For a total investment of roughly 3,000 rupees, he would make around 55,000 rupees – nearly twenty times the initial outlay – which sounded like a huge margin but did not take into account the labour involved in the process. The harvesting took about two days, with Gopeti and his family cutting the stalks by hand and depositing the seeds in the farmers' association office.

But the red sorghum remained in the office for weeks on end, with Mahipal refusing to send his men to collect the seeds. There were farmers from nearly 100 villages facing such a situation, and they eventually banded together and went to meet the collector in Nizamabad. The farmers knew that there were things happening that had made Mahipal's position rather precarious. Gopeti said that there were other dealers who were jealous of Mahipal and who had bought some red sorghum on the sly from a few villages. They took this stock to Mahipal's buyers and sold it at a very low rate, bringing down the market price of red sorghum. Mahipal hadn't anticipated such an event. He had expected to make a handsome profit, given the demand in past years for red sorghum, and he had ordered so much seed that he would need a bank loan to pay all the farmers. The sudden dip in the price of red sorghum scared Mahipal, who began to sense that he would have to sell it at a loss, at a rate well below what he had promised the farmers. Mahipal began to stall, Gopeti said, telling the collector that he needed more time to get the money. The farmers began agitating, and eventually converged in Armoor for a day-long protest, travelling there in trucks and buses.

I asked Gopeti who had burned the government jeeps. He avoided answering the question, and that seemed as good as a confession. He was adamant, however, that the farmers had not set fire to Mahipal's house. He said that it was Anand Reddy, the rival seed dealer, who had hired thugs to mix in with the farmers and destroy Mahipal's house and that Mahipal, in retaliation, had sent his men to attack Anand's house. The farmers, he said, had no part in any of this – in fact, some of them felt quite sympathetic towards Mahipal.

Later, when I was no longer in Andhra Pradesh, I would find some videos on YouTube of Mahipal's house being set on fire. Someone had taken movies with a mobile phone and posted them on the Web. The movies were very short, barely ten seconds each and rather grainy, but they were nevertheless surprisingly evocative: the mob collecting in front of Mahipal's mansion with its oddly imposing pillars; the shabby, unshaven men hammering away at the windows with iron rods; the view up a stairwell that showed flames rising up in the background.

All this seemed a world away from Hasakothur as I accompanied Gopeti to his farming plot, walking along narrow paths skirting the squares of green and looking out for the piles of shit where farmers had relieved themselves in the course of their work day. A teenage boy was bent over the trunk of a short palm tree, shaking an earthen pot. He was tapping toddy, to be drunk at home rather than sold, and Gopeti led me up for a closer look. The toddy was pungent and grey in colour, and large, drunken ants swarmed all over the pot. We walked on, passing a depression in the ground that was overgrown with weeds. It was a water tank, Gopeti said, but it had been dry for over a decade.

Most of the farmers depended for water on electrical pumps that they called borewells. The borewells were expensive, around 50,000 rupees each, and then there was the cost of putting the borewells in. The small companies that the farmers hired for this charged 150 rupees for each foot they went down, and often they had to dig to at least 250 feet to find groundwater. Even then, there was no guarantee that water would be found, and sometimes it was necessary to sink a dozen or more holes in a five-acre plot before striking water, each dig costing the farmers more money and putting them further in debt.

It was a cycle of diminishing returns. The area of Telangana received little rainfall and had only two perennial rivers, the Krishna and the Godavari. But the influence of the market and its tendency towards crop monocultures had made farmers switch from their older practice of growing millets – small-seeded grasses that require relatively little water – to the more commercially dominant and thirsty crops of cotton, maize and soybean. The Congress government that succeeded Naidu had criticized his policies and promised to bring irrigation canals to ten million acres of farmland, but after four years in power, an expert in Hyderabad told me, not a single acre had been brought under irrigation even though 600 billion rupees had been handed out to contractors.

The desperation of the farmers in Hasakothur for water, and their frantic digging to find aquifers, is part of a disturbing national trend. Michael Specter, an American journalist, noted in a 2006 article in the *New Yorker* that after thirty years, two million wells in India had proliferated to twenty-three million. He also pointed out that digging too deep brings in saltwater and arsenic contamination, something that has been happening in West Bengal and Punjab, both highly modernized agricultural states. 'As sources dry up and wells are abandoned, farmers have turned on each other and on themselves,'

Specter wrote. 'Indian newspapers are filled with accounts of …
"suicide farmers", driven to despair by poverty, debt, and often by
drought.' The Planning Commission of the Indian government,
meanwhile, in a recent study on Andhra Pradesh, observed that as
irrigation through canals remained stagnant and tank irrigation
declined, the number of borewells has increased exponentially, especially in Telangana, depleting the water table and leading to 'suicide
deaths'.

For Gopeti, this was all part of his life. Three farmers had killed
themselves the previous year in Hasakothur after incurring debts of a
couple of lakh rupees each. The money had been used largely to sink
borewells to find the water that would have allowed the men to keep
farming. Gopeti's own livelihood was precarious. His working day
began at four in the morning, when he fed his two buffaloes. At six,
he and his wife left for the fields, carrying a lunch of rice, dal and
vegetables. They took one break at nine and another at two to eat,
returning from the fields at six. Gopeti's wife went home to take care
of the cooking while he hung out at the village tea stall with other
farmers till eight. In a good year, Gopeti might make 40,000 to 60,000
rupees, but this was never assured, and he could easily find himself
owing that amount. Even when he made money, that had to be measured against the size of his family, which included his parents, his
wife, and three daughters between the ages of five and fifteen.

By the time Gopeti took me to see his house, it was already past
eight. He didn't seem keen to introduce me to his family, and I didn't
want to press the issue, so we surveyed the house from outside. It was
a two-storey concrete structure arranged around a courtyard, the
rafters stuffed with firewood that Gopeti's family gathered every few
months from nearby forests. The house was nearly three decades old,
having replaced a mud hut that had stood there before. The concrete
house had not been built with money made from farming, Gopeti
said as we walked back to Dr Satyanarayana's house. Gopeti's father
had worked in the Gulf as a labourer for two decades, saving money
that he used to build his family a new house. In fact, Gopeti himself
had stayed out of debt by working in the Gulf.

Although Gopeti had given me the impression of being completely rooted in his village, he had left home at the age of twenty. A middle-man had found him a job in Dubai, the kind of menial labour that is carried out by millions of South Asian immigrants in the rich Gulf States of the Middle East. The middleman's commission for getting Gopeti the job was 50,000 rupees. Gopeti travelled out of Hasako-thur with nine others from the village, all young men leaving their homes for the first time. They went by bus to Bombay, where they waited for a week as their papers were sorted out. They shared one tiny room, but because they had almost no money and a large amount of debt from having to pay the middleman's fee, they avoided going out into the city that they had seen in films and on television. One night, they were driven to the airport and put in the care of a foreman-like worker as they took the flight to Dubai. There, Gopeti went to work at a construction site. He worked for nine hours a day and six days a week, with Fridays off. He slept at a workers' camp in a tent, on what he said was a 'double khatiya', which I, after some effort, translated back into 'bunk bed'. On his day off, Gopeti cooked and did his laundry. As in Bombay, he avoided the city, and after working for two years, he made enough money to repay the loan he had taken to give the middleman his commission. He saved another 50,000 rupees on top of that, which went into buying a borewell for his farm when he came back to Hasakothur.

The electricity in the village had gone out, so we were sitting out-side Dr Satyanarayana's house, hoping to stay cool from the few wisps of wind blowing through the sleepy, dark village. The doctor had been listening to us, accompanied by a small and surprisingly bitter-looking man wearing glasses.

The man spoke up when Gopeti finished his story with his return to the village. 'He's not telling you how bad it really was there,' he said, staring accusingly at Gopeti.

The farmer laughed and shook his head. 'There's no point going into too many details,' he said.

The man, whose name was Janardan, leaned closer towards me. He was the village tailor, he said, and he had spent years working in Dubai and in Saudi Arabia. 'It's horrible there,' he said. 'The Arabs hate us. And after all the money you pay to brokers, after all the work you do, you have nothing.' And yet there was no alternative. He had sent his own son to Dubai in 2004 to work as an electrician, he said, paying a middleman 80,000 rupees. He borrowed the money, which with interest had become 100,000 rupees in a year's time. 'It's like running against a clock that's faster than you,' he said. He slumped back again, staring into the darkness.

I asked him if he earned money in the village from tailoring.

He looked at Gopeti and laughed. 'They never have money for new clothes. My wife makes about five hundred rupees a month from rolling beedis. We live on that.'

## 7

A few days after visiting Hasakothur, I finally managed to see the district collector of Nizamabad. It was Saturday morning when I went to meet him at his house, where I was let in by an armed guard and pointed towards the sprawling bungalow where the collector had a home office. It was a large room, with rows of empty chairs facing the collector's desk, as if he was in the habit of giving lectures or performances from the desk. He wasn't in the room when I was led in, and I sat there for a while, watching the incense sticks on the desk sending their curls of smoke up towards the bright poster of a waterfall.

The collector was a heavyset man, wearing a bright orange shirt, and he surprised me by his candour. The trouble over the red sorghum, he said, was a symptom of the crisis in rural Telangana. The instability in agriculture was something which had been created in great part by the new class of seed dealers. They had connections to politicians, and under the patronage and protection this offered, they often formed syndicates among themselves to manipulate crop prices. The seed dealers made money out of all this, as did their buyers, but the farmers lost heavily in the process.

The price for red sorghum had been rather low the year before, the collector said, and the farmers had wanted the government to intervene on their behalf. He had therefore held an auction in the presence of all the seed dealers where the highest price for red sorghum had come from Mahipal Reddy. The farmers, naturally, had accepted this bid. The collector had wanted to be sure that Mahipal's business was sound enough to handle such a large order, and Mahipal had accordingly showed him a guarantee note from a bank for 40 crore rupees to prove that he would be able to pay the farmers. The trouble began after this, when the farmers had nearly finished growing the crop. A syndicate of dealers opposed to Mahipal had gone to the bank that had issued the guarantee note. They had told the bank that there would be such an excess of red sorghum that prices were bound to be far lower than what Mahipal had offered the farmers. The bank went back on its guarantee note and cancelled its loan to Mahipal. The farmers began their agitation, and the collector was convinced that they were instigated to do so by the rival syndicate. Mahipal then asked the collector for time, promising to pay interest on the money he owed to the farmers. But some of the traders who had originally been part of Mahipal's syndicate now defected to the other side, even as Prabhakar's party began to put pressure on the government, with the farmers beginning a hunger strike. The collector agreed to buy the red sorghum at 12 rupees a kilo, promising that if the state made more than this amount, the excess would be given to the farmers. The cheques I had seen being written out at the municipal office on my first morning in Armoor were part of the government's payment to the farmers.

It was a simple, happy ending to a complicated story, where the government's role was a reassuring, paternal one. But the collector had his reasons for believing that the government had to be active in supporting farmers. They were largely illiterate, he said, and didn't have unions. Only the rich, connected farmers were organized enough to have a union. The collector thought that the problems being faced by poorer farmers had increased since the government stopped subsidizing agricultural commodities – offering a guaranteed rate to farmers if they did not manage to sell their crops to private buyers for a higher price. But support prices were among the practices dismantled by the Naidu-McKinsey approach, leaving farmers to function in the best way they could in the free market with its syndicates, price volatility and speculation.

The collector seemed, for all the trappings of power, to have a

... of the situation in rural India. He had mentioned the ... passing with a note of sympathy, and when I said it was ... to hear a government official not denouncing the guer- ... he laughed. 'I am from a rural background,' he said. 'From a landowning class, that's true. But it's the urban officers and the people at the very top who think of the Maoists as enemies. In many villages, a few families own everything. You can see that, and if you do, then you know that the Naxalites have to be made partners in the national value system.' He paused for a moment and thought. 'If you see the Maoists who are killed by the police in encounters, none of them have more than forty kilos of flesh on them. They're skin and bones. And these are the enemies of the state?'

The collector was reaffirming much of what I had heard in Hyderabad, some of it from a man called Ramanjaneyulu. He ran a non-profit organization called the Centre for Sustainable Agriculture in a house off a narrow lane. He was a rather intense man, vibrating with nervous energy, addressing me in a rapid-fire manner while he answered his mobile phone or checked mail on his laptop. But Ramanjaneyulu was willing to criticize the government as well as the market in his comments about the state of agriculture in India. Until 2004, he had been an agriculture officer in the government. But he left the service when he became convinced that the government's approach towards agriculture, characterized by its cosy nexus with multinationals and its focus on modernization and genetically modified seeds, was quite wrong.

'We don't have the US kind of subsidies, technical support and accountability, which allows you to sue the producer if the seed doesn't work,' he said. 'The first farmer suicide took place in the state in 1986, and that was because the cotton crop failed. There was an incident of white flies, to which the government responded by bringing in new pesticides, which in turn led to new problems, to which GM was proposed as a solution.' He shook his head vigorously. 'The present model is unsustainable. What you need is small farming based on an ecological and sustainable model, which is what our centre tries to encourage in villages. Otherwise, we're looking at a situation where four hundred million farmers will move out of their land by 2011.'

The farmers had been moving off the land in large numbers from the time of the British. I came from a family of farmers too, with my grandfather an unschooled peasant who had grown rice. When my father and his brothers had talked about the past, which was rarely, they mentioned only the good things: the mangoes plucked from trees; the boat taken to school during seasonal floods; the songs sung by my grandfather, who was a strolling minstrel as well as a peasant. I had to look into the edges of these stories to find the darker material: the nameless man killed by my great-grandfather for stealing crops; the death of one of my uncles in early childhood; the earnestness with which my father pursued studies at the village school, convinced even then that farming was a way of the past; the white men who appeared from time to time as spectral representatives of the British Empire; and the silent exodus from that village when independence in 1947 brought with it the partition of the subcontinent into three parts.

Yet even though the life of the Indian farmer had been precarious in the nineteenth and early twentieth centuries, it had required the incredible trauma of famines that killed millions as well as the ethnic cleansing of the 1947 partition to move large numbers of peasants off their land and into slums. But the numbers Ramanjaneyulu was talking about were simply staggering. Four hundred million people made up nearly one-fourteenth of the world's population, and it seemed impossible that the transformation of so many people from rural to urban poor could be achieved without some kind of cataclysm. But there was no doubt that the process was under way, if in a slow trickle compared to the magnitude of the numbers involved. Long after I had left Armoor, I found it surprising when I realized how many of the people I had met there were in transition from farming. The collector was from a farming family, while Devaram, the Dalit agitator, had been a farm worker. Even Mahipal Reddy, the dealer at the centre of the red sorghum story, had once been a farmer.

8

But it took me a long time to get to Mahipal. I had called him soon after my visit to Hasakothur. He was polite but evasive, saying that

he was travelling too much to talk to me and in any case didn't want
to go into the red sorghum story. I kept pestering him and finally,
one Saturday, he agreed to meet me and give me his version of the
events. He asked me to come to his warehouse outside of Armoor
that afternoon. Before that, he would be busy in Nizamabad town,
where he had some business to take care of. I told him I was in the
town and could meet him right there, but he insisted that I come to
the warehouse. 'Just call me before you show up, to make sure that
I'm back from Nizamabad,' he said.

I went down to Armoor around one, intending to take another
look at the burned mansions before I went to see Mahipal. I had
arranged to meet with Saveen, a lecturer in literature at a local college. Saveen was Devaram's nephew, but he could not have been
more different in appearance from the truculent, bearded organizer.
He was a clean-cut, handsome young man who wouldn't have been
out of place in a big city, although underneath the polish, he had an
intensity that wasn't all that different from Devaram's manner.

I found it a relief to wander around Armoor with Saveen and to
discuss something other than red sorghum for a short time. Saveen
talked about a summer he had spent teaching literature in Libya. He
had been impressed by the country, he said, especially the level of
equality it had achieved, and he contrasted it with the scene around
him, where Dalits like him were still treated badly and where, even as
an educated man, he had to be on his guard. We approached Mahipal's
house, empty and gutted, with wind blowing through the gaping
window frames. We went around the back to the spot where the
police had fired at the farmers. Some of the bullets had struck the
wall of a hardware shop, and as I fingered the holes in the concrete
and in the metal shutter, the shop owner came out to talk to me. He
had been terrified when the firing happened, he said, and had hurriedly begun closing his shop. But the farmers hadn't been afraid, he
said. They had laughed at the police.

We left Mahipal's house and headed in the other direction, towards
Anand Reddy's house. The old man I had seen before was still there,
still dusting away. He nodded when Saveen asked him if we could
come inside. We walked past the black Ford to the house, and even

though we could have just stepped in through the gaps where the windows had been, we followed convention and went up the steps to a little porch, through a doorway whose wooden frame had been charred into black coal, and into the living room where the white marble floor was disfigured by great black patches.

Even in its present state, the house seemed opulent. Saveen appeared awed by the wealth it spoke of, and he whispered that it felt wrong to walk around inside the house without permission from the owners. He needn't have worried. Some of the owners were at home, upstairs, and the old man had gone to call them. I turned around to see three people coming in: an elderly lady, a woman in her thirties and a girl in a school uniform.

My attention was drawn to the woman in her thirties, everything about whom suggested that she was the mistress of the house. She was wearing a bright blue sari, from the fringes of which one foot displayed a gleaming golden toe ring. She was slightly plump, and light-skinned – attributes that declared the upward mobility of the man who had married her with as much clarity as the marble and teak in the fittings of the house.

The woman was Mrs Anand Reddy, perfectly poised and quite unperturbed to find two strangers examining her devastated residence. 'It's all because of that Mahipal Reddy,' she said, her fair face darkening a shade as she mentioned the name. She said that her husband and his brother had run a seed business for years in Armoor without any trouble. 'We've never cheated the farmers. This time we didn't even have any business with the farmers. It was Mahipal Reddy who made the arrangement with them. So why did they attack us?' It became clear that her anger was directed at Mahipal rather than the farmers. 'The kharif season is coming up,' she said. 'The farmers have taken out loans and were expecting to clear their loans with the payments for the red sorghum. They wanted to buy seeds to plant rice, for fertilizers and tractors, but they had no money and so they went berserk.'

She had just moved back to the house a couple of days earlier with her mother-in-law and daughter and was living on the upper floor, the least damaged part of the house. 'He grew too big too fast,' she said, still thinking of Mahipal. 'He made his money too quickly.' She lowered her voice. 'There are rumours that the collector got some benefits from Mahipal.'

'What kind of benefits?' I said.

'I don't know,' she said. 'Well, the collector's daughter was getting married. We heard that Mahipal made a gift to the daughter, an *oddalam*.'

'I don't know what that is,' I said.

'It's a gold belt that women wear on their waists in this part of the country,' she said, looking amused. 'The one the collector got was supposed to be worth fifteen lakh rupees.'

I tried calling Mahipal soon after we'd left his rival's house. He said he was still in Nizamabad and would have to cancel the meeting. When I insisted, he asked me to try him again around five. Saveen, who had been listening in on the conversation, said that Mahipal was avoiding me and would keep putting me off until I went away. I said I would just go to the warehouse and wait for him there, hoping that he would show up at some point.

Saveen looked worried when he heard this. 'These are not very safe people,' he said. 'Do you have to meet him?' When he realized I was determined to see Mahipal, he said he would take me to see a friend of his who was a business partner of Mahipal's.

We rode on Saveen's scooter to the outskirts of Armoor, stopping at the fraying edge of the marketplace where the highway curved away from the town. Saveen led me up to the first floor of a shabby concrete building where, in a room that was bare except for a desk and a few chairs, there was a man talking on the phone. He was in his thirties, clean-shaven, wearing an expensive-looking shirt with black and grey circles patterned on the white background. But it was his hands to which he had devoted special attention, with a big gold ring on his right index finger, while above a red sacred thread on his left wrist dangled two thick gold chains.

He was also the first rude person I had met in Andhra Pradesh. He asked me something in Telugu, and although I didn't understand the question, the tone of his voice and the tilt of his head made it clear that he wasn't being particularly polite. Saveen hurriedly launched into an explanation to which the man listened carefully. Then he asked us to sit and switched to Hindi. His name was Rajkumar, and ethnically he was a Marwari, from the western Indian state of Rajasthan. In other ways, though, he could be considered a local man, with his family having settled down in the region many generations ago. The primary family business was in gold and jewellery, Rajkumar said, which meant that they were also moneylenders. 'But don't assume too much from what you see here,' he said a little threateningly. 'This is a small office. Just a front. My business is elsewhere, and it's not only in jewellery. I'm a partner of Mahipal's, among other things.'

'I'd like to meet Mahipal,' I said, 'but it's proving hard to do that.'

'If I take you, he will meet you,' Rajkumar said, snapping his fingers at an attendant to bring us tea. 'But why should I take you? Who are you to me?'

He listened lazily to my answer and then to Saveen's more elaborate explanation. He occasionally grunted in response to Saveen, but for the most part he seemed uninterested in our presence and was busy texting on his mobile phone. I was surprised when he stood up and said, 'Come, the car is here.'

There was a white Toyota Innova van parked outside, its seats covered with white cloth. There was another passenger in the car, a man of about Rajkumar's age who looked like a minor political functionary in his spotless white kurta-pyjamas and dark sunglasses. 'He's one of my business partners,' Rajkumar said as he slid smoothly into the car. 'He's a farmer. A rich farmer.' The rich farmer nodded and began texting as the van pulled out.

## 9

The Toyota sped away from the town, past the black rocks of Navnath and through the countryside. The hum of the air conditioning, the liveried driver, the white covers on the seats and the expressionless faces of the two business partners, both now wearing dark glasses, added a touch of menace to the more commonplace aura of power and wealth in the car. I felt as if I was in the company of cocaine lords, and that impression was only heightened when the Toyota honked at the gates of Mahipal's warehouse and drove in. We climbed out of the car, and as servants ran around to get plastic chairs, we joined a circle of men sitting in the yard, one of them intent on counting a large stack of currency notes.

Mahipal was eyeing me sheepishly, which seemed to indicate that he knew who I was even though we hadn't yet been introduced. Raj-kumar took him aside to talk, and when they returned, Mahipal asked me to sit next to him. Here, finally, was the man at the centre of the red sorghum story, someone who had either been the victim of a conspiracy by other dealers or who was directly responsible for all the chaos.

I had been expecting a hard-edged man, but Mahipal, with his glasses and wavy hair, looked very soft, especially when compared to the villainous Rajkumar. He began to speak quickly, almost airily, as he tried to show me how well his business was doing, his comments supported with enthusiastic exclamations from the surrounding crowd of yes men. 'I am first and foremost a farmer, and the son of a farmer,' Mahipal began, sounding as if he was addressing a political rally. 'Everything I have done, I did it for the farmers.'

He had started as a small farmer, he said, with little education but with sufficient foresight to get into the seed dealing business in the late eighties. By 1990, he had built his warehouse and was dealing in seeds supplied by big companies, including multinationals, and sup-plying buyers from all over India. The other dealers in the area had been in the habit of giving low rates to farmers, who had naturally begun moving to him when he began offering them more money. This year, when the collector called an auction of all the dealers, Mahipal had been the only one to meet the asking price of 15 rupees a kilo from the farmers. It was a reasonable offer for him to make, he said. There was a lot of demand for lal jowar in North India, where many of his buyers were located. 'Not just in North India,' Mahipal said. 'In other parts of India too. Even in Pakistan.' The only condi-tion he had set was that he wanted the entire crop of the area because he was worried that his rivals might buy some red sorghum and dump it on the market to drive down the price. But this happened anyway, he said. 'These other people, they went around and offered twenty-two rupees to the farmers. Five villages sold it to the other dealers at that price. They took it to Delhi and sold it for thirteen, at a big loss. Why did they do that? They wanted to finish off Mahipal Reddy.'

He paused to catch his breath, and the men around him nodded with approval at how well Mahipal was telling the story.

'I applied for a loan of forty crore rupees from HDFC bank to finance the seed purchase,' Mahipal continued. 'The bank gave me a letter approving the loan, and I gave them a bond as security. Then these other people, they went to the bank and said that lal jowar was fetching a market price of only six or seven rupees. The bank called me and said they were cancelling the loan. I asked the collector for his help. He spoke to the bank, then to some of the other banks, but none of them would give me a loan. The other dealers then created a team to make trouble. They wanted to set fire to this warehouse and to murder me. Some farmers, mostly the Maoist party people, began a hunger strike. Then they held a big protest with some antisocial elements joining in with them.

'I was in Hyderabad at the time, and not in the warehouse. I was afraid of what the antisocial elements hired by the other men might do to me. But they came after me in Hyderabad too. I have a house there and I was going home one evening when I got a phone call telling me to turn back. I asked the driver to slow down when we approached my house. We could see two cars parked right outside the house, both filled with men. I called my family to come out quickly and get into the car. We drove away and the cars followed us, but then, when they saw me driving to the Taj Banjara Hotel, they backed off. There were too many people for them to do what they wanted to do. We stayed in the hotel that night. Later, I found out that my house in Armoor had been ransacked and burned down. I took a loss of one crore rupees on the house. They didn't even leave a spoon.'

I asked Mahipal if Anand Reddy was the dealer who had caused all the trouble.

'No,' he said. 'The real villain is a man called Vijender Reddy. He lives in Hyderabad, not here, but he runs Ganga Kaveri Seeds. He's the one who stopped the bank loan. The people who went on hunger strike, he sponsored them. He's the big dealer in the area.'

I had the odd feeling that I had heard Mahipal's story before, but I couldn't quite pin down the source. Later, I would remember the account Arindam Chaudhuri had given me of his father being driven to the campus of his management institute and seeing the men waiting to assault him. It was like an archetypal scene in the lives of men rising upwards in the new India, with similar elements: the mysterious phone call, the shadowy rivals, the view through the windscreen of a car, the thugs waiting at the end of the road and the refuge found in a hotel.

But I didn't make the connection right then. The setting was too different, with an edge to the men who sat around me even if Mahipal himself seemed smooth and polished. I was also busy trying to figure out if I had followed all the parts of Mahipal's narrative: the bidding, the syndicates, the price fixing, the loans, the rumours, the threats, the thugs, the hotel, the car, the arson and the riot. It brought back the feeling that I was tracing a story about cocaine rather than red sorghum. And perhaps there was a relation between cocaine and red sorghum in the way speculation filled the space between the supposedly neutral market forces of supply and demand. If one changed the scale of the profits so that the seed bought for 15 was sold to the wholesale buyer not for 22 but for 2,200, the scene around me would naturally be transformed. The dealers would be tougher, their warehouses heavily guarded and Rajkumar would presumably thrive. Red sorghum, in that sense, was just a very cheap kind of cocaine.

'What is red sorghum for?' I asked. 'Can people eat it?'

'No, no,' the people around me cried out. 'It's for *bhains*, cattle, and for chicken.'

Mahipal smiled and said, 'It makes them fat, makes them produce more milk, more eggs, more meat, so that people in the cities can eat them and get bigger.' He asked one of the attendants to see if there was any red sorghum left in the warehouse. The man returned with a handful that he poured on to my palm – hard, small grains that were reddish in colour, opaque objects that seemed so static and yet whose value went up and down on the market.

I had been leaning close to Mahipal to hear him better, and I suddenly smelled the alcohol on his breath. It hadn't been much past four when we came in, so he must have started his drinking early.

'My business is fine in spite of all the trouble,' Mahipal said. 'Look at all this work going on around me. I'm going to be expanding even more next year. Look at how busy I am!'

He had two mobile phones on his lap which rang incessantly, one of them playing a pop version of the song 'Ain't No Sunshine When She's Gone'. On his left, there was an anxious-looking man with whom Mahipal began to discuss transporting seeds. The man had a creased plastic shopping bag from which he pulled out wads of money.

'This is one lakh,' he said. 'I'll give you two lakhs tomorrow.'

'That's fine,' Mahipal said, looking unconcerned.

The man tied the bag up with a piece of string and handed it to one of the attendants, and after looking at Mahipal with an air of expectation and receiving no response, he left.

Dusk was setting over Mahipal's warehouse, although the sun seemed to hold its light steady for the men sitting in the circle. The engines of trucks roared behind us as they were backed up, one by one, to the loading ramp of the warehouse, while to our left the electric lights came on in the two-storey concrete building where Mahipal lived when he wasn't in Hyderabad. The mood of the gathering seemed to have eased now that the red sorghum story was over, and Mahipal became friendly. Saveen and I got up to leave. I was planning to take a bus from Armoor to Nizamabad, where I was supposed to have dinner with Prabhakar and his family at nine.

'You can't go now,' Mahipal said. 'You must have a drink with us. What do you drink? Whisky?'

I was anxious to go, exhausted now after closing the circle of the red sorghum episode. I knew I could keep pursuing the story, perhaps chasing down the villain's villain, the man in Hyderabad whom Mahipal had spoken of as the biggest dealer in the area. But I also felt done, and I was tired of Armoor and the surrounding landscape. But Mahipal was so insistent that I agreed to have a drink.

An attendant was dispatched to Armoor to buy whisky and beer.

The circle around Mahipal grew smaller and more intimate, and as darkness consumed the yard where we had been sitting, we moved to the house. There were five of us – Rajkumar, Saveen, a man with very small eyes, Mahipal and me – and we sat in a bedroom on the upper floor. There was a television, a bed and a coffee table on which a servant had put plates of pakoras and potato chips mixed with chopped onions and green chillies. The bottles were opened – Kingfisher beer for Saveen and me, Blender's Pride whisky for the others – and the television was switched on to a news channel.

There had been a series of bomb blasts in Bangalore, and the men wanted to hear news of this. But the anchor of the Telugu channel, a woman dressed in a Western suit, hadn't got to the blasts yet, so the attention of the drinkers drifted away from the television. The sleek air conditioner hummed away in the background, the conversation grew louder, while Saveen became ever quieter, uncomfortable in this gathering of men who made money with such ease. The conversation stopped when there was a news clip about a Bollywood starlet called Shilpa Shetty. There was a slight grin on the male reporter's face as he displayed a pin-up of Shetty, the lower half of the picture blanked out by a black square. Somebody made a joke and everybody apart from Saveen laughed.

Mahipal's phone rang. He began speaking rapidly into it in Hindi. I was sitting next to him and I followed the conversation with ease, drawn in by Mahipal's pleading tone. He was begging with the man who had called him, asking him for a loan of 5 lakh rupees. I was surprised by how small an amount Mahipal was asking for, especially given the scale of his business and the tens of crores we had been speaking of earlier. But as Mahipal kept talking, unaware or unheeding that I could understand him, I began to get a sense that things were precarious for him.

'I'm in a bad shape,' he said. 'My jowar seeds are still lying in the godown and I need at least thirty-five to forty lakhs. I've sold off the land in Hyderabad and that'll give me some money, but if you can give me at least ten now, I can then hold out till I get the money from selling the land. That cunt Pappi, he doesn't answer his phone even though I've called him so many times.'

When he hung up, he seemed as relaxed as ever, perhaps even more boisterous. He was going to Delhi next week, along with Rajkumar and the man with the small eyes.

'We'll fly there and then we'll hire a Tata Sumo to go and visit our buyers in Delhi, Uttar Pradesh, Haryana and Punjab.' When Mahipal heard that I was going to be in Delhi too, he became insistent that I meet them there. 'We'll have a nice hotel room, yaar. We can drink as much as we like.'

Since the beer had gone to my head, I spoke as loudly as the rest of them and said that of course we would meet up.

'If we can't meet in Delhi, we'll meet you in America,' the man with the small eyes said. Mahipal and he would be going to Texas, where the latter's son was an engineer with Motorola. Then they would go to Illinois. Then, where should they go after that? they asked me. Las Vegas? Niagara Falls? Atlantic City? New York? Where and how would they be able to spend all the money that they made?

Saveen suddenly leaned over the table towards me. 'You should call and cancel the dinner,' he said, speaking softly but with emphasis.

'No, I can't do that,' I said.

'It would not be good for you to leave at present,' he said. 'I know them for many years. Just cancel the dinner. This is not the right time to leave.'

I was taken aback and looked around the room. Was Saveen saying that these men would get violent if I tried to leave now? They didn't strike me as particularly menacing, apart from Rajkumar, and the way they were speaking, shouting loudly, was nothing more than the slightly sentimental drunkenness Indian men are prone to after a few pegs.

Saveen leaned towards me again and said, somewhat desperately, 'They will smell the liquor on your breath and they will be unhappy.'

I realized that he wasn't worried about me leaving Mahipal's gang, as much as about me going to Prabhakar's house for dinner. The comrades were all anti-alcohol and would be upset with me. 'Okay,' I told Saveen. But I also wanted to get out, and so I finished my beer and stood up. I thought I would walk to the Ankapur market and wait there for a bus to Nizamabad, but Mahipal insisted that his driver would drop me off.

Another white Toyota Innova van was requisitioned. I climbed in next to the liveried driver, feeling slightly drunk. The driver fiddled with the air conditioner to get the temperature just right, put some Telugu music on and drove smoothly along National Highway 16 towards Nizamabad. Before heading off, he assured me that he was a very good driver and that prior to working for Mahipal, he had driven a minister in the state cabinet.

It started raining – not the confetti being sprinkled earlier in the evening, but monsoon gusts that cascaded down the windscreen. Two thin farmers ran down the highway on our right, covering their heads with plastic sheets, one of them holding a torch. Another man wheeled his scooter in the same direction as us, completely soaked in the rain. We kept moving, our big van equal to the challenge of the rain and the darkness, more powerful than our surroundings. A truck suddenly came at us out of the night, and for a second I thought it was going to smash into us. In the blaze of headlights, I saw the name the driver had chosen for his truck and that was painted above the windscreen. It said 'Kranti', or 'Revolution'. Then the trucker adjusted his course and flashed past us, heading towards Armoor.

# The Factory: The Permanent World of Temporary Workers

*The encounter squad – India's first Egyptian resort – the steel factory – Malda labour – the barracks – reading Amartya Sen – the security guards – the Tongsman – ghost workers – Maytas Hill County*

## 1

The highway out of Hyderabad towards Kothur village was still being worked on, with new overpasses and exits being constructed next to the lanes that were open to traffic. Vijay and I were halfway to our destination when we saw the man appear, standing in the middle of the road and waving us down. We were travelling fast, moving much too quickly to understand immediately what the man's appearance meant. A few days earlier, on this same road, we had been stopped by two police constables. Assigned to guard duty at another point on the highway and left to fend for their own transportation, all the men had wanted was a lift. But the figure in front of us now was not in uniform, and his objective was far less clear, although I had the impression that he was part of the knotted confusion of people and cars that had sprung up suddenly on the smooth thread of the highway.

Vijay brought his tiny car to a halt, and the man loomed up in front of the windscreen, a dark, stocky figure dressed in a T-shirt and jeans. He put his right hand down on the bonnet of our car. In his left hand, he held an automatic pistol, its barrel pointing up at an acute angle. His gaze, as it swept over our faces, was intense, scrutinizing us carefully, meeting our eyes for a few seconds. Then he abruptly lost interest in us and switched his attention to a motorcycle coming up from behind, on our right. He advanced swiftly towards the bike, pointing his pistol at the riders. A policeman in uniform appeared on our left, tapped on our window, and asked us to move on.

Vijay drove away slowly, his eyes and mine fixed on the rear-view mirror to get a better sense of the composition of the scene. There was the gunman in front of the motorcycle. Off to the side, next to the uniformed policeman, was a red Maruti car, a modest, everyday model of the kind that might belong to a minor civil servant or a doctor. There was a policeman sitting at the wheel, an officer in a peaked cap, his window rolled down. There was also a man in the back seat, but he was invisible, just a silhouette behind the tinted black window. The gunman had now moved on from the motorcycle towards an approaching bus, which he flagged down, waiting as the passengers slowly piled out on to the road.

From all this, it was possible to come to the following conclusions. The men were hunting for someone. The gunman did not know what this person looked like; it was the invisible man in the back of the car, an informer, who knew that. They expected their target to be coming this way, but they had no information as to how he or she was travelling, which is why they had stopped a car, a motorcycle and a bus. The mix of uniformed men and the armed man in plain clothes, the unmarked civilian car being used by the policemen, and the pistol – rather than rifle – in the hand of the gunman meant that this was not a legal operation. We had just run into one of the encounter squads operated by the police, what Devaram had talked about when he pointed his imaginary pistol at me. If the target had the misfortune of running into the encounter squad, he would probably be gunned down in cold blood, with a report released later to the media to say that the person had been killed in an active encounter and that he had shot first at the police.

Later, I would find out from news accounts that the police had indeed been looking for a Maoist who, fortunately, did not show up that day. At the time, though, the scene felt unreal as soon as we had left it behind, taking on the shape of a dream. And in a way, the encounter squad was a dream, surfacing from the deep regions of the national subconscious where farmer suicides, Maoists and impoverished workers swirled together to form the collateral damage of progress. In a few weeks, the prime minister would announce the dispatching of tens of thousands of paramilitary troops to encircle the Maoists in the 'red corridor' they had carved out in the forests of central India, but although this was one more reminder of the ways in which India was at war with its own people, it would elicit little comment from the big cities.

The truth was that India was being remade forcefully, and some aspects of that remaking were more visible than others. Once the encounter squad had been left behind, it seemed almost impossible not to give in to the pleasure of the new, smoothly tarred highway with its carefully demarcated lanes. It lifted us off the surrounding landscape like an aircraft, and as I looked down at the uneven patchwork of agricultural fields where people toiled ceaselessly in the summer heat, I could not help but think of them as marooned at a lower plane of existence. The highway was the transcendent future, with its straight shoulders and central reservations cradling flowers and topiary bushes, its green signs and electronic boards copied from advanced civilizations in the West. The signs told us that we were driving southwards, in the direction of Bangalore, and that if we wanted to, we could loop across all of India on this highway. It was part of the Golden Quadrilateral project, a six-lane band of modernity embracing the country, with only the occasional glitch of an encounter squad to remind us of those being left behind.

I had last been in Andhra Pradesh a year before, in 2008, when I spent most of my time with the farmers around Armoor. This time, Vijay was taking me to a village called Kothur in the district of Mahabubnagar. It was close to Hyderabad, about thirty kilometres from the city, and change was visible all the way up to the village. We stopped for lunch just before we got to Kothur, driving past a security guard into a walled complex. The area had once been a vineyard producing table grapes, but the land had since been acquired by a property developer. The vineyards had been destroyed and two pyramids put up in their place. They were part of Papyrus Port, which was, as the brochure put it, 'India's First Egyptian Resort'.

The pyramids were not very large, perhaps thirty feet high, and were made of granite. They had names – Khafres and Khufus [sic] – but like all the other proper nouns echoing through the resort ('Lawn of Isis', 'Lawn of Osiris', 'Prometeus [sic] Unbound Health Club'), the names suggested not Egyptian or Greek but an Indian sort of Disneyland. Yet although money had been spent in putting up the resort and effort expended in creating a clean and comfortable complex, Papyrus Port was still more an idea than a place, with the offerings in the brochure far more generous than what was available in the actual resort.

The pictures showed a large swimming pool, a huge conference hall, a zoo, 'multicuisine' restaurants and a list of 'adventurous sports' running from 'Water Zorb' – whatever that might be – to 'Commando Net'. In reality, the swimming pool was small, the 'Prometeus Unbound Health Club' a tiny room with two lonely treadmills, the zoo a cage with some sick-looking rabbits whose fur was falling off, and the multicuisine restaurants of Khafres and Khufus capable at that moment of serving only local food.

But there was something other than the gap between vision and reality that added to the dissonance of Papyrus Port. Apart from a dating couple in the restaurant and a family group enjoying kebabs on the lawn, the place was empty. It had been crowded when Vijay visited it a couple of years earlier, but now, in the summer of 2009, there was suddenly less money in India. The global downturn had come home, and even the middle classes and the elites accustomed to the high-consumption side of globalization were beginning to find things difficult. The campus recruitment conducted by IT companies in engineering colleges was down or, in some cases, had stopped entirely. There were lay-offs happening in many organizations. The building boom that had thrown up condos everywhere had slowed down, and the billboards in Hyderabad offered free rent and discounts to entice customers into buying the half-built units. In my mother's lower-middle-class neighbourhood in Calcutta, the posters offering jobs in call centres had been displaced by signs that said: 'Sick of credit card debt? Tired of phone calls demanding money? Call this number to find a solution.' The downturn was one reason why Papyrus Port was emptier than it should have been.

When an attendant showed us around the 'Live Like a Pharaoh' suites, they too turned out to be empty. Vijay had thought that I might want to stay at the resort, but I decided that I would be better off at his house in the village. The resort was comfortable, but it was hard to picture being there in the evening, all by myself apart from the staff, a middle-class pharaoh protected by security guards and an electric fence from the land and its people.

2

The land was part of the district of Mahabubnagar, and it was teeming with people. Many of them were outsiders, itinerant figures coming from as far north as Uttar Pradesh, Bihar and Madhya Pradesh, or from the eastern segment of India that includes West Bengal, Orissa and Assam, travelling on a long chain of trains and buses to find work in the factories of Kothur. Within that seemingly sparse agricultural landscape, so remote from the highway, there were nearly a hundred factories churning out chemicals, pharmaceutical products, steel bars and metal pipes, places that were discernible only when one got off the highway. The factories weren't clustered together but appeared at random, across a patchwork of fields, near the village market, or next to the old road that had been superseded by the modern highway, and one didn't see the factories as much as the marks they created on the landscape: smoke being belched out from a distant chimney; black heaps of slag that had been deposited on the fields and were being turned over with infinitesimal patience by women and children for a few scraps of iron; the infernal metallic squeaking of machinery from behind walled complexes; and the sickly sweet smell of chemicals that appeared suddenly on the wings of an occasional breeze.

The area around Kothur had been developed as an industrial zone in the eighties, and the name Kothur, which means 'new village', reflected that transformation, replacing the earlier name of Patur, or 'old village'. The industrialization had been initiated, accompanied by subsidies and tax breaks from the government, because Mahabubnagar was considered to be one of the poor, 'backward' districts of the Telangana region. It is home to lower castes trying to eke a living out of agriculture as well as to the Lambada gypsies, a community so impoverished that it often sells its children to shady adoption agencies and sex traffickers.

Two decades after the industrialization of the area, about a million people, or two-thirds of the adult population of Mahabubnagar district, have to travel to distant parts of India to find employment. They end up in Bangalore or as far away as Bombay, often working as construction labourers. In a recent report on migrant labour in India published by the United Nations Development Project, its authors Priya Deshingkar and Shaheen Akhter interviewed Mahabubnagar workers and discovered that even though the middlemen who take them to the construction sites are often paid 4,500 rupees for each worker, the workers themselves get paid as little as 1,200 rupees a month in cash and in food. The workers – most of whom belong to the lower castes, the authors write – are often trapped in debt because of the advances they take to fund the initial expenses of their migration. Their children are regularly coerced into work, the women are often sexually abused, and all of the workers are prone to injuries since India has the highest accident rate in the world for construction workers, with 165 out of every 1,000 labourers getting injured on the job.

While the local people of Mahabubnagar go elsewhere for work, the factories in the area attract tens of thousands of men from other parts of India. It is an arrangement that suits employers everywhere well, ensuring that the workers will be too insecure and uprooted to ever mount organized protests against their conditions and wages. They are from distant regions, of no interest to local politicians seeking votes, and they are alienated from the local people by differences in language and culture.

A few miles from Papyrus Port, diagonally across from it on the other side of the highway, was the Vinayak steel factory. It stood near an intersection, surrounded by high walls and facing a muddy yard where canvas-covered trucks idled through the day. Although unlike Papyrus Port in every other way, the steel factory too had an excellent brochure that I had received when I first went to meet the managing director, Venkatesh Rao. The cover displayed a bouquet of steel rods, and when I rubbed my hand on the rods, I could feel their rough textured surface, contrasting sharply with the smooth paper. A skyscraper of concrete and glass rose towards a cloud-covered sky from the bouquet. It was an advertising agency's rendition of how the rods built at the factory went into the making of condominiums and office towers. The picture eliminated all signs of the human labour that went into creating the rods, but it was nevertheless a reminder of the connection between this nondescript, almost invisible steel factory and the globalized cities. The steel factory was one of the countless invisible nodes of modernization in India, pulling in workers from distant rural areas to create the material that would be used for construction far away, perhaps by men and women who travelled from Mahabubnagar. It was to get a sense of the labour involved in producing the steel rods that I entered the factory echoing with metallic clangs and screeches, the yards smelling of smoke and grease, the sky above cut into thin quadrants by angled delivery chutes that groaned into life without warning and stopped just as suddenly.

The factory seemed a rather bewildering place at first, strangely empty in spite of the noise coming from everywhere. There had been some activity at the entrance, with the security guards patting down workers going out and recording the licence numbers of trucks entering the factory. But once I had walked away from the gate, I saw few people. The administrative building, a two-storey, whitewashed concrete structure, seemed deserted, its small windows revealing nothing of the clerical staff sitting inside. There was a temple as well, equally empty, although it appeared clean and well maintained. There were workshops scattered all around the grounds, each surrounded by black coal dust, places where raw iron ore was worked through various stages into the finished product of the TMT bars, the abbreviation standing for 'thermomechanical treatment'. When I occasionally glimpsed workers inside these workshops, they seemed diminished by the scale of the operations, barely visible through the fire and smoke roaring in the furnaces.

It was when I arrived at the rolling mill, the place where steel ingots were turned into the finished product of TMT bars, that I finally received some sense of what went on in the factory. Here,

finally, was the heart of the place, a vast, open-sided shed filled with
deafening noise and the blast of heat from furnaces operating at 1,200
degrees Celsius. The men visible through the smoke and noise were
infernal creatures, rags wrapped around their faces to protect themselves from the heat, inevitably dwarfed by the extremity of the
place, with everything so large, so fast and so hot. It was as if they
were being worked by the machines and materials rather than the
other way around. There was a man feeding ingots into the furnace
at the very beginning of the mill, using long metal tongs. At the
other end of the vast shed there were two men who were his doubles,
faces similarly wrapped in rags and wielding tongs like his with
which they grabbed the rods that shot out at great speed from the
belt. The rods blazed red as they came out, and the men moved in
unison like drugged dancers, each picking up an end of the rod and
then moving it to the side with a concentrated effort that was broken
only by the expulsion of their breaths.

In between the men with tongs was the steel, turned by the
alchemy of modern engineering and a proprietory process licensed
from a German company into a hot, red liquid. I watched the liquid
twisting and turning through the belts, sizzling as it ran through the
water-filled pipes that cooled down the external surface of the liquid
and gave the material the strength and suppleness that would make it
so valuable as construction material. It was a long tongue of fire,
infernal and alive, claiming the men with the tongs as its servants. If
the rolling mill was the heart of the steel factory, the red, pulsating
liquid was its soul.

3

The changes that have been wrought in India in the past two decades
have not been kind to the poor. Even as the number of millionaires
and billionaires has increased, followed by the aspirers from the middle classes, the poor have seen either little or no improvement at all,
depending on which economists and policy makers one chooses to
believe. The data collected by the Indian government, which has

been subject to some controversy for its tendency to downplay the number of poor people and the extent of their destitution, is nevertheless stark. In 2004–5, the last year for which data was available, the total number of people in India consuming less than 20 rupees (or 50 cents) a day was 836 million – or 77 per cent of the population.

The people in this group belong overwhelmingly to what policy makers refer to as the 'unorganized' or 'informal' sector of the economy, which means that the work they do is irregular, carried out in harsh conditions and offers no security or upward mobility. Many of the people in this category are farmers, but a large number are also migrant workers, people who oscillate between the rural areas where they have grown up and the cities or semi-urban areas like Mahabubnagar where they work. An Indian government report in April 2009 that looked at the 'informal' economy characterized migrant workers, along with child labourers and bonded labourers, as being at the very bottom of all those working in the informal economy. Almost all migrant workers, the report noted, face 'longer working hours, social isolation, lower wages and inadequate access to basic amenities'. They live in slums, are expected to be available to work around the clock and are denied access to the ration cards that would allow them to buy subsidized food from what remains of the country's public distribution system. And although they are everywhere – huddled in tents erected on pavements and under flyovers in Delhi; at marketplaces in Calcutta, where they sit with cloth bags of tools ready for a contractor to hire them for the day; gathered around fires made from rags and newspapers in the town of Imphal, near Burma; and at train stations everywhere as they struggle to make their way into the 'unreserved' compartments offering human beings as much room as cattle trucks taking their passengers to the slaughterhouse – they are invisible in the sense that they seem to count for nothing at all.

It is difficult even to get an estimate of the number of migrant workers in India. The government census of 2001 considered 307 million people, or 30 per cent of the total population, as migrants. In this assessment, however, the census was merely counting people who had moved away from their places of residence, and not the reasons for their migration. The authors of the UNDP report on migrant workers, in contrast, have figured that there are around 100 million 'circular' migrant workers in India. Of these, the report notes, the largest number, some forty million people, is engaged in construction, followed by twenty million workers, mostly women and girls, who are employed as domestic servants. From various case studies around the country, the UNDP researchers found that migrant work was often a way of maintaining the minimal standard of living of rural families rather than improving such standards. They also discovered that middlemen contractors often locked workers into high-interest debts, low pay and abysmal working conditions, including the practice of bonded labour for entire families that is especially prevalent among the ten million workers employed by small factories that make mud bricks.

A few years earlier, in Delhi, I met a man who worked for a trade union attempting to organize migrant workers. Among the things he said was that there was an underclass even in relation to the destitute migrant workers, a group so desperate that factory owners often use them as scabs during a strike. These were the people he called 'Malda labour' after a town of that name in West Bengal. 'If you ask any of these men where they're from, they all say "Malda". Is it possible for a small town like Malda to have so many people?' The organizer explained that the men were from Bangladesh, just across the border from Malda. They were Muslims, crossing into India illegally, without any rights at all and often willing to work for a pittance. He told me about an instance when he had visited some Malda labourers in their shanties because he knew that they had been hired to work the next day at a factory where his union had called a strike. 'We took some food, some cheap liquor and drank them into the ground so that they wouldn't be able to get to work the next day. It was more food and drink than they'd seen for a long time,' the organizer said. It wasn't a terribly ethical thing to do, he admitted, but he didn't have much of a choice in trying to unionize migrant workers.

Overwhelmingly, it was owners who won in such battles with migrant workers attempting to organize themselves. Vijay had told me about what happened at the steel factory when some workers tried, in the late eighties, to form a union. This was a time when the factory did not depend entirely on migrant workers, and its workforce was divided evenly between migrants and local workers, many of the local people consisting of men from the Lambada tribe. Two Lambada men had taken the lead in organizing the workers, managing to win the support of both locals and migrants and getting the union registered. The labour commissioner, in accordance with the laws, asked the factory management to recognize the union, which it did. When the union demanded better wages and improved safety measures, the management refused. The workers retaliated by going on strike.

At this point, Vijay said, the owners consulted the police, and an officer said that he would help them find a solution. He visited the Lambada village and talked to some of the men there, possibly threatening them and perhaps also offering them money. Soon after, one of the women from the village accused a worker of attempting to rape her. The policeman immediately lodged cases of sexual assault against all the organizers, and this terrified the migrant workers, who began returning to their posts. The strike was broken, all local workers dismissed, and since then the factory has hired only migrants. If Lambadas are given any work these days, it is only as daily-wage labourers.

The migrants keep coming, following routes that seem to be both contingent and considered, subject completely to chance in some ways but perhaps also depending on an intermediary who can provide an introduction that might lead to work. For those who come to Kothur and find work at Vinayak steel, the factory becomes their entire world. It is a place where they work twelve-hour shifts, during the day and at night. It is where they eat and sleep and shit, and when they are not in a workshop or in a loading shed, they are to be found in the barracks that are squeezed in between a coal storage shed and the back wall of the factory complex.

The factory did not charge rent, and its workforce of 1,000 people was mostly concentrated into two rows of concrete cubicles that were topped off with an asbestos roof. Because these quarters were sited in the furthest corner of the complex, it was possible to tour the entire factory without going into the workers' area, and for the most part, no one other than the workers went there. There was good reason for avoiding the barracks. It was the most squalid and miserable place I had ever seen in my life, more so than the worst slum I had visited. The two rows of cubicles were separated from each other by a little strip of concrete with gutters on each side. There was trash everywhere in the narrow corridor between the rows, and even the verandahs running in front of the rooms were filled with the carcasses of objects: broken chairs and fans, discarded items of clothing, vegetable peelings, leftover food and empty pint bottles of cheap liquor. There was a constant smell of shit in the air, and the entire place seemed to be cast in shades of grey.

The repulsion I felt on my first visit was accentuated by the unwillingness of the workers to talk to me. I had been given complete freedom by Venkatesh Rao, the managing director, to interview the workers. It was an unusual decision on his part, especially given the fierceness with which factory owners prevent any scrutiny of their businesses. But Rao wasn't an owner. He was an employee, if a very well-paid one, and he'd admitted frankly that while he would never be able to improve the conditions of the workers – the owners wouldn't stand for that, he said – he nevertheless understood how miserable their lives were.

I had appreciated that freedom when it was granted to me. I liked it less the first afternoon I went to the barracks and tried to engage with the workers and found that none of them wanted to talk to me in any detail. I understood why the workers were wary of me. In spite of my telling them that I had the managing director's permission, they felt uncertain about my presence – afraid that I might be a government labour inspector come to see their living conditions – and were determined, in the way of migrant workers, to avoid any discussions that might imperil their jobs. Some of the workers were teenage boys, in the most obvious violation of laws against hiring children, and they were the ones most anxious to avoid me, replying in monosyllables or smiling and walking away when I asked them questions.

But there was more than just caution involved in their refusal to engage. I was so well fed and well rested in contrast to them that I might as well have come from another planet. They encountered men similar to me every day in the engineers and accountants who also worked at the factory. But the hierarchy and division were clear in those encounters, and men from the managerial class did not cross the border into this living space of theirs. This was their domain, and the only people from outside their class who came here were the labour contractors, the tough middlemen straddling the decent, bourgeois world of management and the rough, desperate realm of the workers.

The workers continued to avoid me as I sat on an unoccupied cot, watching the men as they wandered around in the afternoon heat, bare-chested and clad in faded, checked cotton towels or in grimy underpants. The men appeared shabby and their bodies looked worn out by the work, shorn of flab without being muscular. Some of them carried pots of water to go behind the barracks for a shit. Others pumped small stoves to get the fire going for their evening meal. There was no hint of domesticity about the food being prepared, nor any sign of pleasure. They chopped the vegetables mechanically, smoked a cigarette or a beedi, and urinated into the gutter. In spite of the heat and the absence of fans inside the cubicles, the doors were closed. Some of the rooms had television sets, and there was an occasional flicker of colour and noise when a door opened briefly, giving me a glimpse of men huddled around a screen watching a Bollywood film.

But if the place seemed settled in its hard rhythm, around the edges of that was a sense of flux. A group of five workers from Orissa arrived even as I sat there, having got off a train that morning at Hyderabad and then taken a bus to Kothur. They were all boys of thirteen or fourteen, slightly built and holding cheap duffel bags, looking almost like schoolboys playing truant except for their mature, cautious faces. When I approached them, they answered my questions about where they had come from uneasily, refusing to give me their names. They had worked at the factory before, but they did not yet know what work might be available for them this time around. Then they walked away from me, heading for a room that was apparently vacant.

The largest contingent of workers came from the states of Orissa and Bihar, although there were also men from West Bengal, Uttar Pradesh, Madhya Pradesh and Assam. The barracks were divided along ethnic groups, and I was sitting roughly on the dividing line between the Bihari and the Oriya quarters. A man called Rabinder had been getting his dinner ready nearby – the workers cooked early, around four or five, so that those going off to evening shifts could have dinner before starting out – and I tried talking to him. He was from Orissa, a short man with a paunch and a moustache, his gaze shifty as he responded to my questions. He had been a tailor in his village, he said, and he hoped to go back to that when he had saved enough money.

As I was talking to Rabinder, another man came out of a nearby room and stood listening to us. He seemed different from the workers I had come across so far. He looked cleaner, to begin with, less broken down than even the Oriya teenagers who had just arrived. He was wiry in build, dressed in a yellow T-shirt and Bermuda shorts, and his face had prominently Mongoloid features, with wide cheekbones and tapering eyes. I asked him where he was from and he said that he had come from Assam. I have forgotten almost all the Assamese I once knew, but I remembered enough to be able to ask him his name. His face lit up and he replied in a volley of words, sitting down next to me and smiling even as Rabinder curled his lips in a sneer and walked away. The man's name was Mohanta Mising. He was twenty-one years old, and he hadn't been at the factory for more than a couple of weeks.

## 4

In the late eighties, as Mahabubnagar was industrialized, the old village of Patur had been renamed as the new village of Kothur. Now, at the turn of the century, Kothur was neither old nor new but simply a divided village, sliced into two halves by the highway. The marketplace and the steel factory were on one side, most of the houses and fields on the other. Vijay had a small house in the village, a rudimentary concrete building full of cobwebs and beetles that he had built many years ago. He lived in Hyderabad, and I was on my own in the house except for the watchman and his family who lived in a separate hut diagonally across from me. In the morning, it was a pleasant, almost pastoral place, surrounded by agricultural plots and looking out at the settlement of the Lambadas. The women were striking in their independence and manner of dress, always walking in front of their husbands and dressed in bright skirts and a profusion of jewellery.

Yet the rural life was on the retreat. There were factories everywhere, Papyrus Port close by and, a little further away, the new Hyderabad airport. Much of the land between the city and the airport had apparently been bought up by real-estate developers anticipating the expansion of the city, and it seemed just a matter of time before the Lambadas were forced off the land entirely. Vijay's house was separated by the highway from the Kothur market and the steel factory, which meant that I had to cross the highway on foot, like most of the villagers. I did so with some anxiety the first time, walking past paddy fields pockmarked with slag to the ramp leading up to the highway. There I followed the example of two villagers, waiting for a break in the traffic coming from Hyderabad and scampering to the median, then waiting again for a gap in the stream of vehicles from Bangalore before completing my crossing. After that, it was a ten-minute walk to the market arranged along the road that had been the main thoroughfare until it was superseded by the new highway.

The market that was the centre of Kothur was a hard, dusty settlement with carts selling vegetables and fruit, pharmacies, liquor stores that traded mainly in pint bottles of cheap whisky, and a couple of cybercafés where the computers seemed weighed down by all the porn that had been surfed on them. There were concrete houses around the edges of the market, looking as if they had been dropped at random on to the fields, some poultry shacks, a jewellery store that doubled as a moneylending operation, and three restaurants. It was at one of these that I took my breakfast and lunch, a cheap meal consisting largely of potatoes and watery dal. Served by ten-year-old boys, the food was consumed eagerly by the tired-looking workers and farmers who ate at the restaurant.

I went to another place for dinner, a dhaba at the very end of the marketplace. Hidden by a row of parked trucks and sitting next to the squeaking complex of a factory manufacturing metal pipes, the dhaba had different names – 'Bhawani Dhaba' or 'Vijai Family Dhaba' – depending on which sign one chose to read. There were a series of concrete cubicles to one side of a patch of grass, with curtains drawn across them in a suggestive manner, and a hallway at the back with plastic tables and chairs. There were never too many customers at the dhaba, but when they showed up, they preferred the booths, groups of tough-looking local businessmen clustered around whisky and tandoori chicken.

I usually sat in the hallway, surrounded by three or four restless-looking teenage waiters, looking out at the rain falling on the new highway. The rain, which came in fits and starts, suggested that the monsoons would be poor that year. It took the edge off the heat, but it also added to the desolate atmosphere of this place that was neither city, town nor village, the marketplace always deserted by nine or ten in the evening except for the occasional drunken man, while above us traffic sped along on the new highway under a bright orange neon sign that said: 'DO NOT USE CELLPHONE WHILE DRIVING'. There were no women and no children in this world – only men who were either hard, broken-down, or both, a dystopic realm of worker drones producing objects whose purpose seemed unfathomable to me.

It was depressing, and even a little frightening, to cross the highway on my way back to Vijay's house. I could have avoided this by staying at Papyrus Port and hiring a car, but I realized how much I would have missed. The act of walking changed the way I experienced everything around Kothur. My uneasiness while crossing the highway and the diminution I felt as I walked for what seemed like hours across that flat landscape brought me a little closer to the experience of the workers. Walking shrunk me down to the level of an insect, for even as I made my way slowly towards the steel factory along the dirt track that ran under the highway, I could see the cars and trucks speeding past. It made me feel lost, unfit somehow for the new world I could see up there.

One afternoon, as I made my way back from the steel factory through a series of puddles, I needed to take a piss. There was only one other person visible, a man walking in my direction but some distance away. I urinated against a brick wall, feeling slightly embarrassed. I heard the man come closer and expected him to walk on – a man pissing in the open is a common sight in India – but I could feel him stop when he reached me. He was standing right behind me and at first I was worried that he was the owner of the brick wall I was soaking in my piss. But he stayed silent, and I began to grow puzzled and annoyed. When I finished, I turned around and looked at him aggressively.

The stranger was waiting for me with a smile on his face, as unlikely a figure as I could have expected to encounter in that blighted landscape. He was rather handsome, hair cut cleanly and moustache trimmed well, a man in his twenties dressed in a cream-coloured polo shirt and trousers, with strapped sandals on his feet. He had a brown office bag on one shoulder.

'Sir,' he said politely, 'where are you coming from?'

'The steel factory,' I said irritably. 'What about you?'

'I'm looking for work,' he said, gesturing at his bag.

We stood there amid the puddles and the dirt, the man telling me about himself against the sound of cars passing by high up on the highway. His name was Amit Mishra, and he was from Faizabad in Uttar Pradesh. He was working as a clerk at a company in Gujarat and had come to Hyderabad to visit a relative. He wasn't too happy at his job or with living in Gujarat, and when he had heard from his relative that there were many factories in the Kothur area, he had decided to visit them and see if any of them had a position for him.

This sounded quite futile to me, and there were parts of his story that didn't fit. Gujarat was a long way from Uttar Pradesh, I said, but so was Andhra Pradesh. He smiled and nodded when I said this, not contradicting me, seemingly much more interested in my reasons for being in the middle of nowhere than in his own reasons for being there. When he heard that I lived in New York, he asked, in the reflexive manner of poorer Indians, whether I could help him emigrate to America. I deflected the question and asked him about his plans for the day. He had taken a bus to Kothur in the morning, he said. He would try as many places as he could before returning to Hyderabad in the evening. Here, then, was the reality of India, and middle-class India at that. In spite of all the talk about technology and the Internet, the educated, clean-cut Mishra was looking for work the way a man might have fifty years ago, walking the many miles from one random factory to another, hoping that his civilized demeanour would get him an interview with an official, dropping off a CV but in all likelihood never hearing back from any of these companies.

Mishra was an accountant, but before he had done accountancy, he had been a student of history. His head was still full of the books he had read, and standing in the muck, he wanted to have a discussion with me about what democracy meant.

'Sir, have you read Amartya Sen?' he said, referring to the Harvard economist and Nobel laureate best known for his work on hunger and inequality. 'You remember what he said about famine, that it doesn't necessarily happen because there isn't enough food but because the powerful take food away from the powerless? It's still like that in India. Are you going to write that in your book?'

I asked Mishra if he wanted to come to the market and have a cup of tea, but he shook his head. The sun was beginning to drop over the horizon, and he wanted to put in as many job applications as he could before taking the bus back to Hyderabad. He asked me for directions to the steel factory and then left, walking under the highway towards the smokestacks of the factory.

5

The way to the factory led past the security booth, which was Karthik's domain. He was the security supervisor, always present when I entered the factory, painstakingly writing down the numbers of trucks in a thick ledger or answering calls from the office. When I first came to the factory with Vijay, he was reluctant to let us in to meet Rao, the managing director, but he adjusted swiftly to my subsequent visits, slightly amused by my interest in the factory and quite willing to talk about the place.

A tall man with glasses and a neat moustache, Karthik carried himself well, his striped tunic marking him out as higher in rank than the other guards in their solid-grey shirts. Although he didn't seem officious, usually speaking in a quiet voice, he was careful to maintain hierarchy, never socializing or eating with the guards.

The supervisor's position was, nevertheless, a kind of coming down in the world for Karthik. He had imagined other careers for himself and he reconciled himself to a job as a security supervisor only after these other possibilities vanished. He was from a village in Orissa, and his father had died when he was young. Karthik had wanted to join the air force and had passed the exams that would allow him to become a non-commissioned officer on the ground staff. But his mother had become distraught just as he was about to leave, afraid that her only son would die in combat in some distant place. Karthik gave up on the air force job and instead decided to have a business of his own. For five years, he ran a poultry business, buying chicks from hatcheries in Andhra Pradesh and selling them wholesale in his village.

At the time, Karthik thought that he was doing rather well. Now, when he looked back at the time, he said, he could see that the business had been rather precarious. Karthik ran the buying end in Andhra Pradesh and left the sales to be managed by a couple of partners, childhood friends of his from the village. He found out later that they had been cheating him and that his business was running at a loss. But he made things worse for himself by putting a lot of money into building a new house in his village. 'I saw other people doing the same thing,' he said. 'I fell for the disease too, making the kind of house you see in the movies. It had city-style furniture, sofas and all that, a big television. I got into debt building that house and buying so many things. Now I live in a rented shack in Kothur and a tenant lives in the fancy house.'

He laughed as he told me the story. Workers dressed in grease-stained clothes signed off at the booth before going out, submitting first to a body check by the guards. Trucks idled behind them, sending clouds of diesel smoke rolling through the yard. A Bihari guard, striking-looking with his big eyes, carefully twirled moustache and gold earrings, came to ask Karthik for a break. Karthik's manner became reserved and officer-like as he listened, and it struck me that he was living a diluted version of the air force career he had wanted, wearing a uniform while supervising other men in uniforms.

'Does your tenant pay a good rent for the fancy house?' I asked Karthik when the booth was quiet again.

'He doesn't,' Karthik said. 'But it's hard to blame him. No one would pay a high rent for a house in a village. After all, it's a village.' He thought for a while. 'It was stupid to build a house like that there,' he said. 'They belong in cities.'

Three years earlier, Karthik closed down his business and joined a private security company. He was posted to different factory sites around Kothur and had arrived at the steel factory only seven months ago. His duties here involved supervising sixteen guards, one of whom was a woman. 'The factory hires Lambada women on a daily basis to clean and cook,' he explained. 'They need to be checked when they go out. They could smuggle out three or four kilos of iron under their skirts and sell it to a scrap dealer. They would get good money for that.'

In terms of the factory's hierarchy, Karthik was relatively privileged, with a steady job, a decent salary and benefits like annual leave. The guards who worked under him were in a different category altogether, including the Assamese man I had met on my first afternoon at the barracks, and whom I went back to see the following day to get a sense of his story.

Mohanta, or Mohan, as he preferred to be called, was from Dhemaji district in Assam. This was his first time away from home, which might have explained why he had looked so unscathed by the misery of the barracks. Mohan had travelled from his village with two other men, both more experienced than him at making a living as migrant workers. They had taken a bus from the village to Guwahati, the capital of Assam, and then travelled southwards by rail, switching trains once before reaching Hyderabad. Eventually, Mohan and his friends made their way to the steel factory, where they were hired as security guards.

As Mohan told me about his journey to the factory, his companions appeared on the verandah, taking unauthorized breaks from their shifts. There was Dhaniram, older than Mohan at twenty-eight, and Dibyajoti, who said he was twenty but looked about sixteen. They were small, wiry men, looking even smaller in the uniforms that were too big for them. Both of them seemed pleased to discover that I had some familiarity with Assam. 'Here they have no idea of where we're from,' Mohan said, laughing. 'They call us Nepalis.'

The Assamese men didn't mix much with the other workers. All the workers interacted only with men from their own communities, and this might have been one of the things that made the barracks so squalid. It was utterly masculine in its atmosphere, without the women and children who would have been more likely to break ethnic boundaries and perhaps create a sense of a larger community. In other ways too, the barracks were shorn of the softening aspects visible in the worst slum, from the liveliness of children playing to women talking with each other. In a slum, there would have been colourful saris hung out to dry, the smell of cooking that was more than just functional, and small plants like chillies and basil. Here, there was none of that, as if the workers resisted putting down any kinds of roots at all.

The Assamese men too were surprised by the sheer wretchedness of the place they had ended up in. Dhaniram and Dibyajoti had been away from home before but, even so, they found the steel factory to be different, and difficult. Dhaniram had worked in North India, for ten months in Himachal Pradesh and for another ten months in Punjab. His job at these places had been at *dhaga* factories where yarn was made. The pay had been poor, around 3,000 rupees a month, and in Punjab, he had also had to pay 700 rupees to share a room with five other people. In between these jobs at the yarn factories, Dhaniram had returned to his village, living there for as long as he could until the money he had made ran out.

This was a common pattern for the migrant workers. Since there was no security in the jobs they found, and little chance of upward mobility, they extracted from the work a freedom of sorts, cycling in and out of jobs and returning to their villages to recuperate from their hard labour and loneliness before setting out again when the money ran out.

The baby-faced Dibyajoti, only too happy to chat instead of returning to his post, had held an even wider range of jobs than Dhaniram. He had worked at a yarn factory in Ludhiana, Punjab, for a year; in Siang district in the north-eastern state of Arunachal Pradesh, where he had made furniture; and in his home district of Dhemaji for a year on a road gang. He had even lived in my hometown, Shillong, where he had been a mechanic in a small auto repair shop. Of all the different kinds of work he had done, Dibyajoti had liked making furniture the most. If he was ever free to pursue his dreams, he would settle down in his village and have a furniture workshop there. 'He's really good with his hands,' Dhaniram said. 'But no one in the village has any money to buy furniture. Maybe once in several years.'

Dibyajoti's cheerful manner belied the circumstances that had sent him out to work at all these places around India. 'His life is really sad – just ask him,' Mohan said, and then he and Dhaniram began giving me the story of that life. Dibyajoti listened quietly, offering a clarifying detail every now and then.

His parents had died when he was still young, his mechanic father from cancer, his mother from what he said was 'fever'. He had three brothers and a sister, and his eldest brother had killed himself a few years ago by drinking poison. 'He was a poultry farmer,' Dibyajoti said, 'but all his birds fell sick and died. He lost his money and became depressed. Then he drank poison.'

Dibyajoti and the surviving siblings left their village after the brother's suicide. They moved to Mohan's village, where Dibyajoti's two other brothers, one older and one younger than him, worked as agricultural labourers. Over the years, they had saved enough to buy a plot of land, but they earned little money from their farming. Most of the rice they grew was consumed at home and so Dibyajoti had become a roving worker to supplement the family income.

His sister, however, was in school and studying in the twelfth grade. 'She's really talented,' Mohan said with a touch of romantic wistfulness. 'Good in studies. And then she dances so well, you should see her during the Bihu festival.' The three brothers were trying their best to keep her in school. They felt that she had the best chance of breaking through their poverty and unhappy family circumstances to become something other than a farmer or a migrant worker.

I asked Dibyajoti what he thought of his new job. He looked at himself, at the uniform that was too big for him, with the military belt and epaulettes that made him look not tough or smart but like a teenage boy acting in a school play. Then he looked at his surroundings, with the other workers going through their afternoon routines, including Rabinder hunched over a pot, cooking. 'There's nothing here,' he said. 'At least when I was in Punjab, there were temples to see, sometimes even a circus or a mela to go to. Here, there's nothing and I don't even understand the language they speak.'

'It's a strange life, going out to work in other places,' Dhaniram said. 'I remember this thing that happened when I was working in the yarn factory in Himachal.'

'The dead boy, you mean?' Mohan said.

'There was this boy who used to work with us in the factory, and with whom I shared a room,' Dhaniram said. 'He wasn't from Assam, but from some other state. I don't know from where. He didn't come to work one day and when we went back to the room, we didn't see him there either. The next morning, somebody went to fetch water from a nearby spring and he was just lying there, dead. No marks on him, nothing. The police came, asked some questions, went away. Nobody came for him and we didn't know any of his family. So we put money together and burned him, and as for his few belongings, we distributed those things among ourselves.'

The door to the cubicle in front of us opened and a man came out, bare-chested, wearing a lungi folded up to his knees. He was strikingly different from the other workers I had seen so far. He was powerfully built, with muscles rippling on his arms, a broad chest and a tapered waist. I was about to talk to him but I checked myself when I saw his expression, jaws clenched tightly under a thin moustache.

The Assamese men invited me inside their room. It was Mohan's turn to cook because he was on the evening shift, and he began preparing dinner while we talked, chopping vegetables and getting the rice going on the stove. The room was about ten feet by ten, an unadorned cube of concrete with a naked bulb dangling from the ceiling. The only piece of furniture was the single bed on which one of them got to sleep once every three nights, the others taking the floor. They had found the bed when they moved in. The legs at the foot of the bed were missing, and someone had piled a stack of bricks underneath to hold the bed up. There were nails driven into the wall from which hung three duffel bags and three pairs of trousers, while some combs and a broken mirror sat on the window ledge. Other than that, there was the stove on the floor, a pan, a bag of rice, a bottle of cooking oil and a few jars containing salt and spices. Since the men were still waiting for their first month's pay, they had bought their groceries on credit extended to them by vendors at the Kothur market. They had no mobile phones, no other belongings. Human life had been reduced to its very essence in the room, to just the basics required to live.

Karthik later filled out the story of how the Assamese men had come to be hired at the steel factory. There was a colleague of Karthik's, called Chilli, who worked as a security supervisor at the Pelican Rubber factory, close to the new airport. Chilli was also from north-eastern India, from the state of Arunachal Pradesh, and the Assamese had found him through common acquaintances. 'Chilli sent me seven of these Assam people,' Karthik said. 'Three we took in here, four we sent to another factory our security company has a contract for. We gave the three here the room to stay in and their uniforms. They'll have to pay for their uniforms, but we'll take that out of their first month's salary.'

'How much do people make as guards?' I asked Karthik.

'You can get anything from three thousand five hundred to six thousand rupees as a guard. And maybe up to nine thousand as a supervisor.'

The work was seven days a week, in alternating shifts of twelve hours. If people took a day off, they lost that day's pay. It was apparent from talking to Karthik that there wasn't much in the way of training and that the security company was used to people coming and going in these jobs. Mohan had complained that people took the Assamese to be Nepalis, but this had worked slightly to their advantage as far as getting jobs as guards was concerned. In a crude carry-over of colonial stereotypes, the security business tended to be dominated by men from Nepal and from Bihar who were perceived to be good at being guards, and the Assamese had slipped in as faux-Nepalese. The other guards at the factory were all from Bihar.

I asked Karthik what he thought of the Assamese guards. 'They're okay,' he said. 'A bit too *shaukhin*,' he added. He meant that they had a taste for the finer things in life. 'Very careful about how they look, how they dress. If they have money, they'll buy jeans and mobile phones. But the Biharis, they'll save the money to buy land or start a small business. These Assamese fellows, they'll go off home as soon as they've made some money.'

When I spoke to some of the Bihari guards about Karthik's perception that they saved money, they laughed at the idea. The man with the gold earrings, slightly arrogant in his demeanour, said, 'That's what he thinks. He should visit me where I live and see it for himself.'

But there was certainly a difference between the Biharis and the Assamese, and that was in their reasons for working as security guards. The man with the earrings made it clear that he was a Rajput, an upper caste, and so were most of the other Bihari guards. They would not take a job at the loading shed or in the rolling mill, even if it paid more. They needed to preserve their position in the social hierarchy, and being guards allowed them to be a notch above the workers. The Assamese men, by contrast, were tribals, happily outside the caste system. They had chosen to be guards because they thought it was safer than working at the furnaces. Even though none of them had been employed in a steel factory before, they assumed that the smoke of the furnaces was bad for health and that accidents were very likely to happen with the fire and heavy machinery all around.

Mohan talked about his work as a security guard as straightforward and even dull, except when the men had to break up fights between the workers. That usually happened in the barracks, late at night, after people had been drinking. 'There's a lot of scrap metal lying here,' he said, picking up an iron rod and demonstrating. 'It's easy for people to hurt each other if you don't step in right away.' Other than that, he found the night shifts difficult. Sometimes, he fell asleep, and a guard was fined if he was caught sleeping on the job. 'It's hardest to stay awake between twelve and two,' he said, his eyes still reflecting the wonder of a village boy who had discovered this strange fact about the human body. 'It's odd how that's the time when you start nodding on the chair. After it gets to be two, it's easy to stay awake, but I don't know why.'

## 6

Life in the barracks was unvarying, with sleep and work punctuated by activities like cooking and eating. The only change to the rhythm was when people left for their villages or when new workers arrived. Dibyajoti fell sick at one point, and his companions described to me in great detail – even as he listened in, looking embarrassed – that he had dysentery and had to shit every hour or so, running off from guard duty.

As I hung around with the Assamese, I became familiar with two other workers living in the cubicle across from them. Both were from Bihar. One was the muscled man called Pradip, taciturn, unfriendly and somehow different from the rest of the workers. He seemed more confident, perhaps because of his build, and he seemed to have an important job at the factory. I often saw him lying half-naked in bed with the door of his room open. Sometimes, a plump, bearded man who seemed to be a supervisor came running into the barracks, asking Pradip to come quickly. Pradip would grunt in response, put on some clothes and disappear for an hour. When he returned, he would go back to bed and lie in the dark of his cubicle.

Pradip's companion was very young. He said that he was eighteen years old, although, like Dibyajoti, he seemed more like fifteen or sixteen, with just the hint of facial hair. He was friendly until I asked him his name, when he became very agitated, unconvinced by the guards that it was okay to give me this information about himself. But apart from concealing this detail and lying about his age, he was happy to speak, talking in a voice that was high-pitched, just beginning to break.

His life as a migrant worker had started when he ran away from home at the age of twelve. No one had treated him badly, he said, looking surprised that I might think so. He was from a village near Jhajha in Bihar, with three brothers and three sisters. His father had died long ago and he felt that there was no work for him in the village. The land they cultivated was too small for all the brothers to make a living out of it, and he had received little schooling. When he ran away from home, he went north, to Delhi, and then landed up in Panipat, in Haryana, where he worked at a yarn factory. After two years, he left the job and went back to his village. He stayed there for a few months before going to Calcutta to find work. When he couldn't get anything there, he came to Hyderabad and ended up at the steel factory.

'You didn't want to go back to the yarn factory?' I said.

'It's not good to do that work for a long time,' he said. 'There's dust in these factories. It's bad for you. It gets inside you, and you start coughing. You fall sick, and people become old very quickly.'

Dhaniram and Dibyajoti nodded vigorously, recalling their own yarn factory experiences. Now the boy was without work again. He had been at the steel factory for only two months, doing loading work, but he had been laid off a few days earlier, apparently because there were too many men at the factory. He was staying on while he considered what to do and where to go next.

A few days after I spoke to the boy, I had my first conversation with Pradip. I was sitting with Mohan when Pradip came up to me, smiling. He was sorry that he'd been so rude when I approached him before. He had been having a terrible toothache and was unable to talk, but he'd finally been to a dentist and had the bothersome tooth pulled out. He opened his mouth and shoved his finger inside to show me the spot in the back where the tooth had been extracted. Most of his teeth were in bad shape, yellow and decaying, providing a startling contrast with the rest of him, seemingly so healthy and strong. But as I talked to Pradip, I was surprised by how different he looked. Until then, he had seemed like a giant, almost menacing, but walking next to me as we made our way to the tea shack outside the factory, he barely came up to my chest. He was finely proportioned, with strong arms, but quite small, with a voice that was soft, almost feminine.

Pradip was what he called a 'Tongsman', a job that involved pushing iron ingots into the furnace at the rolling mill during the final stage in the production of TMT bars. He said he was twenty-five years old but, like most workers at the factory, he looked about ten years older. He was from Jamui district in Bihar, from a farming family that primarily grew sugar cane. The land wasn't big enough to sustain everyone, so Pradip had left the farming to his elder brother and drifted around the country, spending much of his time in the western part of India.

He had begun by working as a welder on ships in the port city of Surat, in Gujarat, but he gave up that work after six months. He had been falling sick frequently, he said, suffering a great deal of pain in his back. Pradip wouldn't elaborate on his ailments, even though I pressed him for details, wondering how he managed to do the hard labour of a tongsman if he suffered from back pain. Like most workers, and like most members of India's underclass, he seemed to operate at a high level of abstraction when it came to certain things, especially those that had to do with the body. Just as Dibyajoti had said that his mother died of 'fever' and Pradip's young room-mate had been afraid of the effects of 'dust', Pradip would only say that he suffered from 'pain'.

In elite circles in India, this is a sign of the illiteracy of the lower classes, an indication of how they lack intellectual property as well as material property. But as I heard these simple words – 'fever', 'dust', 'pain' – taking the place of any complicated diagnosis or description of symptoms, it struck me that one of the characteristics of being higher up on the class ladder was the specificity with which a person could speak of one's ailments. But there was another way of under-standing the use of such simple words. The workers didn't have access to the kind of medical care that would let them receive complex for-mulations of their illness. So they suffered with a stoicism that was ingrained in their social status. Given the lives that migrant workers lived, someone like Pradip had no choice but to abandon the nuances of illness for a broad, catch-all word. The same was true when it came to telling the story of his life, which was often empty of descriptive detail and rendered in thick strokes.

After Pradip gave up being a welder on ships, he began to work in steel factories around the country, in Bombay, Goa and Bangalore. The place where he had stayed the longest was Goa, where he had been for six years. But he seemed indifferent to the attractions of most of the places he had lived in. He had not found ships and the sea glamorous, and his Goa did not contain the sun, sand and music that drew wealthy Indians and Western tourists to its beaches. Pradip's life had been defined largely by the factories he worked in, and they had more or less been the same everywhere.

He had begun working at the Kothur factory just two months earl-ier. He had been called there by a labour contractor, a middleman who had worked with him before and thought of him as a depend-able person. From these details, and from the way the bearded man had sometimes come looking for Pradip at the barracks, it seemed that a tongsman occupied a relatively high position in the hierarchy of workers at the steel factory.

He had been a tongsman before, Pradip explained, and that had helped him get the job at Vinayak steel. A tongsman's work was dan-gerous and managers preferred to hire a man who was already used to the arduous conditions: the extreme heat, the speed of the line, the physical effort involved in shovelling iron ingots in, and the danger of the heavy machinery and molten steel. In all other ways, however, Pradip was a migrant labourer like most of the other men I had seen at the factory. There was no telling how long he would be there and where he would go once he was done with the work – or, as was more likely, once the work was done with him.

We were sitting outside the factory, drinking tea. The owner of the stall, a man in his forties with grey hair, was a migrant too, from Rajasthan, and he listened to our conversation with interest. Pradip refused to let me pay, taking out a battered purse from the back pocket of his jeans. The jeans were knock-off, as was the T-shirt, which said 'Dolce & Gabbana' in a swirl of embroidered lettering. From the clothes, one could tell that Pradip was careful about his appearance. He was also measured in his habits. He didn't smoke or drink, and was careful about what he ate. None of the workers could afford much more than rice, dal and vegetables, but Pradip tried to eat fish or meat once a week so that he could maintain his physical strength.

Although Pradip had been indifferent to Bombay or Goa, he said that he liked Calcutta, where he had been before coming to Kothur. 'I have a cousin who's a taxi driver there and spent some time with him. I wanted to find work there, but I couldn't get anything.'

'What did you like about Calcutta?' I said.

'It's not so far from Jamui,' he said. 'The food is excellent and it's cheap. I'd gone there during the time of Durga Puja, with idols of the goddess everywhere, and my cousin and I walked around all night, seeing one idol after another.' He smiled as he remembered those nocturnal walks. 'I could have stayed there for ever, doing that, eating the food, walking at night with so many people and music and lights everywhere.'

He stopped abruptly as a man came out of the factory on a motorcycle and rode towards us. It was the bearded man I had seen hurrying into the barracks every now and then, calling for Pradip to come to the rolling mill.

'That's the contractor who called me here,' Pradip said.

The contractor parked his motorcycle and entered the shack. He had a slight swagger, a way of appearing larger than and different from the working-class men scattered around the tea shack. His face was intelligent and alert, and I remembered how I had seen him note my presence when he came into the barracks.

He came over to where we were sitting, listening carefully as I introduced myself. 'Yes, I've been wondering who you are, hanging around the workers' quarters,' he said. 'Well, now I know.'

Sarkar was a Bengali, from a village in the hills of North Bengal area. He was bigger than Pradip, but pudgy rather than muscular. That, plus his greying beard and his occasionally jocular manner of speaking, would have given him an avuncular manner had it not been for the sense he evoked of being a hard man, wary about my presence at the factory and unimpressed when I told him that I had the managing director's permission to be there.

'Pradip's a big man,' he said to me, and slapped the tongsman on his back. 'Are you going to treat me to tea or what?'

Pradip laughed and said, 'No, you're the big man.'

Nevertheless, he had to pay for Sarkar's tea. The amount was small, 2 rupees, and I would have expected the contractor to pay, if only to show me how generous he was towards the workers. Yet he had insisted on the opposite, which meant that he was either very stingy or that he didn't care what I thought and was interested in demonstrating his power over Pradip.

In his own way, Sarkar was a migrant worker too, but at a different level. He was a middleman, a contractor, the person who hired workers for the factory and relieved the management of any responsibility of dealing with them. He too had worked in steel factories around India – in Orissa, Kerala, Maharashtra and Goa. 'That's where I met Pradip, in Goa, and where I got to see that he was a good worker.' Then he added something strange, holding my gaze and speaking in Bengali, perhaps so that Pradip wouldn't understand what he was saying. 'There are many bad things I've done in my life, and which I won't tell you about – even though I can see you want to know about them. What I will say is that I walked a crooked path for all these years but it made my life no better. I'm no wealthier now than when I started out and so I've decided to go straight.'

I was puzzled by this sudden declaration, but Sarkar wouldn't elaborate. When I asked him about the factory, his answers seemed concocted. I wanted to know what made Pradip such a good worker that Sarkar had called him to Kothur from Calcutta.

'He's a tongsman,' Sarkar replied. 'Have you seen him working? It's skilled work and he makes a lot of money. Anything between twelve to thirteen thousand rupees with overtime.'

Pradip, who had fallen silent, had earlier told me that he earned around 9,000 rupees a month.

'How long can a person work as a tongsman?' I asked Sarkar. 'The work looks difficult.'

'Oh, these people can go on for ever. There's one man at the factory who's nearly seventy. What's the name of that fellow, Pradip, you know the one I'm talking about?'

'I don't know,' Pradip said.

I had not seen a single worker over forty, and I wondered how many years Pradip had left as a tongsman. The work available at the steel factory was for the young and so the workers were migrants in another sense — wanderers in the land of youth, from which they would disappear when they got older, to be replaced by another person from India's unceasing stream of labour.

I asked Sarkar if I could meet the legendary seventy-year-old worker, but he evaded the question. Instead, he wandered into a series of non sequiturs. First, he told me about a vacation he was planning to take with his family. He would go to the north-east, he said, and wanted to know of places to visit. Then he abruptly declared that having decided to go straight, he was also hoping to improve his situation in life by going abroad. 'If things go right,' he said, 'I'll be in South Africa by the end of this year. It'll be work at a steel factory there too. I'm still working on the details involved in getting a job like this. But if it comes through, you understand, I'll start making some real money for the first time in my life.' Sarkar finished his tea and walked unhurriedly towards his bike. 'Are you going to the market? I'll give you a lift,' he said.

I wasn't, but I decided to take a ride with the middleman, wondering if he would reveal anything more of himself if it was just the two of us. We rode down the highway, speeding towards the market, and it struck me how class in Kothur was directly related to the transportation one used. For the owners and managers, there were the air-conditioned Scorpio SUVs and Toyota Innova minivans. I had seen such vehicles one afternoon when a group of buyers visited the factory, businessmen wearing sunglasses and leaning back against the white covers of their seats, reminding me of Rajkumar and the rich farmer in Armoor in whose company I had gone to visit Mahipal. For middlemen contractors like Sarkar, there were motorcycles. As for the tongsmen and other workers, they walked or perhaps rode a bicycle, like the battered one Mohan and his friends had found in a garbage heap and put to use for their trips to the market.

When Sarkar stopped his motorcycle, I asked him if he wanted to sit somewhere and talk.

'Some other time,' he said, and his smile was a little menacing as he drove off.

I realized that he had just wanted me away from the factory. He had removed me from the site neatly, without any fuss.

## 7

Neither Pradip nor the security guards had a sense of the steel factory as a whole. Perhaps Sarkar did, but he had been keen to get rid of me rather than show me around. For the overview I wanted of the factory, I had to visit the management. I had met Rao, the managing director, at the very beginning, but I didn't see him again until at the very end, by which time I felt I had come as close as I could to viewing the factory through the eyes of the workers. And yet, from the tongsman to the guards, each worker had only a fragmentary, partial picture of the factory, a cog's perspective of a large wheel. When I put these different fragments together, I got not a whole but a bewildering, cubist image. For Pradip, the factory was the weight of the metal tongs, the heat of the furnace, the repetitive motion of shovelling ingots and the induction furnace. For him, it didn't matter that ingots came out as TMT bars, or that the TMT bars were then used to construct buildings. The end product mattered to Pradip only if the orders tapered off and he got fired, in which case he would pick up his belongings, shove them into his shoulder bag, put his battered purse into the back pocket of his jeans and take a train to the village or to some other city.

As for Mohan and his friends, they occupied the edges of the factory, not only in the sense that they sat at guard posts on the perimeter of the factory where they looked out for sneak thieves or trouble among the workers, but also in that they had nothing to do with producing the TMT bars. Also, they were not only an ethnic minority, slightly vague to the other workers, but they had to keep themselves deliberately apart in order to maintain their authority. The factory's actual functioning was a mystery to them, although all three of them thought the work to be dangerous. They found the surroundings of Kothur a mystery too. With time, they might adapt to the place, but all three had said they were unlikely to stay long.

Towards the end of my stay, I went to see Rao in his office on the second floor of the administrative building. He wasn't in, but the secretary led me into the chamber and asked me to wait. The room felt institutional, with metal cabinets, a couple of desks and chairs, an old desktop computer and an inkjet printer. There was a calendar on the wall with a picture of Lakshmi, the goddess of wealth, and a garlanded photograph of an elderly couple who, I was told, were the deceased parents of the owner of the factory. There was a coconut sitting on one of the filing cabinets, with six dried palm leaves spread out on top of it, a mutant hybrid of palm and coconut.

Rao was a handsome man, with a generous head of hair. He was also surprisingly frank. I would have expected him to be tougher, to have a little more TMT in him, capable of being hard with the workers and eager to keep nosy outsiders away. But perhaps he had people like Sarkar to do that for him, and above him was the invisible owner, who must have been tough too. Rao had a degree in industrial chemistry and had worked at other factories – in Karnataka, Kerala and Maharashtra – before moving to Vinayak steel nearly two decades ago. He had started here as a chemist, analysing the final products for their quality, and had worked his way up to the managing director's position. He said he was paid very well, with perks like a large house and a chauffeured car, but he had to put in long hours in return, often working through the weekends.

In Rao's mind the story of the factory was analogous to the story of contemporary India, a narrative of vast improvements and modernization leading to ever greater profits. He pointed to a plaque on his desk from the state pollution control board to emphasize that *pollution had been cut down considerably at his factory, in contrast* to rival operations. The production method had been vastly improved as well, he said. They had imported a new, efficient technology from a German company, which was paid a royalty per tonne of steel produced at the factory. The factory had been doing excellent business until the end of 2007. There had been a construction boom in the country, Rao said, and he had been supplying TMT bars to a number of construction companies in and around Hyderabad, including a very large one called Maytas Infra.

But things weren't going quite as well since January 2008. Although he didn't say so, I thought that perhaps this too ran parallel to the story of contemporary India, showing how the rise of the new India had, in recent years, become something of a fall. A nationwide downturn had led to a slowing down of construction projects and a consequent cancellation of orders for Rao's products. He had been especially affected by problems in Hyderabad around Satyam, the fourth-largest software and outsourcing company in India at one time, which had links to the construction company Maytas Infra. Rao had received large orders from Maytas Infra, which had won the contract for building a subway system in Hyderabad. But Maytas Infra had run out of money and stopped working on the metro project. Since it owed Rao's factory 3.5 crore rupees and was unable to pay this amount, it had instead offered four 'villas' in a development owned by a sister company called Maytas Properties. Rao had taken the villas, he said, but their property values had declined and he was concerned that the government would seize all assets owned by Maytas Properties.

Rao faced other problems too. I asked him if transportation of material had become easier for him since the construction of the new highway.

'It's become a headache,' he said, laughing.

He wouldn't say more, but one of his managers later explained to me that the new highway had made it easier for government officials to show up at the factory and ask for bribes. 'Before, the roads were so bad that they wouldn't bother coming this way. These days, they're driving along the highway when they see the factory and think they should make a stop, check for ways in which the factory's breaking rules, and ask for money.' But the manager admitted that there were indeed many ways in which the company broke existing laws, including evasion of taxes, although he insisted that other factories were even worse.

The worst of the violations had to do with the conditions of the workers, which, the manager said, was made easy by the fact that the workers were migrants and did not have a union. The owner of the steel factory had at one time considered buying a nearby sponge iron plant run by the government, but he had backed off after learning that there was a workers' union there.

In fact, the factory employed none of the people I had spoken to. It had only 250 direct employees, almost all of whom were in management. The top five people among these white-collar workers made more than a lakh of rupees a month, ten people more than 50,000 rupees, and fifty engineers made about 25,000 rupees each. Below them were roughly 1,000 workers, of whom 70 per cent were from other states, mostly Bihar and Orissa. The factory was not their employer, however. Instead, it had an arrangement with four middlemen contractors, of whom Sarkar was one, to provide the factory with labourers who earned 20,000 rupees at the very top of the hierarchy and 4,000 at the bottom. The contractors were paid on a commission basis by the factory, receiving 220 rupees per tonne of TMT produced, and it was therefore in their interest to see that workers weren't sitting idle or that there weren't more workers than necessary at the factory.

Of the 1,000 workers employed through the contractors, government regulations required payments into a health insurance and disability scheme called the Employees' State Insurance and into a provident fund that provided pensions. But the contractors, with the approval of the management, saved on these costs by keeping 40 per cent of the workers off the books. These men received no provident funds and no ESI payments. They wouldn't get any compensation or health care if they suffered a serious injury, or a pension when they stopped working. They had no future beyond the immediate labour they carried out, and Pradip was one of these men. He was, in effect, a kind of ghost.

When government officials showed up at the factory and discovered these violations, they did not enforce the rules. Instead, they took a cash bribe, got back into their vehicles, and drove back down the highway, so that the lack of a future for many of the workers was converted into the present enrichment of officials and factory owners. It was the shadow transmutation that ran in parallel to the alchemy of converting iron ore into TMT bars.

*8*

A few days after I returned to Hyderabad from Kothur, I went to see the Maytas Hill County development. I had been thinking of Rao's story about being paid in villas for the amount owed his factory by Maytas Infra, and I began to recall scenes from my last visit to Hyderabad. I thought of the bus I had seen a year before, when driving back with Vijay from the chemical village of Qazipally. It had been empty save for the driver, with the logo 'Maytas Hill County SEZ' emblazoned on its side. There had been billboards all over Hyderabad for the same development, saying 'Less concrete, more chlorophyll'.

According to Rao, the downturn had begun by then, but the effects had not been apparent to those outside the industries. Now the cracks were visible everywhere. In January, an Enron-like accounting fraud was exposed in Satyam, until then a flagship of Cyberabad's global ambitions. Its chairman, Ramalinga Raju, admitted to exaggerating the company's assets. He had also, in a reversal of the practice at factories like Vinayak steel, said that the account books had shown many more IT workers employed than was actually the case. Raju had resigned and been sent to prison while the Indian government took over Satyam and eventually sold it to a group of other companies.

The fallout from Satyam, however, continued unabated in Hyderabad. I was told by people that Raju was in prison not as punishment but to be protected from awkward questions that might reveal the extent of even more widespread fraud. Like Bangalore, the boom in Hyderabad had been about land while pretending to be about software – and Maytas, I was told, was Satyam spelled backwards, a doppelgänger of sorts for the more famous company. 'Places like Hyderabad don't become software capitals of the world unless there's a real-estate dividend,' a local journalist told me with a touch of bitterness. 'Maytas was earlier called Satyam Construction, and that company predates Satyam software, which is to say that the Raju family was about real estate and construction before it was ever about software.'

There were in fact two Maytas companies – the construction firm Maytas Infra, and the real-estate business of Maytas Properties – each partially owned by Ramalinga Raju's sons. Just before admitting his fraud in Satyam, Raju Senior had tried to push for the acquisition of the Maytas companies by Satyam. He had apparently known that the Maytas ventures were in trouble and had been hoping to pass on the losses to Satyam shareholders while extricating his sons from the mess.

The move failed, and the Maytas companies became part of the collapsing empire of software, outsourcing, construction and real estate. I had been hearing of wealthy property owners from Maytas Hill County demonstrating in front of the Raju residences, demanding completion of their expensive villas, and I met up with one of these owners one day. His name was P. Sivakumar, or Siva, a friendly but tired-looking man with dark circles around his eyes. He took me to Maytas Hill County, and the drive turned out to be a pilgrimage of the Cyberabad so loved by McKinsey and Chandrababu Naidu. We rode past the Satyam tower and the Microsoft campus, driving along a wide road known as the 'IT corridor'. The horizon was filled with giant yellow cranes standing still over the shells of buildings, and it was apparent that many construction and real-estate firms had run out of money.

We came up to the Maytas development, sited on a slight rise. The giant letters spelling out the name MAYTAS HILL COUNTY were visible from far away, the letters carefully arranged to look like the iconic Hollywood sign. We stopped in front of Siva's incomplete house, a two-storey structure surrounded by others exactly like it. The only difference was in the degree to which the external facades had been finished, with the first few houses almost complete, the next few half finished and so on to the very end of the line where the houses were grey concrete blobs. In the distance was a thirteen-storey apartment building, but here the narrative was vertical, the money having run out after Maytas had completed the third floor.

As I looked around with Siva, a few of the other owners came up to talk, mirroring Siva much in the way their houses mirrored each other. There was a woman in a salwar kameez and sneakers ('from Dallas, Texas'), and a man on a little scooter ('from Virginia'). Their Indian-American accents rang out loudly in the empty development, interrupted occasionally by the sound of hammers and picks. Each of the owners had hired workers independently to finish the villa he or she owned, intending to move in as soon as the houses were liveable. The wind approached, blowing through the empty approach roads to this ghost of an American suburban town, and then it left the area, sending clouds of dust spiralling up towards the apartment building.

Siva took me inside his house, for which he had paid 85 lakh rupees. A group of carpenters, migrants from Rajasthan, worked on the cabinets, while a barefoot teenage worker, his pants rolled up, balanced precariously on a metal frame jutting out from the house. The house would be painted and finished soon, Siva said. He explained why it was so urgent that owners move in as quickly as possible. They believed that Satyam had transferred money to Maytas illegally. Siva was oddly specific about the details – 300 crores had been moved out of Satyam, he said, through an offshore account in Mauritius, to Maytas – and since Satyam had many creditors, the villa owners were worried that the government would seize the Maytas properties. If they moved in, however, they would have a better chance of fighting the case – possession, as the saying goes in India, being one half of the law.

We went and stood on the roof, next to the solar heaters that reflected a rather modern touch. Otherwise, Siva's house seemed dank, and the rooms were quite cramped. It reminded me of the time I had gone to see Chak's house in Bangalore. But where Chak had been optimistic, Siva's mood was darker, just as his house, although quite expensive, seemed like a cheaper version of Chak's place. When

I said I was surprised that Siva had paid so much money for the house, he replied that the properties had gone rather quickly when they were put up for sale at the end of December 2006. The entire stock had sold out in a couple of days. It had been a boom time, after all, with plenty of money everywhere. Siva had paid a 20 per cent down payment, with the rest financed from the State Bank of India, and at that point he hadn't been particularly worried about money.

Now he was beginning to get a little stressed, he admitted. Siva was from Anantapur district in coastal Andhra, but he had moved to Hyderabad in the late eighties to study science. In 1992, he had gained admission to a graduate programme at Bradley University in Illinois. But his visa application was rejected – this being before the Y2K craze led to the generous distribution of US visas for Indian engineers and engineering students – and he worked in Hyderabad as a computer programmer. In 1997, however, he finally went to America, sent there by the Indian company he was working for. He lived at first in a Virginia suburb, sharing a two-bedroom apartment with three other engineers. He got married, had a son and a daughter, worked in Baltimore, and then moved to Edison, New Jersey, where he lived for ten years. In 2007, he became an American citizen, which, as he put it, was 'the trigger for moving back' to India. He had been worried about his daughter growing up in America. 'It's not such a problem for boys,' Siva said, 'but girls, they have only one chance. If things go wrong, they can't ever recover.'

Siva had also wanted to do something of his own in India, and besides, once he had US citizenship, he was no longer tied to the place.

'You don't feel hampered by not having an Indian passport?' I asked.

'See, we're from here. We know how to work this system,' Siva said. 'You don't really need an Indian passport for that.'

Yet although Siva had moved back to India, the attraction of Maytas Hill County had been that it was close to the American lifestyle he had become used to. He said that 70 per cent of the property owners were NRIs (non-resident Indians), sharing a common culture, eager to live in a gated community where things wouldn't be as chaotic as they were in the rest of Hyderabad. Of course, he reflected, most of the things people had paid for had not been put in place. There was no swimming pool, no tennis court, no movie theatre and no 56-acre clubhouse. There was no water treatment plant, and tankers drove in periodically to supply water, workers from individual villas running after them with plastic bottles. There was electricity, but it was a commercial line, charging a higher rate.

But at least the housing development had been built, even if partially. The entire development was 300 acres, with the residential portion spread over seventy-five acres. Of the remaining section, eighty-five acres had been planned for an SEZ, but all Maytas had done with that was dig a hole in the ground. The company had presumably received tax breaks for that part of the property, the rationale being that the factories put up in the SEZ would create jobs, but the SEZ had been far lower on the list of priorities than the expensive private housing that had gone so quickly when offered for sale.

It seemed to reflect perfectly how little of the boom in Andhra Pradesh had been about creating jobs for the working classes, and a report by the Planning Commission pointed out that from 1995 to 2001, at the peak of its growth, the entire state had added fewer than 2,000 industrial jobs. This was an absurd figure, and no doubt more manufacturing jobs had actually been available, but they had gone to migrant workers who were not on the records, who slipped off the trains and buses to work for a few months before heading somewhere else.

At the steel factory, Sarkar had talked about how good the prospects were for migrant workers, especially for skilled people like Pradip. They could go on till they were seventy or eighty years old, he had said. It was a vision of the future that the workers I spoke to hadn't accepted. But they had been unable to give me an alternative future, saying that they couldn't think beyond a few months. Mohan intended to go back to his village. Even though there was little money to be made there, he felt that the drifting life wasn't for him, but before he returned, he wanted to make back the money he had used up travelling to Kothur and perhaps have a little more that he could spend back in the village. Dhaniram and Dibyajoti, both more seasoned, would also return to the village. But they expected to head out again for work, even as Dibyajoti kept dreaming of having a furniture shop of his own. Pradip's room-mate, the nameless boy, would go back to Bihar and recuperate there for a while before going on the road again. As for Pradip, he didn't know what the future held for him, although as long as those muscles held out, or until he was laid off, he would remain a tongsman somewhere or other.

For what happened to workers who fell through the hole, I didn't have a person I talked to, only a vision. It appeared the afternoon I was talking with Pradip and Sarkar at the tea shack. It was the middle of the day, the sun blazing down on the steel factory and its surroundings. A man came walking down the middle of the road, although it wasn't a walk as much as a stumbling dance. As he came closer, the workers who had gathered outside the tea shack and at the factory gate began to stare.

He was young, maybe in his late teens, dressed in a black T-shirt and trousers. His feet were bare, and he moved on those bare feet down the middle of the road, unheeding of any of us. His eyes were bloodshot, staring into the void. He was most likely a Nepali and he was almost certainly drunk. But there was something about him that suggested a terrible violation, as if he had been raped and set loose on the street. Everyone stared, no one moved, either because they were stunned by his appearance or because they were used to such figures. He went past us, drifting towards the new highway. 'Someone should stop him,' I thought, 'he's going to get killed by a car.' But I couldn't move and just stared on with the other men, as if he was our scapegoat, our sacrifice to unappeasable gods. A police jeep was parked near the edge of the highway, but the policemen made no move either, and the man was soon on the road, a barefooted figure plunging into the onrush of cars from Bangalore. I couldn't watch any longer and turned away. When I looked back again, I saw that he had just made it across and was still moving, a small but distinct figure heading towards the green fields pockmarked with black heaps of slag.

# The Girl from F&B: Women in the Big City

*The arms dealer — why Esther wanted F&B — the accident — recession in America — the Delhi Police manual — the momo stand — Manipur — the luxury mall — the boyfriend — Munirka again*

## 1

Esther once worked as a waitress at Hotel Shangri-La, serving breakfast, high tea and happy hour drinks at the Horizon Club on the nineteenth floor. Some of her guests were businessmen passing through Delhi, while others maintained small but expensive office suites along the corridors twisting away from the club lounge. In the evening, these men sat in the lounge sipping Black Label Scotch with lots of ice, appreciative of the quiet, smiling demeanour with which Esther brought them their food and drinks, leaving them to talk to each other or on their BlackBerries while outside the sheer glass windows the sun went down softly over the parliament building and the palatial bungalows of industrialists and politicians. One of the men who sat in the club lounge was an arms dealer. I met him before I met Esther, although the reason I went to see the arms dealer was because I was looking for Esther.

All through these past few years in India, sometimes in Delhi and sometimes in other cities, I had noticed the women who worked as waitresses in cafés and restaurants and as sales assistants in retail stores. They were usually in their twenties, soft-spoken and fluent in English. In the shape of their eyes, their cheekbones and their light skin, I could read their origins in north-eastern India. They were polite but slightly reticent until I spoke to them and told them that I too had grown up in the north-east. Then they seemed to open up, and often there were extra touches of attention as they served me.

I flattered myself that they liked me. After all, I knew where they were from, I was generous with my tips and I thought I understood something of their loneliness in the loneliness I myself had felt when I first began to leave my small-town origins behind and started my drift through cities. But in most ways, I wasn't like them. I had grown up in Shillong, the most cosmopolitan of urban centres in the north-east, while the women were from Nagaland or Manipur, the first generation from these states to abandon their poor, violence-ridden homes for the globalized metropolises of the mainland. Their journey was longer and harder than mine had ever been, and although there were tens of thousands of them in Delhi alone, they were in some sense utterly isolated, always visible in the malls and restaurants but always opaque to their wealthy customers.

Samrat, whom I had stayed with in Bangalore, and who had moved back to Delhi since then, knew I was looking to interview one of these women. He took me to meet the arms dealer because he thought the man might be able to introduce me to a waitress who worked at the hotel. The arms dealer, who did not like being called an arms dealer and referred to himself as a 'security specialist', was also from the north-east. He had grown up in a small town in Assam called Haflong, a picturesque stop on the train I used to take during my college days and where local tribal men often sat on the platform selling deer meat on banana leaves. But Haflong was also a place riven by poverty, ethnic violence and insurgency, shut down from time to time by floods, an ambush by insurgents or a retaliatory rampage by paramilitary forces.

The arms dealer had risen far from such origins, and although he was making a business of the violence that was endemic to his home-town, his role in it reduced violence to an abstraction. He was bald and suave, wearing a black suit and carrying a BlackBerry. Because of our common background, he came across as welcoming and gregarious the day I met him, slipping into Sylheti, the Bengali dialect that we shared, while at the same time emphasizing the rarefied atmosphere in which he now moved. He travelled around the world, he said, including the frequent trips he made to his company's headquarters in Virginia. When he visited New York, he stayed at the Four Seasons Hotel. 'Not bad, right?' he said. 'Is that an okay hotel?'

We were sitting in the Horizon Club, easing ourselves into the atmosphere of soft armchairs, quiet conversation, tinkling glasses and attentive waitresses. The hotel reminded me of its sister concern, the one I had seen being built near Chak's million-dollar house in Bangalore. But this Shangri-La had been around before as a government-run hotel called Qutab, which had been sold off to the Adarsh group as part of India's ongoing 'divestment' process. It had been rebranded since then, and through its windows Delhi looked nothing like the place I knew. It appeared, instead, as a vaguely futuristic city, a settlement on a distant planet where human ingenuity had created a lush green canopy of trees, broken up occasionally by the monolith of a government building or the tower of a luxury hotel. I almost expected, when looking up, to see a faintly visible glass dome that kept the oxygen in, as if the city I was looking at was artificial, its comfort and organization disguising the fact that in reality it was at war with a harsh, alien environment.

The arms dealer's wife joined us soon after we sat down. She too was from the north-east, from a ramshackle border town in Assam where I had last been fifteen years earlier, watching the winking lights of smuggling boats as they made their night-time run between India and Bangladesh. Unlike the arms dealer, however, she spoke only in English. Her stiffness puzzled me until I realized that she was working hard at her language. Sometimes, her accent slipped, and she displayed a moment of confusion before catching herself and moving on. Her father had been a member of parliament, which meant that she was from a fairly privileged background. In spite of this, she said, she had not been sent to an elite school, the kind where English would have been the language of instruction. She revealed this with a touch of bitterness, and I understood that it had made her insecure. She wanted to belong frictionlessly to the elevated world she now moved in, the world that stretched from Hotel Shangri-La in Delhi to the Four Seasons Hotel in New York.

The arms dealer's wife mentioned, very casually, that she had just come from a workout at the hotel gym. She said she had a doctorate and was a fellow at a research foundation, and when the arms dealer handed me his business card, she quickly handed me her business card too. They were both flying to Bangladesh the next day, she said, where they would be guests of the foreign minister.

An Indian man with an American accent came over to say hello to the arms dealer. When he left, the arms dealer turned to me and said, 'That was Boeing.'

'Boeing?'

'All the way from headquarters at Seattle.'

'To sell commercial aircraft?' I said, somewhat confused.

'No, no, defence stuff. Boeing does lots of defence. Missiles, drones.'

He gave me a list of all the arms companies that were in Delhi – McDonnell Douglas, General Dynamics, Boeing, Northrop Grumman – some with offices in Hotel Shangri-La, while others had suites at Le Meridien, another luxury hotel nearby, all of them wanting physical proximity to the politicians, bureaucrats, businessmen and defence officials with whom they carried out their expensive trade. India's arms budget was small by American standards, but it was still worth $30 billion, and according to data compiled by the Pentagon, India had bought weaponry worth $1 billion from American companies in 2008, making it ninth among the top ten nations buying arms from the United States.

The arms dealer took me to see his office. It was a small but luxurious space, with a sitting area that showed us the same futuristic view of Delhi – all trees, neon lights and granite buildings.

'I'm thinking of writing a book,' the arms dealer said. 'Wouldn't it be nice to sit here, with this view, and write a book?'

'Yes,' I said, looking at his desk and at the files arranged neatly around the computer and fax machine. I wondered if there was a stray document lying around that I could steal. I had no idea what I would do with such a document, but it felt like that was what the script demanded.

'If I can't write a book here, with this view and all this nice stuff, then I wouldn't be able to write a book anywhere,' the arms dealer said.

I was examining a low shelf in front of his desk. There were small models resting on it, looking like toys and making me think momentarily of my son. But these weren't toys in front of me. They were scaled-down versions of the products the arms dealer sold. There was an armoured personnel carrier and a battle tank, both of them sand-coloured, as if to suggest that their theatre of operation would be a desert. There was a strange-looking ship too, and Samrat asked the dealer, 'What's that?'

'A littoral combat ship,' the dealer said, dragging out the t's. He led us back to the lounge, pressing us to stay for dinner. When we declined, because we had another engagement, he was insistent that we meet again. Then he remembered the reason I had come. He called over a tall Sikh who was in charge of the club lounge.

'What was the name of that girl who used to work here? The one from Manipur?'

'The girl from F&B?' the Sikh said. 'Esther.'

'Can you get me her cell number?'

The Sikh came back with the number written on a piece of hotel stationery. The arms dealer called, chatted for a while and then handed me the phone. If Esther was surprised, she didn't show it, and we made plans to meet on Saturday afternoon at the 'McD' on Janpath. My friend and I said goodbye to the arms dealer and his wife and wished them a good trip to Dhaka.

'Do you sell to Bangladesh as well?' I asked.

'I sell to everyone on the subcontinent,' he said. 'It's business.'

2

The 'McD' where Esther had wanted to meet me was on the corner of Tolstoy Marg and Janpath (or 'People's Way'), directly across from rows of handicraft stores selling tie-dyed scarves and jewellery to unhappy-looking backpackers. It was walking distance from the magazine office at Connaught Place where I had worked in the late nineties while living in Munirka, and I had often wandered along Janpath, looking at the handicraft stores and the tall office buildings. The neighbourhood had seemed to me then to be the climax of urban civilization, the centre of a fantastically alienating and alluring big city, and it was oddly disappointing to see the McDonald's insert itself into the area. It was meant to emphasize how global Delhi had become, but what it accomplished was a diminution of scale. The McDonald's was a reminder that Janpath was not Times Square. It was no longer even Janpath.

There was a doorman to salute and let me in, a man dressed like a soldier on parade with his peaked cap, sash and boots. The menu had no beef, and mutton had been squeezed in as a replacement for the Mahaburger. The crowd was lively and vocal, gathered in large groups of family and friends, making the place quite unlike McDonald's outlets I had seen in America with their often solitary diners. Numerous women in uniform, mostly from the north-east, circulated around the restaurant, taking away trays when customers were done eating.

Esther and her younger sister, Renu, were sitting next to each other at a table pushed against the wall, watching me with curiosity as I approached. Renu was slender, darker than Esther and dressed in a salwar kameez that made her seem more at ease among the Delhi clientele of McDonald's. She had just graduated from college and seemed full of energy, hurriedly finishing her Happy Meal so that she wouldn't be left out of the conversation.

Esther hadn't ordered any food. She sat pushing around a large Coke, the ice rattling in the cup. There were dark circles around her eyes: she had finished work at two in the morning and not got home till three thirty. She was a couple of years older than Renu, lighter skinned and stockily built, and her hair was cut short. She was dressed in a green top and jeans, cheap and functional clothes, and the only visible decorative touches were a pair of small earrings and the red nail polish painted on to thick, square fingertips.

It was difficult, as I sat across from Esther, to imagine her at Shangri-La. She didn't seem sufficiently polished and demure, unlike the waitresses I had seen when I had been at the lounge with the arms dealer. The women there had been soft-footed and soft-spoken, flaring momentarily into existence with a smile, putting down a saucer or taking away a cup before receding into the background. Unlike them, and unlike the bubbly Renu, Esther exuded both tiredness and toughness. She was a worker, clenching her fist occasionally to make a point as she told me about her journey from the north-east to the imperial centre of Delhi.

Esther had grown up in Imphal, the capital of the north-eastern state of Manipur. Her father was a Tangkhul Naga from Ukhrul district, while her mother was from the Kom tribe in the Moirang area. To the people sitting in McDonald's, Esther probably looked no more than vaguely Mongoloid, perhaps a Nepali, or perhaps – in the pejorative language commonly used in Delhi for all Mongoloid people – a 'Chinky'. Yet the different backgrounds of her parents indicated a coming together of opposites, a meeting between a Naga from the northern mountains of Ukhrul and a Kom from the watery rice valley of Moirang that had produced the contrasting looks and personalities of the sisters in front of me.

Esther's father was a minor government official, now retired, while her mother taught Hindi at a school. The background of her parents, along with her mixed tribal heritage, meant that Esther had grown up in a way that was quite cosmopolitan, interacting with people from other communities. Her best friend, she said, was from Bihar, and as a student she had travelled with her friend to Patna, the capital of Bihar, and across the border to Nepal. It also meant that there were ways in which Esther felt removed from her own ethnic background. 'I don't know how to speak Tangkhul,' she said. 'If I mingle with them, I feel different. They're not bad people, Nagas. But I want to move ahead. I don't want to look back. I want to see the world. If I was at home now, I'd be married and with two kids.'

In Imphal, Esther had received a relatively high level of education. She had studied biochemistry in college and then gone on to complete a master's degree in botany. She had wanted to be a doctor, she said, but she had settled instead for a one-year tourism course in Chandigarh, Punjab, in 2004. Her time in Chandigarh went by quickly, and she had seen little of the city by the time she finished her course and moved to Delhi.

Her first job, in 2005, was doing ticketing for a travel agency in Malviya Nagar. She was living near Delhi University in an area called North Campus, and the office was in south Delhi, which meant that she had to take a series of buses across the city to get to work. The men in the buses were aggressive and uncouth and she often lost her way. But soon she found a better job at the front desk of the Taj Palace Hotel, and her salary increased to 6,000 rupees a month from the 4,000 she had made as a travel agent.

The Taj Palace Hotel was a very different work environment from the travel agency. It was a five-star hotel, the place where I had heard Vijay Mallya give his talk on luxury brands a couple of years earlier. In the plush surroundings of Taj Palace, Esther found herself serving wealthy Indians and foreigners, who were luxury brands of a kind too, and it was while working among them that Esther began to feel that there were better jobs at such places than serving on the front desk. 'I had a friend who worked on a cruise ship. She made so much money, yeah. Every time she came back, she had one lakh rupees in her pocket,' Esther said, her tone more of wonder than envy.

The friend worked in 'F&B', Esther said, by which she meant 'Food and Beverages'. She always used the phrase in its abbreviated form, and she used it often, so that it ran through our many conversations like a potent code, generating positive or negative meanings depending on how Esther was feeling that day about herself, her work and her life.

At that first meeting of ours, Esther was cautious. She was opening up her life to a stranger and she was understandably anxious to portray that life as a success. She therefore depicted F&B in a particularly optimistic light, emphasizing how much it had given her and how it had allowed her to move away from the narrow life – married and with two kids – that she would have had if she had stayed in Imphal.

Esther's cruise ship friend convinced her that she should move from the front desk position to one in F&B. The work was harder, but the money was better, largely because of tips. 'I wanted F&B so badly,' Esther said, and although there were no openings for her at Taj Palace, a manager there helped her get an interview at Hotel Shangri-La. She began working at Shangri-La in 2006 and remained there for over two years, earning a salary of 7,500 rupees before tips. At first, she was stationed at the 'Thai-Chinese restaurant' on the first floor. Then she was moved upstairs, to the Horizon Club. 'The food and drinks are complimentary for club members,' she said, 'and there's a fixed budget from the hotel for the costs run up in the club. We're supposed to manage within that.'

For the most part, the clients had been fine, she said. 'Sometimes, the general manager's friends would come and we had to be extra nice to them. There were some Australian guys, some French guys from the embassy. If there's no Perrier, and we give them some other soda water, the French guys would get impatient. Sometimes, people are strange, like a US client who swore at me in Horizon. I abused him in Hindi, but I kept smiling while I did that so that he wouldn't know. Sometimes, in the restaurant downstairs, we would have Asian customers. Now, if the customers are Chinese or Japanese, we'll never get a tip. Rain will come down from the skies if one of them tips.'

On 13 February 2009, Esther said with sudden specificity, she left Shangri-La to work in Zest, a new restaurant located in a mall in south Delhi. The salary, at 13,000 rupees, was almost double what she was making at Shangri-La, although money was not the only reason for her changing jobs. The hours were far longer at the new place, starting at noon and finishing at two in the morning, and she worked six days a week. 'But it's okay,' Esther said. 'In F&B, every day you learn something new.'

A sudden burst of 'Happy Birthday' from an adjoining table drowned out Esther's talk. I looked at the busy tables around us. No one was paying us any attention, although I wondered what they would see if they looked in our direction, at the two young women sitting across a table from me, an older man. We had been talking for a couple of hours, and Esther and Renu needed to leave. Although it was Esther's day off, she had to go to Shangri-La to pick up some papers from the human resources department. We made plans to meet again, and I offered to give the sisters a lift to Shangri-La. The driver of the car I had hired that day, a young man from Rajasthan, was parked across the street, and he reached around to open the door for me when he saw me coming. I registered the sudden shock on his face when he saw the women accompanying me and realized that they were coming with me. He went numb as I let Esther and Renu into the back of the car and came around and sat next to him. He hadn't said a word, but I knew what he was thinking. He had assumed that the women were prostitutes and that I was going home with them. When we stopped at Shangri-La to drop off Esther and Renu, his expression changed. But I could see, as we drove homewards, that he was puzzled by what I had been doing with them in the first place.

### 3

The land of F&B, where Esther lived much of the time, was a place of reversed polarities. I began to understand this as Esther and I met over the course of the next few months. Since she worked six days a week, we had to squeeze our meetings into her workdays, mostly at three in the afternoon when there was a lull in the rhythm of the restaurant.

Esther usually sent me a text message to let me know that she could meet. The messages arrived at three or four in the morning, when she had just clocked off for the day and was in a van heading home to North Campus, trying to stay ahead of the early summer dawn. I got used to my phone vibrating under my pillow, displaying messages that were oddly cheerful and bouncy for that time of the night but that seemed to reveal only one facet of Esther's personality.

I was living with a friend in Vasant Kunj, not far from where Esther worked. I would meet her at the mall in an auto-rickshaw or taxi, and we would drive to an older, smaller shopping complex in Vasant Vihar fifteen minutes away, where we sat at a café and talked.

When I first went to pick her up, Esther had asked me to wait for her at a nearby bus stop rather than at the mall itself, and I wondered if she felt self-conscious at being met by a man, or if the bus stop was part of a familiar routine. After the initial occasions, however, she seemed to mind less if I went right down to the mall. When I got there, I always found it hard to spot her. She tended to hug the wall, staying away from other people, looking small against the vast facade of the mall with its granite, glass and luxury-brand logos. The heat was fierce, about 110 degrees at the peak of summer, and Esther seemed utterly isolated from the swirl of activity at the mall entrance: uniformed guards shoving their metal detectors under vehicles being taken to the underground parking garage; attendants rushing to take over those cars whose owners wanted valet parking; shoppers in sunglasses making the transition from air-conditioned cars to air-conditioned mall in a burst of perfume and jewellery.

Esther was always dressed the same way, wearing either a blue or green top, jeans and strapped sandals that, with their thick soles, were rather masculine. Her eyes slid blankly over the cars going past her, her face withdrawn and remote, and when she registered my arrival, always a few seconds after she actually saw me, she gave a quick, nervous smile. She then walked hurriedly towards me and dived into the back seat.

When we arrived at the Barista café in Vasant Vihar, Esther stood out among the carefully made-up women meeting their dates or friends. Even though she was the same age as these other women, mostly in their twenties, she looked older, more worn down. She also didn't know what to order the first time we went to the Barista. When the waitress came to our table, Esther looked self-conscious and said she wanted a Coke. The waitress eyed her with surprise, puzzled that Esther didn't know that you couldn't get a Coke at a Barista.

But it made sense, in a way. The view from F&B was about serving, not about being served. It was about what one was able to offer to the customer sitting at the table, across that almost invisible but impregnable barrier of class. At the Barista, Esther happened to be on the wrong side of the table. She would have known everything on the menu, down to the minute details, if we had been at Zest, or at Shangri-La. She would be able to advise customers on what mix of drinks, appetizers and entrées to order. But she hadn't waited tables at a Barista, and so the menu there became an unfamiliar, alien document, something she hadn't studied sufficiently.

Esther finally chose an iced drink, frowning at the menu with its abundance of superlatives. Then she asked the waitress, a slender nineteen-year-old, 'Where are you from?'

'Manipur,' the girl replied.

'I'm from Manipur too. Where's your home?'

'Churachandpur,' the waitress said, easing up a little in her posture.

The three of us chatted for a while about Churachandpur and Imphal, the Barista waitress telling us that this was her first job and that she had been in Delhi for just four months.

'How much are you making?' Esther asked.

'Four thousand,' the girl said.

'That's not bad,' Esther said.

'She looks barely sixteen,' I said when she had left.

'Oh, she's not so young,' Esther said.

Although a franchise café was so intimidating to Esther, she herself worked in probably one of the most expensive restaurants in Delhi. It had been described to me by Manish, the cigar dealer I had visited recently, as 'the most happening place' in the city. Manish was less enthusiastic about the Emporio Mall, where Zest was located. 'It's a bit imitative. Dubai in Delhi, you know?' he said.

At the beginning of our interaction, Esther had appeared quite dazzled by the glamour of working F&B at Zest. It was a 'forty-four crore' restaurant serving 'seven cuisines', she told me, with twenty expert chefs, a 'mixologist' from Australia, four dining rooms and a 1,800-bottle wine cellar. The bricks had been imported from China, the marble from Italy, and even the music in the restaurant was sent over the Internet by a company based in the UK. 'It's so beautiful,' Esther said.

There were 408 'girls' who worked at the restaurant, all of them reporting for work at noon and most of them finishing their shifts at two in the morning. Only the hostesses got to leave slightly earlier. The restaurant was divided into seven divisions, one for each cuisine, each division having a staff of seventy and with a hierarchy that started with the manager, continued through assistant manager, hostess, various levels of waitresses who were called 'station assistants', and finally 'runners' who were at the very bottom. There was a similar hierarchy among the kitchen staff as well, and one's position in the hierarchy determined how many 'points' one had, with more points translating into a greater share of the tips. In the past fifteen days, Esther said, her division had received 75,000 rupees in tips, of which she might receive around 500 rupees.

Esther was in the middle of the hierarchy. She was a station holder, one of nine in her division. 'The others are all guys,' she said, 'so I have to challenge them all the time.' Her job was to explain the menu, take orders and serve the food, which brought her into close contact with her customers. 'They come in with bags and bags of stuff,' she said, 'with Louis Vuitton, Cartier, all these names written on them. Sometimes, a customer drops a receipt on the floor and when I pick it up to give it back to her, I'll see that the amount of money she has spent runs to tens of lakhs.'

The restaurant, in spite of its long hours and stream of wealthy clientele, wasn't technically open. It was still waiting for its liquor licence from the government, but that hadn't stopped it from functioning unofficially for the Delhi rich who constituted the restaurant's patrons and many of whom knew the owners. Zest was part of the holdings of DLF, India's largest real-estate company, and which owned the Emporio Mall as well as the restaurant. DLF is 'primarily engaged', as the Reuters India profile of the company puts it, 'in the business of colonization and real-estate development'. Like other large Indian companies, it is, in spite of being publicly traded, more or less a family business, and the owner or chairman, K. P. Singh, was in 2008 rated by *Forbes* as the eighth-richest person in the world and perhaps the richest real-estate businessman in the world. But the global downturn had come to India since then. Vijay Mallya, whom I had last seen talking about luxury brands at the Taj Palace Hotel, had fallen off the list of billionaires, losing $900 million of the $1.2 billion he was valued at in 2008. Singh's fall was less precipitous, down to number seventy-four in the list of the world's billionaires in 2010, but that still left him one of the richest people in India.

Esther's part in such wealth was a very tiny one, something like the role of a serving maid at a great imperial palace, one of history's unrecorded, unremembered millions, a barbarian in Rome. Yet Delhi as an imperial capital was also a postmodern, millennial city where Esther traversed different layers of history every day on her way to work.

She left home at ten in the morning, taking a 10-rupee ride on a cycle rickshaw from her flat to the metro station of North Campus. This was an area dominated by Delhi University but contained within the walls of the old city that had for over two centuries been the Mughal capital of the Indian subcontinent. From North Campus, Esther took the metro, built in the past few years, to Central Secretariat, not far from Shangri-La and sitting at the heart of Lutyens' Delhi, so called after the Edwardian architect who planned the neighbourhood as a centre for the British Raj in the first decades of the twentieth century. After independence, this stretch of Delhi with its juxtaposition of ministerial buildings, luxury hotels and private mansions became the heart of the Indian government, although a corporate presence has been added to the neighbourhood in recent years. From Central Secretariat, Esther travelled on a bus that took her south, into a wealthy, post-independence part of the city that was expanding into the suburbs of Gurgaon. Her journey across these layers of history involved two hours of travelling, 30 rupees in fares, and three modes of transportation.

Nothing of this long journey and transition through the different worlds of Delhi would be evident once Esther stepped into the locker room of the restaurant. There, she changed into her uniform and put on her make-up of kajal eyeliner, eye shadow and blusher – required by the restaurant of its female staff but items that each employee had to provide for herself. Finally, she would arrange her hair in the mandatory zigzag pattern that represented the letter Z for Zest. At one thirty, she would have lunch along with the other staff. It was usually Indian food, but if the chefs were feeling good, they would throw in a special dish. Since evening happened to be the busiest time in the restaurant, there was never any opportunity for dinner. Nor was there much chance of a break. When Esther was really tired and could steal some time from being on the restaurant floor, she sat and dozed on a chair in the locker room. 'I could lie down on the floor and go to sleep right there, but they'll come and wake you up even if you're dead,' she said.

Esther's journey home was easier because an office van dropped her and other workers off, cutting down her travel time by thirty minutes. She reached her flat at 3.30 a.m., barely enough time to sleep and get ready for the next morning. 'I feel like a thief,' she said. 'When I come home, everyone's sleeping. It's a strange job that requires you to be up when everyone else is in bed.'

Esther's long working hours left her little time for reflection. Yet whenever we met, she liked to talk about who she had become, and was still becoming, in the course of her long journey from Imphal to Delhi. In this vast city, she found herself among a wide range of strangers, and her experience of these people through F&B had given her a body of knowledge that was a blend of prejudice and wisdom, sometimes perceptive and sometimes contradictory.

I asked her if there were women from other parts of India among her colleagues.

'There are, but you know, I think, those of us who are from the north-east, we're stronger. I can fight, like that day when I had a quarrel with the manager. The women who are not from the north-east, they won't challenge authority. But also, they won't mingle with other people, the way we can. We girls from the north-east are independent, strong.'

'And what about the men?'

'The guys are high-profile people,' she said, laughing. '*Chota kam nahi karega.* They won't do small work. But me, what to do? I was not born with a kilo of gold. I have a cousin brother in Imphal. He's a three hundred and sixty-five drunkard. You understand? He's drunk every day. When I go home, he asks me for money. What to do? I give him money, but he doesn't know how much I sweat to earn the money. In Delhi, I have fifty-four cousin brothers and sisters. Most of the girls are working. The guys are all home ministers. They stay at home, do nothing. They're looking for a good job, the right job.'

In Delhi, Esther often felt conscious of her difference from other Indian people. 'We have small eyes,' she said. 'They can tell we're from the north-east. Sometimes, the way they think about us, the way they talk about us, makes me not think of myself as Indian. I want them to accept me the way I am, not the way they want me to be.'

She thought for a while and then told me of the event that had led her to leave Shangri-La. 'I worked hard there, and pushed myself to learn F&B. Then, on 23 November 2008, I was working the afternoon shift. At 10.30 p.m., I finished work. The rule is for the hotel to drop you off if you're working late, so I took a hotel car, with a new driver. In north Delhi, a drunk man in a cream-coloured Maruti Esteem jumped through a red light and rammed into our car. The hotel driver, he just ran away, leaving me there.'

Esther was in the back seat, writhing in pain. She dragged herself out of the car on to the road, but although there were people around, no one came to her help. Finally, a couple walking by stopped and approached her. They asked her where she was from. They were from Manipur too, and the woman was a nurse at the Ram Manohar Lohia hospital. They took Esther to the hospital, where she needed twenty-three stitches in her head.

She still had a scar on her forehead. She lifted her hair so that I could see the bunched-up tissue on the right side of her forehead. She had lost three teeth. 'The ones I have now, they're all duplicates,' she said. 'The people from the hotel came to see me and the first thing they wanted to know was when I was coming back to work. I said, "I can't even get up from bed by myself, and you want to know when I can work?"' She was in the hospital for a month, and the hotel, after some initial fuss, covered her medical costs. 'They put me on painkillers, on a saline drip, and for one month I just lay in the bed. I got fat, and my weight went up from fifty kilos to sixty-five. That's how much I weigh now. My back hurts if I stand for long, and of course, in this job you have to do that all the time. When I went back to work, I began to feel bad about being at Shangri-La, and that's when I started looking for another option.'

4

One day, I met up with Esther in the morning. Instead of going back home, she had stayed over with a friend in Munirka, my old neighbourhood. She had permission to report at work a little later than usual and the plan was for us to visit her flat in North Campus, then come back south together.

I picked her up near the Rama Market, the spot where for years I had waited for the 620 bus to take me to my office in Connaught Place. I remembered how I would walk through the alleyways of Munirka, passing an open-air auto repair shack where, in spite of wanting to avoid the sight, I would invariably find my gaze drawn towards a man whose entire nose was missing, possibly eaten away by syphilis. I remembered taking a bus back from work that, just before it came to Rama Market, ran over a bicyclist while speeding through a red light. The bus hit the man, braked, skidded off its path and jumped across the divider into the opposite lane, careening through the traffic and the pavement on the other side, slowing down a little when it hit some trees and bushes before slamming into a wall, the shattering windows sending shards of glass through the bus.

Esther was silent as the taxi driver began the drive towards North Campus. We left south Delhi behind and began crossing the central stretch of Lutyens' Delhi. The sun was bright and harsh, but the trees and flowers around the bungalows of the area made everything look cool and comfortable. We crossed the entrance to the Santushti Shopping Complex, where Manish was no doubt sitting in his cigar store, being pleasant to his wealthy clients. We approached the Delhi Gymkhana Club, and Esther asked, 'Are we near the prime minister's house?' We were indeed, as was evident from the armed men and police jeeps everywhere. She looked out of the window as if she hoped to catch a glimpse of the prime minister himself, but then she sank back into the seat and became quiet. When she spoke again, she sounded wistful.

'Some day I would like to have a car,' she said. 'My father has a bicycle. He's old, but that's what he uses to ride around the town. Sometimes, he'll double-carry and take my mother out on the bicycle. My mother doesn't like it. She's quite fat now, and it's hard for him to pedal with both of them on the bicycle. One day, they fell down, and my mother was so angry.' Esther started laughing. 'She said, "I'll never go with you on your bicycle again."'

We entered the northern end of Delhi through the walls of the old fort city. The wall retains little of its former glory; it may still be impressively thick, but the strength of a fort wall doesn't mean much in a modern age. There were bricks missing in the wall, and when we came to the old city, there was no imperial splendour, just poor people negotiating a series of crowded streets and alleys.

Esther's flat was at the end of a narrow alleyway, on the top floor of a building. From the faces of the pedestrians, I could tell that this was one of the areas, like Munirka in south Delhi, where people from the north-east were concentrated, bunched together for a greater sense of safety. It was also an area where, because of its proximity to the university, the landlords were willing to deviate from the marked preference in Delhi for well-off, upper-caste Hindu tenants. The flat, up a narrow flight of stairs, was small, with two rooms in a railroad arrangement opening out to the roof. There was a narrow passage-way leading out from the last room, with a kitchen and bathroom on one side, the view from the roof overlooking houses crammed close to each other.

The rent was 6,500 rupees and the Punjabi landlady, Esther said, was quite nice, although that depended a little on her moods. It seemed to me that, even though Delhi was expensive, Esther was paying more than the market rate for her place. The extra amount was a sort of unofficial tax imposed upon ethnic minorities and the poor by the landlords of the city, who know that such people aren't welcome in most neighbourhoods and can therefore be charged a higher rent while being provided with fairly rudimentary facilities.

The flat had been decorated in a functional manner. The room I sat in was crowded, containing a bed, an old-fashioned CRT television and a refrigerator. This was where Esther and her two sisters slept, while in the outer room, far more bare, a brother made his bed at night. The brother, five years older than Esther, was not home when I visited. Esther had an older half-brother who was married and lived in Imphal as well as a younger brother who was studying engineering at a private college in Bangalore, an expensive education into which the parents had directed most of their savings. The brother who lived with Esther had a master's in sociology, but although he had applied for many jobs and taken countless exams, he remained unsuccessful in finding employment.

Mary was the eldest of the three sisters, four years older than

Esther, and she had a job at a call centre in Gurgaon. Unlike Renu, who was excited to have me visiting and seemed eager to show me around, Mary looked tired. She was lying on the bed fully dressed, watching television as she waited for the call centre van to pick her up.

I thought of my own brief foray into the call centre world and the sinking feeling with which I had clocked in, sitting down at one of a row of computers and reaching reluctantly for the headphones that would connect me to angry or upset people in England. That was a time when call centre work was talked up as an exciting profession, part of the new India. The media no longer referred to call centres in this manner, and few of the people who worked there saw it as more fulfilling than being a clerk in a government office. The outsourcing business wasn't doing quite as well either, Mary said. She had received a smaller salary increase this year than in the past, and the kind of calls she made had changed in nature.

Mary worked in collections these days, and when she arrived at the office in Gurgaon, she would start calling American customers, threatening them with repossession of their cars because they had fallen behind with their loan payments. It was a sudden, reversed camera shot of the American recession, viewed from a flat in a slum-like neighbourhood in north Delhi. It was unpleasant work, Mary said, but she did it to earn a living. I would later find out from Esther that Mary was a disappointed person. She had left call centre work, hoping for a different life, and she had returned to it only because her dream hadn't come true. But I didn't know this at the time, and as Mary headed out to work, I thought of the strangers she would connect with, people who were falling behind, who were part of a wave of foreclosures and job losses, and who would never know anything of the young woman calling to remind them of their failures.

Renu had been waiting impatiently to show me her plants. 'Even the landlady admires them,' she said. 'I give her seeds and plants, but then she comes back in a few weeks and says that they've all died. I don't know what she does with them.' Renu's plants sat in earthen pots along the narrow passageway leading out to the roof. They looked healthy, a gathering of aloe vera, spinach and what Renu called 'Naga coriander'. Sometimes, she said, she bought celery from the market and replanted the roots. She had gathered seeds from a lemon tree on the street and planted those and although it was still small, she was hopeful that it would eventually start producing fruit. In order to make sure that her plants grew well, Renu went to the municipal parks in the winter, to the areas where gardeners burned dead leaves, gathering soil that was therefore rich in ash. It was Renu's way of creating a touch of Manipur in the alien city in which she found herself.

Renu also did much of the cooking. She looked at Esther and said slyly, 'She's telling you about her problems and how hard she works. You should see her when she comes home from work in a bad mood. They fight at work, we suffer.'

'You, you have a good time at home, what do you know?' Esther said. 'I'm so tired sometimes. I don't have the energy to go out and get a recharge card for my mobile. I have to beg Renu to go and get it for me. She won't do it unless I bribe her. A hundred-rupee note.'

Renu laughed and began serving us the rice and fish curry she had cooked. 'There's some pork in the fridge too,' Renu said. 'Do you want some?'

She served me the pork, cubes with fat glistening on them, the way I liked it. I felt relaxed and lazy after the meal, and thought about how paradoxical the situation was. The warmth and hospitality the sisters displayed was characteristic of the north-east, but it was the urban anonymity of Delhi that had allowed them to entertain me, a man from a different ethnic group, in their house.

As we talked, I also noticed how much more optimistic Renu was about the future than her sisters. She didn't have to work long hours like Esther or Mary, and she was in that sense not yet worn down by the world. She talked about how she occasionally went to church, something neither of the other sisters did. She visited the Methodist Church on Lodi Road, which rented out the space every week to the Tangkhul Baptist Church to which the sisters belonged. Renu sang in the choir, but what she really liked about church was the way it created a home-like space, with feasts that involved familiar food. In other ways, however, Renu seemed to have adapted far better to

Delhi than her sisters. Her Hindi was more fluent and she dressed with ease in a salwar kameez, looking much like any middle-class young woman from Delhi. Her ambitions too revealed a sense of freedom in how she imagined her future. She wanted to become a journalist and was interested in doing a one-year course at the YMCA.

The course seemed rather expensive to me, with the fees amounting to 37,000 rupees. 'Who'll pay for it?' I said.

Renu laughed.

Esther, who was sitting sleepily in the chair after her meal, pointed at herself. 'Who'll pay? Me. Who else is there?' Then she looked at her phone and said we should head back south. She had to report for work in an hour.

5

Women did not have it easy in Delhi, whether they were local or from other parts of India. The recent globalization of the city had indeed created new opportunities for some women, especially those working as waitresses and sales assistants. The same globalization had also allowed the use of ultrasound technology to abort some 24,000 female foetuses every year, resulting in a skewed sex ratio of 820 to 1,000 in Delhi. It was into this contradictory realm that women from the north-east arrived in their search for work, and the media was full of stories of them being assaulted, molested and killed, of mobs encircling the rooms they rented and beating women up while the police looked on. For its part, the Delhi Police had issued a 'manual' for people from the north-east living in the city, whose guidelines included:

- Bamboo shoot ... and other smelly dishes should be
  prepared without creating ruckus in neighbourhood.
- Be Roman in 'rooms' ... revealing dresses should be
  avoided.
- Avoid lonely road/bylane when dressed scantily.

One afternoon, I met up with Lansinglu Rongmei, a lawyer who had started the North-East Support Centre in 2007 to help people facing violence and discrimination. We went to the same café where I usually talked with Esther, and the waitress from Churachandpur served us. Lansi was stocky and energetic, her lawyerly cautiousness alternating with a sense of regional pride that made her talk about the cases she took up of people who had been bullied or violated. She was from Dimapur, a small town in Nagaland, but had gone to high school and college in Calcutta. She had moved to Delhi to study law and now practised in the Supreme Court, but after fifteen years in the city, she still didn't feel fully at home.

'Going from Nagaland to Calcutta wasn't so much of a culture shock,' Lansi said. 'I felt they didn't judge you as much. In Delhi, they do. They size you down and they size you up. What kind of a gadget do you have? What kind of a dress are you wearing? What kind of a car do you have? When I was a law student in Delhi University, I had friends from southern India, and from Bihar. I felt that Biharis, whom they call "Haris", are sometimes targeted no less here than people from the north-east.'

I asked her what it was like to be a lawyer in such a place.

She thought about it and said, 'The racism is very subtle sometimes, but it's there. Still, the Supreme Court is a pretty cosmopolitan place. When I am presenting a case there or at the High Court, I can wear shirts and trousers, and they won't judge me for it. But if I'm at a district court, I have to wear a sari or a salwar kameez or they'll be prejudiced against me.'

Lansi's confidence and legal profession allowed her to deal with the city in a way that wasn't possible for many of the women who arrived here from the north-east. Lansi could voice her anger, as she had done in an article where she had described eloquently how 'both boys and girls [from the north-east] are grabbed from behind and asked: "Chinky, sexy, how much?"' The article had made me want to meet her and find out more about the kind of cases she dealt with at the support centre, but Lansi was less combative in person, more reflective and funny.

The support centre had been set up, Lansi told me, with the help of local church leaders. She herself was a practising Christian, but she emphasized that the cases of harassment they came across were not limited to Christians and neither was the assistance provided by the centre. They had a helpline that people could call at any time, but the helpline was really the mobile numbers for Lansi and a colleague of hers. Lansi took out a few visiting cards with the numbers on them, pausing briefly to pass one on to the waitress from Churachandpur. The waitress looked surprised but slipped the card into her apron, and Lansi began talking about the kind of cases she dealt with.

She told me about two women working for a Pizza Hut outlet who had not been paid their salary for three months, and who, after repeated complaints, were informed that their dues would be released in instalments; of a woman locked inside her apartment by the landlord; of another woman taking Hindi lessons from a man who insisted that she make him her boyfriend – a euphemism for wanting sex – in order to improve her Hindi. The harassment moved easily along the bottom half of the class ladder, targeting semi-literate women who worked as maidservants as well as the more educated ones with jobs at restaurants.

It was possible to see a pattern in Lansi's stories, of the clash between women from the north-east and local men, two disparate groups thrown together by the modernity of the new India. It was the sudden explosion of malls and restaurants that had created jobs like the ones at Pizza Hut where men and women worked together; it had drawn thousands of women from the north-east, prized for their English and their lighter skin; it had also stoked the confused desires of men from deeply patriarchal cultures. From the names of the Delhi neighbourhoods that Lansi mentioned – the areas where women had been harassed, assaulted, raped and even murdered by landlords, colleagues and neighbours – it was possible to tell how they had been villages not too long ago and had been haphazardly absorbed into the urban sprawl of Delhi. These were neighbourhoods where the local women went around wearing veils while the men eyed the outsiders, lusting after them and yet resenting them, considering themselves to be from more superior cultures while also feeling that they were less equipped to take advantage of the service economy of globalized cities like Delhi.

But just as not all men in such neighbourhoods were violent towards women, there were also men who were seemingly more modern, more capable of benefiting from the new economy and who still turned out to be predators. The case that bothered Lansi the most was that of a young Assamese woman who had worked at a food stand in Gurgaon with her boyfriend. It was a stand selling the Tibetan dumplings called 'momos', ubiquitous in all Indian cities these days. One of the customers at the momo stand, a middle-aged executive working for a multinational, offered the woman a job cleaning his apartment.

'The girl had come straight from a village,' Lansi said. 'She was so naive. And I think the boyfriend encouraged her to take the job. She went to clean the apartment and the man locked her up and raped her. He kept her there for days, raping her while going to work every morning as usual.'

Eventually, the woman managed to escape and approached Lansi. Because this had happened in Gurgaon, Lansi had to fight the case at the High Court there, something that worried her. The Gurgaon High Court was not as cosmopolitan as the Delhi High Court, Lansi felt. She thought it was more patriarchal, more prejudiced against women from other parts of the country. In the end, it didn't matter because the woman refused to testify in court and the charges were dropped. Lansi assumed that something had gone wrong between the filing of the case and the trial. She thought that the executive had very possibly paid money to the woman's boyfriend and used him to put pressure on the victim, but this was a guess, something Lansi had been unable to verify. When she went to talk to the woman again, she found the momo stand locked up. The couple had apparently left Gurgaon and gone back to Assam.

Esther's experience of Delhi had been nothing like the people Lansi had talked about. She was smarter, tougher and perhaps more fortunate. Yet the initial sense of optimism she had conveyed to me, especially about F&B, gave way gradually to a more complex reality.

If Esther had left home, she had done so as much out of a strong sense of independence as out of a need for employment. 'I'm a graduate,' she had told me the first time we met, clenching her fist to emphasize the point. 'Why should I have to depend on my husband for money?'

But Esther's independence in Delhi had turned out to be a strange thing, with others depending on her. 'Most of my friends in Imphal didn't finish graduation,' Esther said to me at the Barista café a few days after I had talked to Lansi. 'I did my degree and came here to work. But still, in spite of the money I make, I have to think twice before I do anything. I am not a hi-fi type, you know. I have a prepaid phone, on which I spend about three thousand rupees a month on refills. That's the only luxury. I don't have money to buy new clothes or even a pair of chappals.'

Although Esther's salary at Zest was 13,000 a month, the money was not just for herself. She paid a major share of the rent and household expenses. Mary contributed too, but she earned less than Esther. Renu didn't work and neither did the elder brother.

I asked Esther if she resented her brother.

'How can I be angry with him?' she said. 'He's so good to me. He massages my neck, clips my nails, washes my hair. Sometimes, he'll get aloe vera juice from Renu's plant for me to put on my hands.'

Yet Esther couldn't help getting frustrated with her situation and how all her hard work hadn't resulted in a significant improvement in her life. She talked resentfully at times of her bosses – all men – and sometimes even of the women who worked with her. 'There's this friend of mine who works at the restaurant, but she's also a call girl,' Esther said. 'I asked her why she does such a thing and she said she needed money. But I need money too, yeah? I don't stoop to selling my body because of that. If you go to Munirka, you will see some of these girls from the north-east waiting around. They have the taste of money and do these things to get the money. It feels so shameful. I can't even look at them. I keep thinking that other people will consider me to be just like them.'

Her attitude was unsympathetic towards the women who might be working as call girls. 'Look, you have to be extra careful if you're a woman. It's not like it is for boys. At work, these younger girls who do F&B, they have no sense sometimes. There are staff parties, and the boys try to get you drunk and come on to you. The younger ones, they let them. Me, I have a sharp tongue. I say, hey, stay away from me, but these young girls just don't care.'

Even though Esther had earlier talked about how she resented the way people in Delhi were prejudiced against women from the northeast, she herself sometimes exhibited a similar attitude. 'Sometimes, I wish I looked different,' she said. 'I wish I had bigger eyes. That I looked more Indian.' She began to tell me about how when she had worked at Shangri-La, she had seen the most beautiful woman in the world.

'Who was that?' I asked.

'Priyanka Gandhi,' she replied dreamily, naming the heiress apparent of the Congress Party, a woman descended from a long line of prime ministers, part Indian and part Italian. Esther had been filling the water glasses at the table where Priyanka Gandhi was having lunch with her husband. 'She was so beautiful,' Esther said, 'so fair that she looked transparent, as if she was made of glass. I watched her drinking water and it felt like I could see the water going down her throat.'

6

The home that Esther had left behind was a long way from Delhi. She had told me that her family lived in a rented house near the RIMS hospital in Imphal, and even though I hadn't seen the house, it wasn't hard for me to picture the setting. The last time I had been in Manipur was in December 2007, flying in from Delhi with a short stop in Guwahati, the capital of Assam. Those of us going to Manipur weren't allowed to get off the plane at Guwahati. While the Guwahati passengers disembarked, the rest of us sat on the plane while policemen came on board with metal detectors, checking that every piece of luggage in the cabin belonged to a passenger still on the plane. Then the aircraft took off again, flying low over hills and ridges thick with forest cover until it came down over Imphal Valley with its small, rectangular agricultural plots and slender bodies of water edged with dark conifers. The airport was new and clean, but as soon as I stepped outside I found myself facing soldiers in black bandannas bristling around a ring of armoured jeeps with gun turrets cut into the roofs.

Imphal hadn't changed much since the last time I had been there some ten years earlier. In the cool winter afternoon, people picked their way past the rubble and refuse on the streets, surveyed at every corner by armed policemen and soldiers. The electric supply in the town was intermittent, and the small generators chugging away in buildings that looked on the verge of collapse added their diesel fumes to the squalor, the grey of the streets rising to meet the grey of the sky until you could no longer see the hills surrounding the valley. When dusk came, there was a final, frantic burst of activity around the marketplace, creating traffic jams along the main avenue, but by seven in the evening everyone was off the streets, leaving behind a ghost town.

Even by the standards of north-eastern India, where the un-employment rate is twice the national average and the per capita income 30 per cent lower than the rest of the country, Manipur is an especially failed state. The periodic infusions of cash from Delhi seem only to have lined the pockets of local politicians and bureaucrats, leaving Manipur bereft of the most rudimentary infrastructure. Such neglect has been accompanied by the harsh authoritarianism of the government in Delhi, which has subjected the state, since 1958, to the Armed Forces Special Powers Act, which gives security forces the right to detain and to kill without having to answer to the local government.

Half a century after the imposition of this act, Manipur remains as violent a place as ever, with at least twenty-three insurgent groups operating among a population of only 2.5 million people. Some of these groups owe their allegiance to the Meitei culture of the valley, while others represent the diversity of tribes up in the hills, but all of them offer one of the two main employment options for young men in the state, the other being to join the police or paramilitary and fight the insurgents.

When I last came to Manipur, I had just quit my job in Delhi. I took my final pay cheque from the magazine in Connaught Place, locked up my flat in Munirka and headed out of Delhi. I was sick of the city and filled with longing for the north-east. I travelled cheap, going sleeper class on the slow Brahmaputra Mail, making one of the longest train journeys in India, some 2,000 kilometres from Delhi to Guwahati. Then I took a bus to Shillong, my hometown, and another bus to Silchar, a small town in Assam where my sister lived. From Silchar, I flew to Imphal, a flight of some fifteen minutes with the ticket, subsidized by the government, costing me only 600 rupees. It was my first time in Manipur, and there was a dusk-to-dawn curfew in Imphal, the only sounds at night being the rumbling of paramilitary convoys heading for the hills. In the morning, I read or heard about young men suspected of being insurgents who had been picked up from their houses by jeeps that had their licence plates covered. In the countryside, there were battles going on between the Naga and Kuki tribes, the latter apparently supported by Indian intelligence agencies to take on the separatist Nagas.

The violence wasn't quite as overt when I arrived in Imphal in 2007, but there were still 'encounters' between security forces and young insurgents, with the corpses of guerrillas being dragged out feet first from the hotel rooms or houses in which they had been shacked up. A few days into my stay, a bomb went off in an Imphal marketplace, killing eight people. In the countryside, meanwhile, the paramilitary was engaged in operations in Chandel district, bordering Burma, pushing back insurgents from a landmine-strewn area where they had successfully maintained a base for some years. All this seemed to happen silently, like a film with the sound off. Not a word of any of these events appeared in Delhi. It was all too far away, too remote, and since few of the insurgents were Islamists, they evoked no interest from those obsessed with the clash of civilizations.

One day I headed south-west of Imphal, travelling along National Highway 150 towards the hill district of Churachandpur. This is classified as a backward district, the epicentre of the clashes between Kukis and Nagas when I had last been in Manipur. The ethnic violence had simmered down since then, giving way to a more everyday combination of grinding poverty, skirmishes between security forces and insurgents, and an especially high rate of HIV infection. In fact, Manipur has the highest concentration of HIV-affected people in India, with 17 per cent of total cases in the country. Among those particularly vulnerable to HIV infection are drug users who share needles and women who are sex workers, and I was going to Churachandpur to interview some of these women.

Although 150 was called a highway, it was little more than a narrow track built on an embankment raised above paddy fields. The driver of the jeep I had hired came to a small village where there seemed to be a roadblock of sorts. A car was parked on the road, with a group of scruffy-looking boys gathered around the driver's window. Another boy straddled a wooden bench that had been placed on the road. My driver tried to squeeze past the makeshift barrier while everyone was busy with the other car. He accelerated, the bench shot out and closed the gap, and the boy sat back again on the bench, his hard gaze meeting ours. The driver sighed and reached for his wallet.

After an hour of driving along the valley, we reached the hills and the town of Churachandpur. It was built on a slope, a crowded settlement of run-down two-storey buildings, with shops on the ground floor, many of them selling wrinkled, second-hand clothes. In one of those buildings – a warren of rooms connected by narrow wooden staircases – a local group ran a centre for sex workers. The man in charge of the centre was in his mid-twenties, short and tough-looking. He had been a thug in his teens, he said, working for one of the many 'voluntary' organizations that indulged in petty extortion and moral policing and often beat up sex workers. He hadn't realized at the time that the women were driven into prostitution by poverty, violence, drugs and the lack of employment. Now, he helped run the NGO that focused on HIV prevention and provided facilities for the sex workers, including a 'daycare room' where women could leave their children or take a break from work. 'If there's trouble and the insurgents or police start beating them up, they come running to the daycare room for shelter,' the man said.

Manipur has traditionally been a matriarchal society, with women possessing far greater autonomy than their counterparts in the plains.

Yet this does not seem to have helped those who become sex workers. They are among the most invisible groups in this invisible corner
of the country, but they are also constantly subject to violence from
the police, local churches, insurgents and vigilante groups.

The room that offered the Churachandpur sex workers shelter
from such storms was small, with wooden walls, a low ceiling, and
windows looking out to the bus station where the women often went
to solicit clients. I sat with my back to a wall with posters of Jesus and
Norah Jones, facing a 23-year-old called Luni. She had straight hair
down to her shoulders, a snub nose and large eyes, and although it
wasn't cold, she stayed huddled in a shawl as she told me about her
life.

What a life it was, filled with struggle and aspiration, with a search
for happiness and the discovery of failure. She was one of countless
young women drifting to small towns like Churachandpur from
smaller, even more anonymous villages. Luni's parents had separated
soon after she was born and she had grown up with her mother in a
village. She had not been happy with her mother and, at fifteen, she
left home and travelled to Aizawl, the capital of the neighbouring
state of Mizoram. She had wanted to track down her father, she said,
hoping to find in him the affection she felt missing from her life. She
worked as a maidservant for a year while she looked for her father.
When she finally met him, she discovered that he was married and
had other children. He had been happy to see Luni, but he was also
afraid of his wife. One morning, he left a note for Luni saying that
she could no longer stay with them.

Luni moved again, this time to a village in Manipur where she
worked as a labourer in the rice fields. There, she met a farmer whom
she eventually married and with whom she had a daughter. But
Luni's husband was an alcoholic and frequently beat her, and she ran
away again, abandoning her daughter and coming to Churachandpur, where her maternal grandparents lived. The elderly couple had
not been pleased to see her, but they grudgingly let her stay with
them. In Churachandpur, she found friends of her age, youngsters
who eked out a miserable living through jobs as daily-wage labourers
or as petty criminals. One of them introduced Luni to heroin, and

when she became addicted and needed money for her fix, he found her the first of her clients.

She had tried to break the habit once when an NGO took her and other addicts to Delhi for a detox programme. When I asked her what it had been like, this being her only time out of the north-east, she laughed. 'I saw nothing,' she said. She had been curled up on her bunk as the train made its way through the Gangetic Plains, suffering from severe withdrawal symptoms. When she got to Delhi, she was kept inside the detox centre before being put on the train back home.

Luni had relaxed a little as she talked. Around us, the other women were drinking tea and smoking, their laughter lively but not intrusive. Luni took her hands out of her shawl and began rolling cigarettes at great speed. It was a little side occupation of hers, something with which to supplement the money she made from prostitution. I asked her to come out to lunch with me and some of the NGO workers, and her wariness returned.

She was silent as we drove to the only restaurant in Churachandpur, a surprisingly pleasant and airy place called 'Fat Jame's' [sic] that offered a wonderful view of the rooftops and the surrounding hills. But although Luni had lived in Churachandpur for so many years, she had never been there. When we went inside, walking past the modern-looking kitchen with glass walls, she went off to a balcony and stood there on her own, her back towards everybody. I went up to her and asked if she wanted to listen to music, handing her my iPod and headphones. She had never seen one before, but she quickly figured out how to use the menu and I left her there, looking out at the town with the headphones on.

Luni joined us at the table when the food arrived. Fat James came over to ask how we liked lunch, and to tell me that he had learned the business of F&B in Delhi, where he had worked at a restaurant as a cook. Luni seemed more at ease, participating in the conversation, and it suddenly became apparent that not only did she understand English, but that she could speak quite a bit of it too. I asked her if she would show me where she worked, and she said she would as long as the pimp and the madam who ran the place didn't mind.

There are no red-light areas in Manipur, and most sex workers practise their trade near stalls on the highway and in houses and hotels. Churachandpur was too small for hotels, and Luni worked at what she called a 'wine store', a stall selling locally brewed liquor. We left Fat Jame's and walked back past the daycare centre, entering an alleyway that led through a marketplace. There was a butcher's stall, empty but buzzing with flies, the cement floor covered with congealed blood. The stalls in the market, their roofs made of nylon sacks, were filled with plastic trinkets, necklaces and dolls. Even though there were only a few days to go before Christmas – and Churachandpur was primarily Christian, unlike the Imphal Valley – there wasn't much activity at the stalls. Men in tattered clothes loitered around, some of them looking at Luni with appraising glances.

The wine store was a stunted little shack on one of the side streets. I waited outside while Luni went in to get permission. A plump, middle-aged woman slipped out a few minutes later. This was the madam, careful to avoid having to talk to me. Then the pimp emerged with Luni to ask me what I wanted. I had been imagining the kind of villainous figure one sees in Bollywood films, the sort who goes around slashing the women who work for him. But the pimp was the same age as Luni, his sweater full of holes and his aggression barely masking his anxiety. He was worried that whatever I was writing would lead to trouble for him from the insurgents or the police. A policeman had come in just a little while ago, he said, threatening to arrest the only client in the place until he was paid off by the pimp.

I reassured him that whatever I was writing was unlikely ever to make its way to Churachandpur, and he invited me inside eagerly. The wine store was a dark, low-roofed room cobbled together out of plastic sheets, bamboo matting, wood and tin, with a couple of benches and tables pushed against the walls. A few translucent bottles stood on the rough dirt floor, next to an aluminium pot. It was still early in the afternoon and business was slow, and three women sat on a bench, one of them fifteen years old and in a daze. The other women were friendly and welcoming, looking like spectral versions of the young people I taught at a college in New York. I almost felt that I should ask them if they had completed their assignments.

Luni led me out through the back and up some rickety stairs to the room where she met her clients. It was bleak and to the point, with four beds in the room, each separated from the other by curtains. The sheets on the rough wooden cots were old and stained, and I wondered what it was like to make a living like this, offering sex on one of those beds for a few hundred rupees. There wasn't enough room to walk around, so I didn't do much more than stand in one spot and turn, trying to understand the lives that converged in this space. Luni stood by and let me look around, but after a while she suggested that we go down. It was the week of Christmas, a busy time for her, and her clients would be coming in even as I took the highway back to Imphal.

## 7

The restaurant Esther worked in was a long way from Fat Jame's in every way. It was located on the top floor of the Emporio Mall, a granite monstrosity that had been a work in progress for many years. It sat on the foothills of the Delhi Ridge, a forested area that ran all the way from south to north Delhi. The construction of the mall had been temporarily held up by environmentalists taking the developers to court, but theirs was a losing cause in the new India. Now that the mall was complete, apparently the largest in Asia, it prided itself on being home to luxury brands, with four floors of designer outlets topped off by the experience of dining at Zest.

Although I had often stopped by the mall to pick up Esther, I had never been inside and decided to take a closer look one afternoon. I stepped in through the door and wandered around for a while, increasingly puzzled by what I saw. The people around me were middle class, no doubt fairly well off, but they didn't look like the luxury-brand clientele Esther had spoken of, purchasing items worth lakhs. The shops too were run-of-the mill franchises. Finally, when I asked one of the attendants where Zest was, I discovered my mistake. I was in the wrong mall. Although it looked like one vast complex from outside, there were actually two malls next to each other, both owned by DLF. I was standing in the more downmarket one. If I went outside and made my way along the winding walkway to the next building, I would reach Emporio.

The luxury mall was like a five-star hotel, with a fountain, brass railings and marble floors. The impression of a hotel was emphasized further by the open lounge on the ground floor where people sat on couches eating pastries and drinking tea. I went up and down the mall, sometimes using the stairs and sometimes the elevator, wondering what it was like for Esther to work here. The luxury stores around me seemed quite empty. I decided to go into one, a Paul Smith outlet, but I lost my nerve at the last moment and veered away from the door. Instead, I continued on my circuit of the corridor winding around the atrium, puzzled that I had been unable to go inside the shop. Below me, in the lobby, I saw a woman stride out to the middle of the marble floor, pirouetting on high heels and sticking out her hips. She was tall and slender, and as I looked more closely, I could see the group of people she was posing for. It was some kind of a fashion shoot.

I was still wondering why I had been unable to enter the Paul Smith store. I didn't normally go to designer stores, but when I had ventured into some of them in New York out of curiosity, I hadn't felt such unease. Somehow, I was more exposed and vulnerable in Delhi. This wasn't because it would be apparent to everyone in the shop that I couldn't afford to buy anything – because that would be pretty obvious in Manhattan too – but it mattered to me in Delhi that people would know, as if the very objects would sneer at me for daring to enter their space. In the West, with its long excess of capitalism, it might be possible to scoff at luxury brands. They had been around so long that they had lost some of their meaning. But in India, luxury brands still possessed power.

I went up to take a look at Zest. Earlier, I had thought of going in and having a drink there. But now I felt uncertain, remembering what Esther had said about how it wasn't officially open. And who knew how much a drink there might cost? Instead, I loitered near the entrance, staring into the dark interior of the restaurant while trying not to be too obvious. I could see the bar, generic with its dim lighting and polished wood. The dining areas were much further back and I couldn't see anything of the places where the seven cuisines were served. It was still early in the evening, and in spite of the music playing softly (piped over the Internet from the UK) and the waitresses walking around looking fresh in their crisp uniforms, there seemed to be few customers. It was like a stage set before the opening of the play, holding no meaning yet for the audience. It was alive at the moment only for Esther and her colleagues.

I went back down the stairs. When I reached the lobby on the ground floor, I passed the woman I had taken to be a model. But now I understood that I had been mistaken. She had been trying a pair of shoes on, using the vast expanse of the lobby to check out how they looked and felt on her feet. The people I had taken to be photographer and make-up artist were just her friends.

8

Esther had a boyfriend, someone she had come to know while working at Shangri-La. He had been one of the extroverts in the F&B crowd there, handsome, with an eye for women. In the beginning, Esther had turned down his many requests to go out with him. She had found him attractive, she told me, but she had been uncertain about his intentions. He was too fond of women, and she wasn't sure if he would be loyal to her. She became his girlfriend only after he stopped flirting with other F&B women, reassuring Esther that he was quite serious about her.

It was natural that Esther would want a companion. But she was also a cautious person. She didn't want to become like some of the other women in F&B: a few were call girls; there was a colleague at Shangri-La who went out regularly with a Japanese businessman whenever he stayed in the hotel; and there were those who gave in too easily to their male colleagues and then got dumped by them.

Esther proceeded slowly, going out with the man, the two of them gradually becoming involved enough to start thinking about marriage. But Esther hadn't told her parents about her boyfriend. Her sisters knew him and liked him, but her brother was disapproving. The boyfriend wasn't from Manipur. He was a Bengali from Orissa, and a Hindu as well, which bothered Esther a little. 'I don't want him to become Christian,' she said. 'How can I ask someone I love to change his faith? On the other hand, I believe in the Church. That is my way. So we will each stick to our own religion, but the children, I want one boy and one girl, I want them to be brought up as Christians.'

Two years earlier, not long after they started going out, Esther's boyfriend had received a job offer from a hotel in the United Arab Emirates. His parents came from Orissa to Delhi to see him off, and Esther met them briefly. The parents did not know she was seeing their son, but he called them from UAE and told them that Esther and he were thinking about getting married. The parents, according to Esther, were surprised. 'His mother said, "Oh, I should have guessed from the way you were looking at each other."' But the parents accepted their son's decision, and although Esther and her boyfriend weren't certain about where and when to get married, they began talking more decisively of their future together.

It was a long-distance relationship, hard for Esther in many ways, but she had encouraged him to take the job at UAE. 'I miss him, but I don't want to hold him back,' she said. 'It is important for a man to go out into the world.' He was coming back on a brief visit that summer, and she was excited at the prospect of seeing him after so long. She had arranged to take a week off work to spend time with him.

I wanted to be around to meet the boyfriend, but I had already made plans to go to Andhra Pradesh during the week he was going to be in Delhi. When I finally returned to the city, the boyfriend was already back in UAE.

Esther and I met at the Barista café. She had a new mobile phone, a bright red gadget that she played with as we talked, but she looked even more tired than usual. The visit had begun very well, she said. Her boyfriend had been tender and loving. He had brought gifts for her sisters and for her, including the new mobile phone. He had also spent an entire afternoon with Esther and her sisters at their flat, high-spirited and entertaining as he told them about his life in UAE. He'd talked about wanting to come back to Delhi, but Esther had insisted that he stay on in UAE because he was earning much more there. He had also brought up the prospect of Esther getting a job there, but she had said that wouldn't be possible because she couldn't leave her family behind.

'But all the time while he was talking to us, he was on his mobile phone, you know, always texting,' Esther said. 'So when he went to the bathroom, I picked up his phone and looked at the messages to see who he was texting with so much. I couldn't believe it. It was this girl at the UAE hotel who had written to say she was missing him, and he had written back saying that he loved her. Imagine that, he's sitting with me, having a good time with me, and all along, there's this other girl he's thinking of and whom he loves.' Esther stared into the distance. 'The guys are not satisfied with just one,' she said. 'It's like that with the ones I know at Zest. They're flirting with one girl at work, with another on their mobiles, and with one more when they leave the restaurant. "What is it with you guys, yeah?" I tell them. They say, "Just enjoying life, yeah. Come on, Esther, relax." I tell them go to hell with their enjoying life.'

When Esther confronted her boyfriend, he was contrite, asking her to forgive him. Esther returned all the gifts, including the jewellery he had given her and the phone, but he left everything with Renu, asking her to pass them on to Esther after he had gone back to UAE. Since then, he had been calling and texting Esther to ask if they could be together again.

Esther took out the new phone and showed me a picture of the boyfriend. He was quite handsome, and I could see why women might be attracted to him. Esther tapped through the menu to show me one of the messages he had sent her. I had been expecting something transparently fake, but the message was quite touching: 'Just one more chance, Esther, and I'm yours for life, I promise.'

'I don't know what to do,' Esther said. 'Whether to get back with him even though I don't trust him any more, or to break up even though I miss him so much. Sometimes, it seems to me that this just keeps happening over and over again to all the women in our family.'

Esther's elder sister, Mary, had been engaged to a man in Imphal. She had left her call centre job in Delhi and gone back home, where the wedding preparations had been in full swing when they discovered that the fiancé was engaged to another woman at the same time. Mary cancelled the wedding, came back to Delhi and took up another call centre job. She no longer talked about getting married, Esther said. Renu too had had a boyfriend in college, someone she became quite attached to, and who suddenly broke up with her. Esther talked about her mother, who had been with another man and had a son with him before being abandoned by the man. She had married Esther's father later.

'How was your father about that?' I asked.

'He's a very good man, he loves my mother and my half-brother. My half-brother is as much a part of our family as any of the other siblings.' She wanted my advice about what to do with her boyfriend. 'I've never done anything like that to him,' she said. 'I have opportunities too. I work, I am independent. I look at boys, sure, and I think, "Oh, that one's nice. That one's bad." But it doesn't go beyond that.'

### 9

One afternoon, Esther took me to meet a friend of hers in Munirka, someone with whom she occasionally stayed over. I had been curious about how the neighbourhood had changed in the years since I last lived there. There had been plenty of people from the north-east when I was a resident of Munirka, but few of them were single women. It had been an unsafe area for women, with sexual assaults not uncommon in the deserted stretches of land between the crowded village and the university campus.

As Esther and I approached Munirka, there was much about the neighbourhood that seemed immediately familiar, from the unkempt park on our right to the garbage dump that sat at the beginning of a row of concrete buildings. Some of the buildings had become larger, with decorative flourishes like fluted metal bars on the balconies, but they still stood cheek by jowl, with little alleyways separating them from each other. People could still jump from one balcony to another if they wanted to.

I slowed down when we came to the building where I had lived. It was unchanged, the passageway in front of it deserted at that time in the afternoon. I felt no sense of triumph that I had seemingly moved up since I lived inside that one-room flat, its back door opening to a sheer drop. The neighbourhood became more crowded as we went further in. There were little groups of local Jat men and those from the north-east, keeping their distance from each other. The men from the north-east worked night shifts at call centres, while the local men were either unemployed or running small businesses that did not require their presence at that hour. The street running past the buildings was still a dirt track, but the buffaloes that had wallowed there had vanished, giving way to cars and motorcycles. The young Jats who stood around looked like prosperous street toughs, wearing branded jeans and sneakers, occasionally sending a glance sliding up the body of a young woman emerging from a building.

Esther's friend Moi lived a couple of buildings down from my former residence, up on the third floor. We climbed the narrow stairwell of the building, passing flats whose doors had been left open because of the heat. Moi's single-room flat was almost exactly like mine, from the size of the room to her belongings. There was a cheap mattress on the floor, probably bought from Rama Market; a portable red gas cylinder with a burner attached to it, something easier to get than the regular gas cylinders that required an immense amount of paperwork; and an odd mishmash of crockery, cooking utensils and clothes.

Moi was from Churachandpur, slim and stylish in jeans and T-shirt. She shared the flat with two of her siblings – a brother who worked at a laundry and a sister who was a waitress at a café in IIT Delhi. We sat on the floor and chatted about how Moi had come to Delhi. She had moved around a lot, working in Arunachal Pradesh as a teacher and a warden at a school, in Calcutta for a Christian charity, and in Chennai for another charity doing relief work for people affected by the tsunami in 2004. She had moved to Delhi the year after with a job at a children's home in Noida, which she had followed with a position at a call centre for two years. It had been hard going, she said, working evenings and nights at a call centre while living in Munirka. One evening, while waiting for a van to pick her up, she had been harassed by men in a car asking if she was available for the night. On another occasion, two men on a motorcycle had grabbed her arm, trying to drag her on to the bike and letting go only when her screams attracted attention from passers-by.

At work, Moi had been a 'precollector', making calls to American customers falling behind with their payments.

I asked her what it had been like.

She responded with a surprisingly good rendition of a deep masculine growl. 'Tell me the colour of the panties you're wearing,' she said.

The two women started laughing.

Moi eventually left the call centre because her employers wouldn't give her the two weeks' leave she needed to go home. Since then, she had been looking around for work without much success, and she was considering returning to a call centre job since it was relatively easy to get one.

Moi's life sounded to me like a strange combination of Victorian and millennial motifs: on the one hand, there were all those children's homes and boarding schools she had worked at; on the other, there was her job as a precollector talking to men on the other side of the world. But the same was true of Esther, I thought, as we left Moi's flat and walked out of Munirka. She was so modern in some ways, with her job at a fancy restaurant and a text-messaging boyfriend from a different religion and ethnicity who worked in a faraway country. Yet there were other forces acting upon Esther's life that made her look back home, towards possibilities that seemed to have little in them of the new India.

The break-up with her boyfriend had left Esther worried and depressed. When I had first met her, she had been confident about her F&B work. She had said she was better at the work than many of her peers. She knew the menu inside out, knew what to suggest to customers and how to serve the food correctly. Even when she talked about quarrelling with the manager, that was part of her ambition, of wanting to become an assistant manager.

These days Esther spoke differently about her job. 'I wanted to be a doctor, not this F&B. Sometimes, I want to go back home, but what is there back home? If I go home, what will I do? But this job has no security, no pension.' She told me that she had taken an exam for a government schoolteacher's job in Imphal. The salary was 14,000 rupees, and it came with benefits like a pension, as well as a form of security that did not exist in F&B. Her mother was a schoolteacher too, and what Esther sometimes wanted, after all her independence, striving, exposure and mobility was a simple repetition of her mother's life.

'My mother wants me to take the job if I get it,' Esther said. 'I got through the exam, but the interview is still left. I'll take the train home, which will take three days, give the interview, get back on the train for another three days, and come back to this F&B. If I get the interview call, that is.' She began talking about home. 'You know, once I flew home to Imphal, and my parents came to get me at the airport. They had become so old that it was painful to see them. I feel scared about them, I think, "*Kitna din wo rahega?*" My mother has a nerve problem, she shakes her head like this.' Esther demonstrated how her mother's head shook. 'My father has memory loss sometimes. And me, after all these years in Delhi, I have forty-two rupees in my bank account. At times I'm fed up. I think I'll go back. At least I won't have to pay rent in Imphal. Then sometimes, I think I won't go back to Imphal, but maybe just get out of Delhi. I want to go to Simla.'

I remembered how I used to feel that way when I lived in Munirka, when I felt the need to get out of the city and went for a brief holiday to the nearby hills of Uttaranchal or Himachal Pradesh. But Esther didn't have that option. 'I haven't been able to go to Simla even for a week's holiday,' Esther said. 'I made plans so many times, but every time I had to cancel. At work, I sometimes get sick of the people I am serving. Sometimes, there are fights at the station because no one wants to go and serve a party that's come in. Everyone can tell they'll be difficult. Once, a Korean couple left a two-rupee coin for us as a tip. At least that allowed us to have a good laugh. Last night, a party of Delhi ladies came in. They ordered the Indian appetizer platter. The platter weighs two and a half kilos. I had to hold it with one hand, while with my other hand, I held the tongs with which to pick up the food. My back was hurting, the platter was so heavy, and when I got to the ladies, none of them would let me put food on her plate. They were doing that Indian thing, "*Pehle aap, pehle aap.* No, no, serve her first," and so I would go to the next lady, who would refuse and send me on to the next one and it went on and on until I was so sick of all of them.'

Esther had now begun looking for other jobs, even in Delhi. She wanted something that offered permanence and regular hours, something that demanded less of her body and was not as susceptible to the whims of rich customers. On the last day I met her at the Barista café, she told me that she knew a man who was a member of parliament. He was from the Congress Party, she said, one of the youngest MPs in the country. She had come to know the man through his Mizo girlfriend, and he had hinted that he might be able to get her a job in the parliament.

It was a possibility that excited Esther, but she was worried that he might ask for a bribe in exchange for the job. She was expecting to meet with him later that afternoon. 'If he wants money, I'll have to say no. I don't have any money,' she said. Esther decided to call the MP to find out when he wanted to meet.

The conversation was brief. 'You're too busy today?' she said. 'You want me to try again in a few days?' She put the phone down and shrugged. 'Sometimes, I really regret why I joined F&B,' she went on. 'My elder brother wanted me to study further and get a job with the central government. Sometimes, I think I want to do that, study something, maybe get an MBA through correspondence. But that would cost me at least eighty thousand rupees. And the problem is that now I know the taste of money, I cannot go back to the student life. I called a friend recently who works in Taj Mansingh. She's also fed up with F&B. But we were talking, and I got scared. If I change jobs, what if, in the future, I regret leaving F&B?'

I dropped her off in front of the mall, watching as she vanished inside that vast building. It was nearly dusk, and the lights were on everywhere, each luxury-brand logo carved out on the wall bathed in its own glow. When I went home, I decided to look up the Congress

MPs from Agra to find out more about the man who had held out the prospect of a job in the parliament for Esther. It would be nice if it came true, I thought – if a young woman from the border provinces who was smart, hard-working and good ended up working in the building that was the symbol of India's democracy.

I looked for a long time on the Internet, sifting through the names, political parties and constituencies of the various MPs. There were no young Congress MPs from Agra.

No one at all with the name Esther had given me.

# Acknowledgements

Because the names of a number of Indian cities have been changed in the past decade, I would like to clarify that the place referred to in the introduction as Gauhati is now known as Guwahati, just as Calcutta is known as Kolkata, Madras as Chennai and Bombay as Mumbai. I would also like to note that some of the material in this book has appeared, in a different form, in the *Guardian*, *n+1*, the Review section of *The National* in Abu Dhabi and in the anthology *AIDS Sutra*. The book itself was written in a superb programme called Scrivener, which I cannot recommend highly enough.

I am grateful to an extremely large number of people for making this book possible. I would like to thank everyone who spoke to me in the course of four years of interviews, especially the people who appear in the narrative and to whom I am grateful for their willingness to open up their lives to a stranger. I have interpreted those lives in my own subjective fashion, of course, and further straitjacketed them into the themes and movements of the narrative. I would therefore like to note that the minor role occupied by Vijay Gudavarthy in the book in no way does justice to the major role he played in my journey through Hyderabad and Andhra Pradesh. I am glad that I found a generous, knowledgeable and perceptive friend like him in a place so new to me.

Pankaj Mishra started me off and believed in this book well before I did. Sanjay Reddy shared his knowledge and humanism with me while Hartosh Singh Bal shared, among many other things, his whisky. Chitra Padmanabhan shared, among many other things, the antidotes required after too much whisky.

I met many people in India for contacts and suggestions in the course of researching this book. Some of them provided me with far more than that, often hosting me in an old subcontinental spirit of generosity. For that, I would like to thank Samrat Chaudhury, Mary

Therese Khurkalang, Anita Roy, Vivek Narayanan, Gautam Mody, Nilanjana Roy and Devangshu Datta, Alam Srinivas, Sanjoy Narayan, Jehangir Pocha, Umesh Anand and Jai Arjun Singh in Delhi; Sugata Raju, Anjum Hasan, Zac O'Yeah, U. Ananthamurthy, Arjun Jaydev, A. R. Vasavi, Roy Sinai, Aravind Adiga, Jeet Thayil and Achal Prabhala in Bangalore; Chinnaiah Jangam, Krishna Reddy, R. Limbadri, Ram Karan, N. Venugopal and Sridala Swami in Andhra Pradesh; and Jinendra Maibam and Kingson Shimray in Manipur.

For institutional support, I would like to thank the Society of Authors in the UK for a travel grant that came at a very early stage of research and helped get this book off the ground. I would also like to thank the Nation Institute in New York, especially Esther Kaplan, for a research grant that helped me finish some of the reporting. I am grateful to the Radcliffe Institute for Advanced Study at Harvard University, and in particular Judy Vichniac, for a year-long fellowship that allowed me to write this book. I am grateful to Barbara Grosz and Lindy Hess at the Radcliffe Institute, and to my superbly competent research assistant, Abigail Lind, for making my stay there such a productive experience. I am grateful to Eugene Lang College at the New School for providing me with an institutional base in New York, and to my colleagues and students there for providing a human superstructure to that base. I am especially grateful to Neil Gordon for bringing me to the New School and for believing that I had something special to contribute there.

Among editorial colleagues at magazines and newspapers, I would like to thank Katharine Viner and Helen Oldfield of the *Guardian* for starting me off with the call centre story. I am grateful to Sam Leith, Lindsay Duguid, Jennifer Szalai, John Palattella, Albert Mobilio, Jonathan Shainin, Peter Baker, Vinod Jose, and the team at *n+1*, especially Marco Roth, Benjamin Kunkel and Chad Harbach for editorial interventions – some of which, sometimes, took the form of cheques. I am grateful to David Miller at Rogers, Coleridge and White for doing the needful. I am in debt to Mary Mount for her early support for the book and for editing it with her usual clarity and confidence.

In the year that I spent in Cambridge writing this book, there were a select few who handled my obsessiveness with grace. I am grateful to Marlon Cummings for beer and laughter, to Ananya Vajpeyi for vegetarian dinners, to Russ Rymer for shared confidences, to Suneeta Gill for confident cooking and to Balraj Gill for camaraderie. I am grateful to Basharat Peer for the energy and enthusiasm he provided in New York and in New Delhi. I am grateful to Adam Shatz for his unwavering loyalty. I am grateful to Amy Rosenberg for, among other things, her decade-long perseverance and for being a superb mother to my son. I am more grateful than I can say to my mother, to whom this book is dedicated.

But above all, I am grateful to Ranen Lal Deb, for being there and for being himself.

# *He just wanted a decent book to read ...*

Not too much to ask, is it? It was in 1935 when Allen Lane, Managing Director of Bodley Head Publishers, stood on a platform at Exeter railway station looking for something good to read on his journey back to London. His choice was limited to popular magazines and poor-quality paperbacks – the same choice faced every day by the vast majority of readers, few of whom could afford hardbacks. Lane's disappointment and subsequent anger at the range of books generally available led him to found a company – and change the world.

*'We believed in the existence in this country of a vast reading public for intelligent books at a low price, and staked everything on it'*
**Sir Allen Lane, 1902–1970, founder of Penguin Books**

The quality paperback had arrived – and not just in bookshops. Lane was adamant that his Penguins should appear in chain stores and tobacconists, and should cost no more than a packet of cigarettes.

Reading habits (and cigarette prices) have changed since 1935, but Penguin still believes in publishing the best books for everybody to enjoy. We still believe that good design costs no more than bad design, and we still believe that quality books published passionately and responsibly make the world a better place.

So wherever you see the little bird – whether it's on a piece of prize-winning literary fiction or a celebrity autobiography, political tour de force or historical masterpiece, a serial-killer thriller, reference book, world classic or a piece of pure escapism – you can bet that it represents the very best that the genre has to offer.

**Whatever you like to read – trust Penguin.**

read more
www.penguin.co.uk